Francis Bacon

The Temper of a Man

SIR FRANCIS BACON, LORD CHANCELLOR OF ENGLAND
By John Vanderbank

Francis Bacon

The Temper of a Man

CATHERINE DRINKER BOWEN

INTRODUCTION BY DOMINIC J. BALESTRA

Fordham University Press
New York
1993

LC 93-32785
ISBN –0–8232–1537–7 (*hardcover*)
ISBN 0–8232–1538–5 (*paperback*)

Printed in the United States of America

Library of Congress Cataloging-in-Publication Data
Bowen, Catherine Drinker, 1897–1973.
Francis Bacon : the temper of a man / by Catherine Drinker
Bowen; introduction by Dominic J. Balestra. — 2nd ed.
p.   cm.
Includes bibliographical references and index.
ISBN 0–8232–1537–7 (hard) : $30.00 — ISBN 0–8232–1538–5
(pbk.) : $20.00
1. Bacon, Francis, 1561–1626. 2. Philosophers — England —
Biography. I. Title
B1197.B6   1993
192 — dc20
[B]   93–32785
CIP

for

John H. Powell

Authority and place demonstrate and try the tempers of
men, by moving every passion and discovering every frailty.

PLUTARCH, *Lives*

CONTENTS

Introduction by DOMINIC J. BALESTRA   xi

Prologue: Lord Bacon's Reputation   1

I • An Elizabethan Eden, 1561–1579

An Elizabethan Eden   21

II • The Struggle to Rise, 1579–1613

1. Two Conflicting Ambitions   45
2. Bacon and Essex   68
3. Bacon Begins to Write   81
4. The Ambition of the Understanding   97
5. The Ambition of the Will   111

III • Bacon Ascending: A Time of Glory, 1613–1620

1. Lord Coke's Defeat   133
2. Lord Chancellor   151

IV • Impeachment, 1621

Impeachment   175

V • A Noble Five Years, 1621–1626

A Noble Year   205

Author's Note   235

Index   237

Illustrations appear between pages 118 and 119.

INTRODUCTION

Dueling Ambitions

IN THE 1560s England saw the birth of two geniuses, William Shakespeare and Francis Bacon. One, the son of a leather tradesman of modest means, went to the local grammar school, and by chance and natural endowment realized his genius in the theater. The other, the son of learned and wealthy parents, went to Trinity College, Cambridge, and by birth and design realized his genius in Court, despite his slow rise through thirty-six years of public service and sudden fall in less than two years as Lord Chancellor. Francis Bacon played many roles in the English Renaissance. He was a courtier, an essayist, parliamentarian, jurist, historian, Lord Chancellor and, through it all, a philosopher. His achievement in each is more than impressive, and the constellation of accomplishments is truly stellar.

Throughout his life Bacon was hampered by recurring bouts of poor health. Yet his persevering determination to fulfill two lifelong commitments succeeded in earning him a permanent place both as philosopher and as public servant. In a famous letter[1] of 1592 to his uncle, William Cecil Burghley, who was Secretary of State and first minister to Elizabeth, Bacon, at the age of thirty-one, "confesses" his dual ambition:

for the *vita activa* in service to the queen and to England, and for the *vita contemplativa*. "Lastly, I confess that I have as vast contemplative ends, as I have moderate civil ends: for I have taken all knowledge to be my province." When Bacon wrote to his uncle, he already had served eight years in Parliament. Reading Bacon's life and his writings strongly suggests that these competing ambitions did not conflict, except in the very practical order of time.

There is a nascent pragmatism in Bacon's epistemological stance. For him any legitimate theory must serve human practices. Further in the letter, after distinguishing these contemplative ends from the "verbose disputations" of abstract philosophies or the aimless results of "blind experiments," Bacon identifies his contemplative ends as knowledge useful for and in service to humanity: "I hope I should bring in industrious observations, grounded conclusions, and profitable inventions and discoveries; the best state of that province. This, whether it be curiosity, or vain glory, or nature, or (if one take it favorably) *philanthropic*, is so fixed in my mind as it cannot be removed."

At this juncture, five years before the publication of the first edition (1597) of his *Essays* and well before *The Proficience and Advancement of Learning* (1605), we find Bacon implying that the only worthwhile and genuine theoretical knowledge is that which serves the realm of human action. This is the seed of a vision which was nurtured and protected in *The Advancement of Learning*, and further developed and supported in the *Novum Organon* (1620), and which blossomed fully in his *New Atlantis*. The last was written in 1624, but published in 1627, the year following Bacon's death, by his chaplain, William Rawley, who introduced the work, reporting: "This fable my Lord devised to the end that he might exhibit therein a model or description of a college instituted for the interpreting of nature and the producing of great and marvelous works for the benefit of men, under the name of Salomen's House, or the College of the Six Days Works."[2]

Bacon's prophetic vision in his *New Atlantis* follows upon his theme of useful knowledge to outline an imaginative anticipation of today's research university, with its supporting network of various scientific and professional associations.

In addition to signaling that knowledge is a power to control the kingdom of nature in service to the kingdom of man, the letter to Burghley alerts us to a much more subtle aspect of Bacon's *Essays*. In providing some of Bacon's most perceptive analyses of and insights into the human condition, the *Essays* fill in the gaps in the study of human nature noted in Book II of *The Advancement of Learning*.[3] Consider, for instance, the question of what Bacon means by "philanthropic" in the letter, then turn to the essay "Of Goodness and Goodness of Nature" for an essential element in his answer. Feigning any self-seeking advantage, he says directly "I take Goodness in this sense, the affecting of the weal of men, which is what the Grecians call *Philanthropic*."[4]

Bacon continued to serve in Parliament for another twenty-six years, while taking on a succession of additional roles: as jurist, as minor counsel to Queen Elizabeth, as King's Counsel to James I (in 1604), then Solicitor-General (1607), Attorney-General (1613), later (1617) Lord Keeper like his father, and finally (in 1618) Lord Chancellor of England. Bacon paid a high price for sustaining the *vita activa* on so many fronts.

Perhaps Bacon played too many roles. His dueling ambitions seemed to generate an ambivalence that may have worked toward his downfall. Achievement in so many corridors fueled the resentment of his enemies during his life; after his death it inevitably invited a maze of divergent opinion about this genius of the English Renaissance. There is a history of disputed judgments by biographers, historians, literary critics, and philosophers. On the one side, he has been hailed as a maker of modernity in multiple ways: as a founding contributor to a new, experimental scientific method, a new philosophical standpoint; as a maker of a new literary genre, the modern essay; and as a modern historian. On the other, he has been belittled as unoriginal in his scientific thinking and condemned as a hypocritical public servant whose impeachment as Lord Chancellor in 1621 betrays the author of the *Essays*. Until the formidable scholar James Spedding published his *Evenings with a Reviewer* (1848), Bacon's reputation had been minimized by a genre of incriminating biography.[5] It is to be regretted that such biography has continued well beyond Spedding's well-documented, scholarly correction. Bacon is still claimed to be the secret author of the writings of Shakespeare, or charged to be the illegitimate son of Queen Elizabeth. Indeed, as recently as 1987 Alan Dodd repeats the latter claim in his *Francis Bacon's Personal Life-Story*, characterized by one critic as "a lamentable pantomime-horse of a book . . . [whose] six hundred pages of half-truth, tendentious inference and unsupported assertion are not worth six minutes of anyone's time."[6] A public servant extraordinaire, a constructive critic of the *status quo*, a philosopher-citizen tried and convicted by those he served—more than any other modern, Bacon comes closest to realizing a life of Plato's philosopher-king. "Controversial," "disputable," and "ironic" are the adjectives that inevitably describe the various accounts of his career or his thought.

The thought of Renaissance philosophers and commentators forms an eclectic tapestry woven out of various Platonic and Augustinian or Aristotelian and Scholastic fibers. Bacon addressed that audience in his philosophical writings, forging a rhetorical wave intended to break once for all not only from the older Scholastic systems but also from the humanist retreat into the untested authority of the classical authors. He formed a watershed marking the end of the Renaissance and the beginning of the modern. Indeed, Bacon's title for his philosophical project, *Instauratio Magna*, "The Great, New Beginning," was a trumpeting call to others to join in the project of a total reconstruction of human knowledge. Its stated purpose was to seek "whether that commerce between the mind of man and the nature of things, which is more precious than anything on earth, or at least than anything that is of the earth, might by any means be restored to its perfect and original condition."[7] Its grandiose program was to be worked out in six phases. Bacon could complete only the first part on the "Division of the Sciences," and make contributions toward the second and the third, "The New Organon, or Directions Concerning the Interpretation of Nature" and "The Phenomena of the Universe." The *New Organon* contains, in aphorisms, Bacon's now-familiar negative critique of Aristotle's syllogistic method and its four-cause interpretation of nature, the powerful imagery of the idols of the mind, and the positive program of a new inductive method for the proper interpretation of nature. Later, in the *New Atlantis*, Bacon captured the promise of the *New Organon* in the vision of "Bensalem," a city of man scientifically liberated from bondage to nature, whose image has come to eclipse Augustine's "City of God" on our eschatological horizon. His *Essays* opened a path into a new, modern genre for subsequent writers—Addison and Steele in England and, later, Emerson in America. And, finally, his histories are among the first in modern times; his legal writings, including various judicial decisions and opinions, warrant study by students of jurisprudence. Assessments of Bacon will always be affected by his dueling ambitions. He will be criticized for doing philosophy or science, as William Harvey had charged, like a Lord Chancellor, or faulted for a philosopher's naïveté in coursing his way between Parliament and a demanding queen and king. Whatever the assessment, there can be little doubt that Francis Bacon deserves study, and no intellectual consideration by philosopher or literary critic or intellectual historian can do it responsibly without a look at his life, at the character of the individual or the temper of the man. Because Bacon's writings do not disclose enough of the man—the *Essays* offer opaque glimpses, the legal writing less, and the philosophical works seem silent—we need biography. And this need is underscored when one recognizes the essential role and telic position, according to Bacon's philosophy, of the *vita activa* relative to the *vita contemplativa*.

In 1962 there was a flurry of lectures, conferences, and works to celebrate the 400th year of the birth of Francis Bacon. Some paid ceremonial tribute to this well-known Englishman. Others, such as Loren Eisley's *Francis Bacon and the Modern Dilemma*, made an attempt to offer an appreciation of Bacon from the perspective of the modern science he had helped spawn. These cannot be recommended today. But some have weathered the last thirty years with little wear. Fulton H. Anderson's *Francis Bacon: His Career and Thought* immediately comes to mind, as does Catherine Drinker Bowen's *Francis Bacon: The Temper of a Man*. Bowen did not write about the life of Bacon merely because 1962 was convenient or opportune. The roots of this work lie in one of her earlier, best, and most acclaimed biographies, *The Lion and the Throne*, which examines the career of Bacon's lifelong nemesis Sir Edward Coke. In that work Bowen sketches an unflattering picture of a crafty and ambitious Bacon, who eventually falls with little to redeem him. With a charitable but disciplined openness and an integrity that is recognized as characteristic of her work, Bowen returns to reconsider the life of Bacon. As a result she softens the harsh lines of the quick sketch in the Coke book. The outcome is a sympathetic and fair investigation that transforms the sketch into a balanced portrait of a fallen Chancellor who had served his king and his public better than most of his contemporaries. Bacon readily admitted to having accepted gifts from parties whose cases were before him. Though he pleaded guilty, he always maintained that the favors never corrupted his legal judgment. In the end, Bowen escorts the reader to "A Noble Five Years" which offers a redemptive look at this impeached and disgraced Lord Chancellor and an opportunity for the reader's own assessment of this lifelong public servant of humanity.

Though this is not a scholarly work, Bowen's well-earned reputation as a reliable biographer, one whose writings are the fruit of serious research, widespread reading, and careful investigation, recommends it to scholars, teachers, and students of Renaissance and early modern Europe. Its engaging, fluid, and easy prose, its sense of history with drama, and its balanced narrative judgment recommend it to all readers. Its secure grip on history and honest awareness of its own interpretive dimensions only confirm the trust already carried by reputation. All readers will simply find this an engaging, dramatic narrative of the life of one of modern England's most significant geniuses. Mrs. Bowen has not attempted a definitive biography. At the end of her work in an "Author's Note" she says that her aim is "evocation" and "an accurate title would be *An Invitation to Francis Bacon*." Upon reading this "Invitation" the curious reader might well turn to Bacon's own writings, perhaps beginning with the *Essays* if inclined to the literary, or *The Advancement of Learning* if inclined to the philosophical. The scholar or teacher who is familiar with Bacon's thought will revisit his writings to discover something missed the first time around or to reconsider and reform easy, long-standing and, by now, stale interpretations of Bacon's career or thought.

In the course of reading Bowen's biography three reflections came readily to this reader's mind, two short and immediate, the third a bit more lengthy and mediate. The first is prompted by the irresistible question: "What might have been written had Bacon devoted his entire life to his thinking and writing"—or even had he devoted as much time and energy to it as he had given to Parliament, law, and service to a queen and then a king at a time when English royalty demanded almost heroic service? But the question here is anachronistic. We must remind ourselves that only recently have philosophers, scientists, historians, and other intellectuals done their work *as professionals*. Our age of the professional is relatively new. Though Bacon's critiques of Aristotelianism and his rhetorical visions in the *New Atlantis* have contributed significantly in bringing about organized societies of learning, he belonged to a quite different time—an age of the bourgeois gentleman—educated, relatively well provided for in an economically, socially, and politically advantaged family. Consider Montaigne and Descartes, Hobbes and Locke, among others; none of these thinkers and writers was a university professional!

The mention of Montaigne brings to mind the ready parallel between him and Bacon. The comparison is salutary if we remind ourselves that Francis' brother, Anthony, was a personal friend of Montaigne's. In many ways Bacon was England's Montaigne. Both were lifelong public servants and jurists, of privileged birth, well educated, critical, and pioneering authors of a new literary genre, the essay. But caution must be exercised especially with respect to the philosophy. Unlike Montaigne, Bacon moved beyond a negative critique to a positive founding of a new philosophical program, one which would contribute toward establishing the Enlightenment's trust in the human capacity to know nature. He attempted this in two ways: through his shaping of and advocacy for a new, inductive method, one that he intended to be used in all legitimate spheres of human inquiry, including the social and political; and through the initiation of an original philosophy of man and nature. The second has been less apparent because of three features of his philosophical writings: his pattern of combining negative and positive critique; his various styles of communication—the aphoristic mode of delivery in *The Advancement of Learning* (1605) and especially in the *Novum Organon* (1620), and the iconographic symbolism of *The Wisdom of the Ancients* (1609), the didactic use of Biblical and classical allusions in all the works, and the allegorical, fabular form of the *New Atlantis* (1627); and, finally, the overall mix of grandiose plan and incomplete execution.

Finally, appreciation of Bacon's role as a maker of modern science and the fact of his trial direct notice to a curious similarity between Bacon and Galileo. Each wrote masterpieces of rhetorical argument;, each sought to serve aristocracy; each authored some of his most significant writing after a trial and fall while under house arrest. But as with Montaigne, there is a conspicuous absence of mathematics in Bacon's writings. As a result Bacon's contribution to modern science cannot be considered comparable to a Galileo's or a Descartes'. His failure to explore fully the role of mathematics in the newly emerging approaches toward a study of nature has always haunted his reputation as a man of science. In the seventeenth century Seth Ward, who proposed Newton for membership in the Royal Society, observed that "it was a misfortune to the world that my Lord Bacon was not skilled in mathematics." Present-day scholars echo Wards's damning remark. The physicist-turned-historian-of-science Dijksterhuis counted Bacon's "undervaluation of mathematics as one of [his] easily recognized defects," and the historian Thorndike held his "total disregard of mathematical method" to be his greatest defect. In spite of this, Bacon has been praised as a founder of the modern inductive method of empirical scientific inference. Indeed, a long-standing interpretation has construed his method as an infallible, mechanical means of generating true theories from observations systematically collected. But the naïve inductivist reading of Bacon has contributed to a steady decline in his reputation since eighteenth-century thinkers accorded him the title of "Father of Experimental Philosophy." Nonetheless, twentieth-century histories of philosophy or science often include such an account of Francis Bacon's inductive method. However, sophisticated developments in the philosophy of science (especially those of Karl Popper and Thomas Kuhn) have nearly eliminated any serious consideration of Bacon's contribution to scientific method. Such an elimination would be an intellectual travesty. To avert such scholarly travesty Peter Urbach's *Francis Bacon's Philosophy of Science* (1987) leads us away from such a mistake of intellectual history by reinterpreting Bacon's program of induction as a much more sophisticated form of inductivism than the long-standing, naïve inductivist interpretation. Whether Urbach succeeds in retrieving for Bacon the once accorded title "Father of Experimental Philosophy" is left to readers of the history and philosophy of science.

Why this kind of reading on Bacon? The explanation lies with the certitude found in mathematical knowledge, and the refuge from the skeptic. Had Montaigne eschewed mathematics because it might withstand his Pyrrhonian criticisms? Modern physics has always been at the center of modern science, and modern physics is through and through mathematical physics. Accordingly, some kind of certitude has often been associated with modern science. Bacon was an animated and powerful critic of the limits and shortcomings of the human mind. The negative critique of his *New Organon* takes aim at Aristotelian and other abstract philosophies that give epistemic primacy to theory. But its positive program of a new method makes it clear that Bacon is no skeptic. In its trusting attitude toward a future built on the new method, the *New Atlantis* reiterates Bacon's optimism about human inquiry about nature. Unlike Descartes, Bacon never sought for certainty in knowledge. He never needed it. In reading Bowen's account of Bacon, we learn that he studied law at Grey's Inn, practiced it for forty years, and reformed it in a major way. We are likewise reminded that Bacon labored under the lawyer's imperative, not that of the mathematician, which commands: claim nothing, even between two dueling conjectures, unless there is certain proof. In contrast the lawyer's imperative commands: the better of the alternative, even if not for certain. This should come as no surprise for understanding a philosophy that always has the *vita contemplativa* in the interest of the *vita activa*.

The Author

Catherine Drinker Bowen died of cancer in 1973—but not before she had authored eight biographies, a number of histories, and various books on the biographer's craft. Her father, Henry Sturgis Drinker, was a lawyer and president of Lehigh University; her mother, Aimée Ernesta (Beaux) Drinker, was a musician. Most of her writings are biographies of extraordinary historical figures. It is interesting to note that the bulk of these treat musicians and lawyers, including Tchaikowsky and his teachers, Anton and Nicholas Rubenstein, in *Free Artist*, Oliver Wendell Holmes in *Yankee from Olympus*, Sir Edward Coke in *The Lion and the Throne*, and Sir Francis Bacon.

Each biography is marked by a vitality that springs from one who managed to have defied time's arrow. Perhaps being born, the youngest of six children, at the end of the nineteenth century, having studied music at the Peabody Institute and Juilliard, and having written her first major biography, *Be-*

loved Friend: The Story of Tchaikowsky and Nadejda von Meck, on nineteenth-century musicians, established her capacity to touch the past as it lived. She wrote about the biographer's craft as a calling. "Yet writers, male and female," are artists, said Bowen. And no artist, she insisted, "can operate lacking belief in her mission." No doubt this sense of vocation produced a care and sensitivity that make the list of awards—the Philadelphia Award, the Phillips Award, the National Book Award, and others, and honorary doctorates from the University of Rochester, the University of North Carolina, Temple University, and others—no surprise. Whatever the explanation, we are the beneficiaries of this writer's power to dramatize history. I wish that I could have heard Catherine Drinker Bowen speak about the "adventures of a biographer" and could have met her to express gratitude for making Francis Bacon, the philosopher, live today.

DOMINIC J. BALESTRA
Fordham University

NOTES

1. *Francis Bacon: A Selection of His Works*, ed. Sidney Warhaft (New York: Macmillan, 1982), pp. 460–61.

2. Ibid., p. 418.

3. See Ronald S. Crane, "The Relation of Bacon's *Essays* to His Program for the Advancement of Learning," in *Essential Articles for the Study of Francis Bacon*, ed. Brian Vickers (Hamden, Conn.: Archon, 1968), pp. 272–79.

4. *The Essays or Counsels Civil or Morall*, in *Bacon: A Selection*, ed. Warhaft, p. 75.

5. See "Bacon's Reputation," the opening chapter of Fulton Anderson's *Francis Bacon: His Career and his Thought* (Los Angeles: University of Southern California Press, 1962).
6. *The Times Literary Supplement* (March 1987), 287.
7. *Instauratio Magna*, in *Bacon: A Selection*, ed. Warhaft, p. 298.

BIBLIOGRAPHY

BACON'S WORKS

Francis Bacon: A Selection of His Works. Ed. Sidney Warhaft. New York: Macmillan, 1982. A convenient, reliable collection of the major works, it includes the original 1597 *Essays* and the two successively enlarged editions of 1612 and 1625, as well as the major philosophical works, *The Proficience and Advancement of Learning*, the *Instauratio Magna*, the *New Organum*, and the *New Atlantis*.

The Works of Francis Bacon. Edd. James Spedding, R. L. Ellis, and D. D. Heath. 14 vols. London, 1857–1874. Repr. New York: Garrett, 1968. Vols. I-V: *Philosophical Works* (English translations of the Latin works are in vols. V, VI). Vols. V-VII: *Literary and Professional Works*. Vols. VIII-XIV: *The Letters and Life of Francis Bacon, Including All His Occasional Works* (chronologically arranged, with bibliographical commentary).

CRITICAL STUDIES

Anderson, Fulton. *Francis Bacon: His Career and His Thought.* Los Angeles: University of Southern California Press, 1962.

Essential Articles for the Study of Francis Bacon. Ed. Brian Vickers. Hamden, Conn.: Archon, 1968.

Urbach, Peter. *Francis Bacon's Philosophy of Science.* LaSalle, Ill.: Open Court, 1987.

Vickers, Brian. *Francis Bacon.* London: Longmans, 1978. A very useful introduction to Bacon's writings and their themes with an annotated bibliography.

PROLOGUE

Lord Bacon's Reputation

PROLOGUE

Lord Bacon's Reputation

FRANCIS BACON'S LIFE, with its slow rise to political power and its sudden awful fall, is a drama on the heroic scale of the old Greek tragedies. The world knows the famous last will and testament, where Bacon left his "soul to God above, his body to be buried obscurely, his name to the next ages, and to foreign nations." The world knows his writings, or the titles of them, at least. But there is a composition of Bacon's which the world has lately forgotten or overlooked. In the fullness of his power and reputation as Lord Chancellor of England, Bacon was impeached by Parliament for taking bribes in office, convicted, and banished from London and the law courts. At the depth of his fall, at the lowest reach of public disgrace and private agony, Bacon wrote a prayer, confessing to God that he had not used his talents to best advantage. Born to be a philosopher, a contemplative man, he acknowledged that he had lived too much in the world and had misspent his talents in things for which he was least fit —"so as I may truly say," he wrote, "my soul hath been a stranger in the course of my pilgrimage."

On the face of it, does the world offer more tragic confes-

[3]

sion? For a Francis Bacon, what more terrible than to know that he had been the instrument of his own betrayal? It is said that a man of genius has been seldom ruined but by himself. *My soul a stranger* . . .

Three and a half centuries have passed since Bacon's death, yet the rumors multiply, and among scholars his name still provokes dissension. His character, with its duality, its yin and yang, its evil and good, its dark side and its light, is not solved by his self-condemnation. This was a mercurial nature, quick — almost shockingly quick — to recover from disaster. This soul which at midnight felt itself so tragically a stranger, on the morrow was ready with new plans and ideas, ranging from grandest intellectual visions to wily schemes for political self-advancement. Bacon's frail body housed a vast imagination, powerful nervous energy, limitless ambition and a naïve vulnerability in the face of the world's unkindness.

Bacon's life is well documented; his writings bear his stamp upon them word for word. Yet this brilliant, complex being has become, over the centuries, a riddle, an enigma. His name is legend, he stands on the far side of the moon. Certain enthusiasts, digging below the spring, even had Bacon writing Shakespeare's plays — a transmutation which is accompanied by smoke, necromancy, cryptography and the fanaticism of a religion. With it this book will not be concerned.

But has any man in history been so variously bespoken, so loved and hated, admired and despised, venerated and damned? Ben Jonson, who knew him, said that he loved Francis Bacon not only for his eloquence but for his virtue — and said it when the Lord Chancellor was in disgrace with all his world. A century later, Alexander Pope referred to Bacon, in a memo-

rable couplet, as "the wisest, brightest, meanest of mankind."
Lord Macaulay condemned Bacon out of hand as treacherous
to his friends, a time-server, magnificent of intellect and cold
of heart. Whereas Shelley the poet said flatly that for his part
he would rather be damned with Plato and Lord Bacon than
go to heaven with Paley and Malthus.

Let me confess I am on Shelley's side, and heartily. The
great Sir Francis Bacon, Lord Verulam and Viscount St. Alban, in despite of tragedy and misfortune, was a cheerful,
hopeful, at times even a playful man. He loved the word
felicity. "Grave solemn wits," he said, "have more dignity than
felicity." Surely there was felicity in Francis Bacon? Without
pompousness, without arrogance or undue humility, this man
addressed himself to the eternal verities, weaving these large
angry topics easily into the opening lines of his essays. Take
the opening of the essay on truth: *"What is truth?* — said
jesting Pilate, and would not stay for an answer." Or on death:
"Men fear death, as children fear to go in the dark." Or on
atheism: "I had rather believe all the fables in the Legend, and
the Talmud, and the Alcoran, than that this universal frame
is without a mind." Consider the opening line of the essay
on gardens, in lighter vein but bearing again that touch of
grace: *"God Almighty first planted a garden."* Bacon's friends
gave evidence that in conversation also, he could approach with
simplicity any subject, themes lofty or themes abstruse.

Bacon once remarked that "by all possible endeavours" we
must "frame the mind to be pliant and obedient to occasion."
A dangerous dictum. Yet pliant though Bacon's own mind
may have been, there is about his thinking something merciless and inexorable. Call it the quality of originality. Say that
Bacon was one of those men who, in Thomas Carlyle's phrase,

[5]

"in some measure converse with this universe at first hand."

Francis Bacon's literary works — notably the *Essays* — have remained where they belong, on the summit. His legal writings are proportionately and surprisingly slim. None were published during Bacon's lifetime save the ninety-seven brilliant and prophetic legal aphorisms in the *Advancement of Learning*. After his death, Bacon's early writings on the law were collected and published in small volumes called *Use of the Law,* or *Elements of the Common Laws.* I have seen copies, well thumbed and marked by members of the profession. During the Great Rebellion and interregnum (1641-1660) there was a lively demand for reprints of Bacon's speeches concerning the legal aspect of the union with Scotland, a demand also for anything Bacon had said on treason, on the jurisdiction of courts, or on kingship and its powers. His one hundred and one ordinances for the regulation of Chancery business endured, as we shall see, for centuries.

Yet compared with his philosophic or scientific works, Bacon's legal writings reached a limited audience. Bacon told King James that he was "in good hope that when Sir Edward Coke's Reports and my Rules and Decisions shall come to posterity there will be question who was the greater lawyer." This remark has been much quoted. Bacon made it long before Coke's four volumes — *Institutes of the Laws of England* — were written. On the courtroom floor, Bacon was a competent lawyer. As time passed he developed indeed into a deep student of the law in its constitutional and philosophic aspects. Yet his published output in the law cannot be ranged against Coke's *Institutes* and his thirteen books of *Reports.*

Francis Bacon's true greatness lay elsewhere. His philosophical works: the *Novum Organum,* the *Advancement of Learn-*

[6]

ing, the *New Atlantis* and the rest, are magnificent, greatly conceived and greatly achieved; it is here that Bacon's reputation rests. Yet even these volumes have suffered periodic triumph and eclipse. The titles are formidable; for the most part the world is satisfied to have them relegated to college survey courses in philosophy or in the history of science and epistemology. Yet pick up these books, read them and we are at once enchanted. "I will now attempt," writes Bacon, "to make a general and faithful perambulation of learning, with an inquiry what parts thereof lie fresh and waste, and not improved and converted by the industry of man. . . . My hope is that if my extreme love of learning carry me too far, I may obtain the excuse of affection: for that it is not granted to man to love and to be wise."

In 1961, the four-hundredth anniversary of Bacon's birth was celebrated on both sides of the Atlantic. The American Philosophical Society held a two-day conference of commemoration, in the course of which a scholar mentioned "the patronizing deflation that Bacon had been subject to in recent years." It is true. Bacon's *Instauratio Magna,* his vision of a new Atlantis where scientists might share experimentation in colleges and workshops — all this has become so much part of modern life that we can scarcely fix our minds on it. We are used to such ideas, we forget the courage and the vision needed to propound them in Bacon's day. We forget that to challenge the accepted epistemology — let alone to challenge God's cosmology and the mysteries of His universe — was to query also the established social and religious order. For this impudence, Bacon's Italian contemporaries — Galileo, Campanella, Giordano Bruno — were imprisoned as heretics, and one of them was burned at the stake.

If too much had not been claimed for Francis Bacon, there would be no need for so many disclaimers. He seems, indeed, not to have belonged strictly to the company of scientists. It is a pity he was ever placed there. Bacon was no mathematician, and for all his prophetic insight, was blind to the potentiality of pure mathematics in the science of the future. Dr. William Harvey was his contemporary in London. Yet Bacon never mentions Harvey's discovery of the circulation of the blood, though this was announced publicly in 1616, when Bacon was at the height of his powers. Bacon met and talked with William Gilbert, when the latter was Queen Elizabeth's physician. But he passes over with a few words Gilbert's great work on the magnet. Nor is Bacon by any means ready to accept Galileo's new cosmos. It is true that Bacon notes it might be well to engage Sir Walter Ralegh's friend, Thomas Hariot, the mathematician, for certain experiments — but nothing comes of it.

Bacon was not a scientist but the propagandist of science. He was the prophet who urged men out of sterile scholasticism into the adventurous, experimental future. In his own words, he rang the bell that called the wits together. At his country houses, in Gorhambury or Twickenham, Bacon carried out, over the years, persistent, patient experiments in natural philosophy. His *Natural History, Novum Organum, History of the Winds, Of Dense and Rare, Of Hot and Cold, Of the Ebb and Flow of the Sea,* his *Description of the Intellectual Globe* are filled with observations and conclusions concerning things of touch, sight and sound. But it is the questions Bacon asks which are valuable, not the answers — and this applies to his legal writings as to his philosophical ones. Certain of Bacon's scientific queries suggest in startling fashion the findings of the twentieth century. Let us inquire, he writes, "how, and how far the humours and affects of the body do alter and work upon the mind; or again, how and how far the passions or apprehensions of the mind do alter or work upon the body. . . . This league of mind and body hath these two parts; how the one discloseth the other, and how the one worketh upon the other."

In our own times, did Sigmund Freud happen upon this paragraph? It has been said that in science, true genius lies in staring long at familiar, age-old patterns — and seeing suddenly a new import, a fresh direction and road to follow. So with Francis Bacon on mind and body, and on dreams. "The exposition of natural dreams," he continues, "discovereth the state of the body by the imaginations of the mind."

It is the scope of his inquiry for which we have to thank Francis Bacon. In science he made no single discovery. His celebrated "forms" have proven useless to laboratory workers. Moreover it is nonsense to claim him as father of the inductive method. The inductive method goes back as far as Aristotle. Yet it is to be remembered that the seventeenth century was an era not of definite discoveries but of inspired guesses, large speculations impossible to prove experimentally until the necessary precision instruments and mathematical techniques should be developed. These inspired leaps and guesses were actually the forerunners of theories which later became accepted and part of general knowledge. To read Bacon on the winds, on heat, light, the ocean currents and the cosmos is to find oneself bewildered by the conjunction of folklore, notions from the ancient Greek philosophers, medieval superstition and inspired sudden reaches into the scientific future.

It is startling, for instance, to read Bacon's surmise that heat is not a substance in itself, but motion: "A Motion expansive, restrained and acting in its strife upon the smaller particles of bodies . . . Heat itself, in its essence and quiddity is Motion and nothing else." Two centuries later, von Humboldt would speak of being "astonished" at Bacon's "happy conjecture" concerning the velocity of light. Bacon writes that he has been bothered by "a strange doubt; viz. whether the face of a clear and starlight sky be seen at the instant when it really exists, and not a little later; and whether there be not, as regards our sight of heavenly bodies, a real time and an apparent time . . . So incredible did it appear to me that the images or rays of heavenly bodies could be conveyed at once to the sight through such immense space, and not take rather a perceptive time in travelling to us."

Bacon's description of his own mind seems the very definition of a scientist. "Being gifted by nature," he writes, "with desire to seek, patience to doubt, fondness to meditate, slowness to assert, readiness to consider, carefulness to dispose and set in order." So eager is Bacon to have us, as he says, "think *things,* not words," so fearful is he lest thinkers revert to the sterile rhetoric of the scholiasts, that he frequently disparages his own gift of words. Let there not be, he cautions, a too "affectionate study of eloquence," so that men begin "to hunt more after words than matter, and more after the choiceness of the phrase, and the round and clean composition of the sentence, and the sweet falling of the clauses, and the varying and illustration of their works with tropes and figures, than after the weight of matter, soundness of argument, life of invention or depth of judgment."

What a happy circumstance, that Bacon himself could not abjure temptation! For it is upon these sentences, round and clean, and upon the sweet falling of his clauses that Bacon's essential reputation rests. Your truly successful propagandist does not exhort, he beguiles.

Thirty-four years after Bacon's death there was founded, in 1660, the Royal Society of London for Improving Natural Knowledge — an institution which during three centuries has been the breeding place of invaluable scientific work. A learned and witty member, known as "fat Tom Sprat" — actually Bishop of Rochester — was deputed to write the Society's first history. The Bishop makes no doubt of Francis Bacon's influence toward the Society's foundation — Bacon would have said its instauration. Robert Boyle the chemist — Oldenburg — Comenius of Moravia — these seventeeth-century scientific thinkers held Bacon in high esteem. To Oldenburg, Bacon was "the great architect of experimental history." During his lifetime Europe was perhaps more receptive to Bacon's ideas than England, as his chaplain, Dr. Rawley, prophesied when he wrote that his master's "fame is greater, and sounds louder in foreign parts abroad, than at home in his own nation." In Italy, Galileo took time to write a refutation of Bacon's treatise on the ocean tides — though it happened that Galileo's conclusions proved even more in error than Bacon's. In France the *Novum Organum* was known; later, the Encyclopedists and members of the Académie Royale des Sciences, notwithstanding Descartes's continued reputation, gave credit to Bacon's empirical thinking. In Germany, Leibnitz, mathematician as well as philosopher, declared, "We do well to think highly of Verulam, for his hard sayings have a deep meaning in them."

Because Bacon made, as we have said, no single "discovery," modern scholars ignore the vigor, elegance and magical persuasiveness of his philosophic writings. A doctoral thesis (1934) — an exhaustive and creditable work, entitled "The Reputation and Influence of Francis Bacon in the Seventeenth Century" — agrees that Bacon was the outstanding figure to whom all members of the Royal Society looked back with some reverence. This statement is followed, however, by careful qualification. But Bacon's "oft-quoted expressions," the author says, "were largely convenient vocalizations of ideas which seem to have been characteristic of the British scientific temperament, inborn and not acquired."

A curious myopia at times besets the academic mind. *Convenient vocalizations of characteristic ideas* . . . In the name of art and intellect, what is more difficult, what more significant than to give voice to the ideas of an era, be they acquired or inborn? What genius does it not demand to perceive these ideas and set them on paper in such form that readers will experience at once the fire and surge of intellectual recognition? It was Leibnitz again who said that, compared with Francis Bacon, Descartes seemed "to creep along the ground." Yet Descartes, Leibnitz — were not these also men who made convenient vocalizations?

Over the centuries, much ink has been spilled to show that Bacon did or did not influence John Locke, thereby laying claim to the title of the first pragmatist. It is noted also that Thomas Hobbes, who walked and talked with Bacon, mentions him but seldom in his writings, and then slightingly. Sir Isaac Newton acknowledged no debt to the Baconian empiricism, though two centuries later Charles Darwin, falling under scientific criticism, protested vigorously that he had "worked on true Baconian principles." Bacon's detractors declare that in natural philosophy his reputation was due to the importance of his position as Lord Chancellor, and that a world primed and ready for empirical thinking would have gone ahead as readily without him.

However that may be, it was Francis Bacon's voice that men heard crying in the wilderness. He has been accepted by the English-speaking world as a familiar of the literate; the Elizabethan era is known as the age of Shakespeare and Bacon.

In his own time Bacon's friends helped to make the legend — those genial brilliant gentlemen, young and old, with whom he corresponded, dined, wined, talked away the summer afternoons, lounging in the canopied chair he had invented against the English wind. There is a fascination to Bacon's friendships because they range so far afield, from the great minds of the age to doubtful but entertaining hangers-on. There were Bishop Lancelot Andrewes and Sir Henry Savile, both of whom helped translate the Bible into King James's English. There were Sir Thomas Bodley and Sir Robert Cotton, the great antiquaries and bookmen; George Herbert the poet; John Selden the legal scholar; Ben Jonson; Count Gondomar the wily, worldly Ambassador from Spain; Fulke Greville, fastidious courtier and litterateur; Archbishop Matthew's son Tobie, who, to the vast embarrassment of his Anglican father, turned Roman Catholic, was imprisoned and banished the realm, and whom Bacon never abandoned, though the friendship was hazardous, to say the least. Then there was Sir Thomas Meautys, Bacon's secretary, who raised a marble monument to his master and who himself lies buried nearby at Saint Michael's Church in St. Albans, Hertfordshire. There was Dr. William Rawley, his chaplain, who after Bacon's death saw to the editing and publishing of his works. And there was also Thomas Bushell, the talented engineer who taught King

[13]

James I how to pump water from his flooded Cornish mines. "Button Bushell," he was called — in his youth ingratiating, a borrower of money and a busy fellow at the horse races, as bright as he was unreliable — and always amusing.

These were Bacon's friends. One and all they wrote about him or corresponded with him — and kept his letters. In his capacity as parliamentarian, politician, Attorney General and Lord Chancellor, Bacon knew everybody, as the saying goes. We hear of him strolling with Sir Walter Ralegh in Gray's Inn gardens. The ill-fated friendship with the Earl of Essex is part of history. Bacon's enemies also contributed to the legend, and his enemies were powerful. Foremost among them was Sir Edward Coke of Norfolk, Queen Elizabeth's Attorney General and Chief Justice under James I. For almost a lifetime, Bacon and Coke were bitter political rivals, in Parliament and the law courts. They even contended for the hand of the same young woman, Lady Elizabeth Hatton, born a Cecil — beautiful, widowed, and rich.

For myself I can almost claim to have added to the legend. Writing Coke's biography, I had much to say of Francis Bacon, and little of it complimentary. The word *crafty* figured, and the words *clever, restless, ambitious.* I cannot retract these words. Francis Bacon was clever, restless, crafty, ambitious. Those who knew him and those who came after saw in him a hint of the reptilian. "He had a delicate, lively hazel eye," said Dr. William Harvey, "like the eye of a viper." Two centuries later, Thomas Carlyle described Sir Francis on his way to be created Baron Verulam: "There rides the great Lord Chancellor. There rides he sublime, with his white ruff, with his fringed velvet cloak, his steeple hat and 'liquorish viper eyes.' Undoubtedly a most hot seething, fermenting piece of life, made of the finest elements, a beautiful kind of man, if you will, but of the earth, earthy."

This earthiness, the brown liquorish viper eyes — all are part of the legend. Henry Hallam the historian made the serpentine comparison in politer form, when he said that Bacon possessed "adroitness and incomparable ductility." No one can argue Hallam's statement. The sinuous mind could indeed twist and turn, loop and reloop, slide, untie and re-cover. The clear cold passionate eye could see two ways at once, could see three ways and beyond; the agile mind could coil and curvet before it struck. In this ductility is our riddle, our paradox of personality. The world sees a Lord Chancellor Bacon who took bribes in office — yet he cannot be called a dishonest man. The world sees him betray his friend and patron Essex — yet Bacon's nature was neither mean nor base. Bacon married, but he never loved a woman. To all intents and purposes he loved, after his father, but one human being upon earth: his brother Anthony, lame, frail, and doomed to die at forty-two.

After Bacon's death and indeed while he was alive, his prime champions were found not only among the worldly but among the virtuous — scholars, clergymen whose lives were blameless and devoted. Is this part of the riddle, or was Ma-caulay right in his verdict that Bacon's champions, dazzled by the effulgence of this brilliant mind, forgot the standards of ordinary decency and morality? The proof is at hand; ma-terials for biography are readily available. Many of Bacon's letters survive in manuscript, and the letters of his brother Anthony, of his mother, his father, his uncle the great Lord Burghley, of his aunts and maternal grandfather and his cele-brated, busy cousin, Sir Robert Cecil. These can be seen at

Lambeth in the Archbishop's library, or in the British Museum and in various muniment rooms, record offices and research libraries here and abroad. By far the best edition of Bacon's private papers, speeches, public utterances and writings was made by James Spedding, published at intervals between 1857 and 1874, the first seven volumes being the *Works,* the last seven, Bacon's *Letters and Life.*

Spedding was thirty years preparing this edition. What set him off initially was Macaulay's celebrated essay of 1837, reviewing a biography written by a fervent partisan of Bacon's. Macaulay's essay was long and angry, eloquent, caustic and deplorably convincing in the muscular, hammer-blow manner that brooks no argument — all to the effect that Bacon was a brilliant, expedient, and thoroughly dishonest man. James Spedding read it, abandoned a government career and spent the rest of his life presenting Bacon's own words to the public, convinced that these words by themselves would prove Macaulay in the wrong. When the first seven volumes appeared, Carlyle characterized them as the "hugest and faithfullest bit of literary navvy-work" he had met with in this generation. "Bacon," he said, "is washed down to the natural skin."

No scholar has known Bacon so thoroughly. And it is pertinent that James Spedding was much beloved in English literary circles. There was a gentleness about him, an intrinsic goodness; Edward FitzGerald called him the wisest man he knew. But Spedding's friends — Carlyle, Thackeray, Tennyson and the rest — were uneasy concerning his project. Why, from all history, had "dear old Spedding," as they called him, chosen to champion the character of Francis Bacon, and against so mighty a paladin as Lord Macaulay? Before Spedding died

he answered the question. Nothing less than affection for
Bacon's character, he said, had made him undertake the task.
Then he quoted something Bacon himself had told a friend,
apropos a contemporary: "I will not question whether you
. . . pass for a disinterested man or no; I freely confess myself am not and so I leave it."

The drama of Bacon's life falls of itself into five separate
parts. Five acts, I call them. The first act comprises Bacon's
childhood and youth, the joyful acceptance of a pleasing inheritance. In the second act, Bacon plots to rise by Queen
Elizabeth's favor and fails signally. Act three shows our hero
at his worldly best and spiritual worst, as Attorney General
and Lord Chancellor under James I. The fourth act is Bacon's
parliamentary impeachment and conviction. In the fifth act
we see Bacon dishonored, banished from London and the
company he loved, yet rising to heights of courage and cre-
ativeness which caused an eighteenth-century writer to name
this final span the *nobile quinquennium,* the noble five years.

A historian has said that the immensity of Bacon's genius
has been a sore trial to his biographers. It is true. Here was
a Renaissance man, as many-sided as da Vinci. Volumes have
been written on Bacon and Sciences; learned treatises on Bacon
and the Law. The British Museum Catalogue is thick with
monographs on Francis Bacon — in English, French, Italian,
German — *Seine Stellung in der Geschichte der Philosophie.*
Yet Lord Campbell, writing his famous series entitled *Lives of
the Lord Chancellors,* remarked that "no writer has yet presented Bacon to us familiarly and naturally, from boyhood to
old age — shown us how his character was formed and de-

veloped — or explained his motives and feelings at different stages of his eventful career."

This was said in the 1840's, but the statement holds. And if the immensity of this man's genius has been a sore trial to his biographers, something else, I think, is even more of a trial; namely, the darkness of Bacon's life. In the midst of courage we see irresolution, and over against transcendent intellect a personal weakness that skirts very close to evil. Bacon yields when he should withstand. We see him content to be in the power of inferior men, content to take aid from such men and even to sue for their favor. "Let me know your mind," he writes, "and your Lordship shall find I will go your way." And again, to the shrewd yet blundering James I: "I will be ready as a chessman to be wherever your royal hand shall set me."

We shrink from the evidence; it is painful to see genius stoop for a mean prize. Perhaps the times were to blame. To live in the shadow of a Queen's favor, to strive continually for a King's smile, is not pretty work. It drove Sir Walter Ralegh to fantastic plots, to despair, egregious lying and the executioner's block. Outside the circle of royal patronage there was no way for an ambitious man to rise in government, no way at all.

Our opening scene, however, is all innocence, domestic happiness and trust. The records point to Bacon's boyhood as an idyl of family affection, of youthful promise encouraged. Unfortunately this Eden no more prepared young Francis for what was to come than if it had been paradise painted on a canvas. There was unreality to those first eighteen years, a deceptive perfection of scene. Petted, caressed, young Francis grew to manhood in the role of perpetual recipient. For him the milk flowed full and sweet — would it not flow forever? Honey slipped facile on the tongue, the prize of place and greatness seemed surely to await this son of a notable father.

With these early scenes, this seeming paradise, our narrative begins.

CHAPTER I

An Elizabethan Eden
1561–1579

An Elizabethan Eden

FRANCIS BACON was born into his Eden in the third year of Queen Elizabeth's reign — January 22, 1561. The place of his birth was an already ancient mansion on the Thames, a mile beyond the western wall of London. York House, the mansion was called. Francis's father, Sir Nicholas Bacon, occupied it by virtue of his station as Lord Keeper of the Seal — the same position, actually, as Lord Chancellor, though the more resounding title went only to clergy or those of higher blood. Sir Nicholas's father had been a yeoman farmer. York House was the Lord Keeper's official dwelling — a romantic old place, walled and turreted, with stables and kitchen gardens behind, and green lawns stretching to the water. To the north an arched gateway gave onto the Strand, a busy, muddy roadway lined with shops, inns and victualing places. Nobody knew the age of York House, but it was ancient enough to be damp in gouty weather, and there were complaints about the drains. Bishops had lived there until Henry VIII, ruthless depriver of clerics, presented the place to Charles Brandon, Duke of Suffolk, during whose tenancy it was described as including "fifty messuages, ten cottages, four stables

and seven gardens in the parish of St. Martin's in the Fields."
Situated at Charing Cross, where the river turns abruptly
southward, York House windows had a clear view up and
down the Thames. Over the wall to the eastward was Durham House, where in Bacon's time Sir Walter Ralegh would
enjoy his turret study. Beyond Durham House the river's
north bank was lined with splendid mansions and green gardens all the way to Temple stairs and the crowded narrow
streets of London. To the west, only the fields and trees of
Scotland Yard and a lane or two separated York House from
the Queen's sprawling palace of Whitehall. At the palace
stairs a boy could see the royal barge, high-bowed and gaudy,
slide to water when her Majesty went citywards, see it hauled
to rest when Majesty returned, and hear the trumpets sound
when Majesty walked on the leads by summer moonlight.
Beyond the trees and pleasances of the palace park, within easy
sight was Westminster Great Hall, where Parliament met and
the law courts kept their terms in the four seasons. At sun-
set the Abbey towers rose against a river sky; the chimes of
St. Margaret's rang near, clashing against the deep reverbera-
tions of the Abbey bells.

Is it coincidence that one finds, so often, great men of history born in the place and scene best suited to their genius?
An Edward Coke, raised in the harsh East Anglian country-
side, where the North Sea beat upon bleak shores and a boy
learned to stand against the weather as he would one day
stand against a king's displeasure . . . A John Adams of
Braintree, child of a scrubbed New England farmhouse, set
among pastures that proclaimed the Almighty's purpose: that
the son of man, being sinful, must wring his harvest perpetu-
ally from the stones . . . A Francis Bacon, who first saw light

in a great house richly furnished — chambers "hanged with tapestry, and tapers burning in stretched-out arms upon the walls." A child reared in close neighborhood to the royal palace, to Parliament and the law courts where his destiny was to unfold. Bacon it seems was born sophisticated. His is a story set in scenes of splendid color and fantastic luxury, out of which he characteristically erupts, now and again, burdened with debts, dyspepsia and incipient failure — then rises and with bounding optimism pursues his way.

Grandeur was Francis Bacon's birthright. His father owned land in six counties; from Sir Nicholas's ledger books we know that at least seventy servants attended him. Like many another gentleman employed in his time about the courts of Henry VIII and Edward VI, the Lord Keeper had grown rich on confiscated monastery properties. King Henry's break with Rome had been extremely profitable to the English gentry. If the monastery lands had not been so extensive, it is more than possible the Reformers would not have been so busy. Church lands, church monies were the base from which the gentry rose. I have said that Francis Bacon was born to grandeur, and so he was. But this is not to say that he was born to the aristocracy. Francis Bacon was a gentleman and the son of a gentleman; his father was a knight, not a peer.

It was from the gentry that Elizabeth chose her councilors of state: shrewd men who had made money in confiscated church land, or burghers who dealt in wool, leather, wine. After their names, in lieu of the word *Goodman,* they wrote the pleasing abbreviation, *Gent.,* or *Knt.,* then paid a herald to draw a pedigree, tracing their lineage back to William Conqueror, as he was called. Better at bargaining than at fighting, these men understood the value of compromise;

Elizabeth could count on them. And she knew exactly how to portion her rewards — not too much, not too little — keeping a man's loyalty on an effectual level with his self-interest. Very rarely she created a new baron, as with Francis Bacon's uncle, Lord Burghley, her first minister. Never mind if the old names, the old great families were jealous; the English Crown had had its fill of warring hereditary lords and barons. The old order was changing, in law, in government, in religion. And the impulse stemmed not from the common people or any discontented mob, but from the new professional class: lawyers, merchants, City traders who had grown rich on Tower Street, as the phrase went, or were "great men on London Bridge," where shops rose three stories high above the arches and the tide. Neither Francis Bacon nor his rival, Edward Coke, were to range themselves on the side of the commonalty, as champions of what they would have called the meaner sort. "I do not love the word People," Bacon wrote to a courtier.

Consider, then, this England of Elizabeth, where the old is being elbowed out by the new, yet where feudal customs still survive. No standing army exists, beyond the caparisoned yeomen of the Queen's guard and such liveried pikemen as are paid followers of nobles or great prelates. Nor has the Queen a navy, only a few frigates and privateersmen to harass the Spanish treasure ships. King Philip owns a fleet of fighting galleons, he has thousands of men under arms. He has offered to marry Elizabeth, to whom the thought of marriage, she says, makes her feel as if someone were tearing the heart out of her bosom.

Consider a government which pays its public servants, its first secretaries and lord treasurers and lord chancellors, a mere nominal sum, then asks them to live like princes, because to keep great state is a matter of honor, breeding respect in the multitude. London has as yet no bourse and no exchange; rich merchants are the official moneylenders. Cash is scarce and the great are forever in debt. The money they owe would ransom a prince. Day and night they lament the situation, if their letters are proof. For ready cash they pawn their jewels, borrow from the London goldsmiths or from their county neighbors, raise their rents or ask legal permission to alienate a piece of entailed woodland, groaning as if they were selling the hand from their wrist. In terms of shameless sycophancy they write wheedling letters to Francis Bacon's uncle, Lord Burghley. Or they apply to Francis's father, the Lord Keeper, beseeching his influence with the Queen, that she may grant them land lately forfeited by treason, or some small pension or place at court.

Sir Nicholas Bacon was a careful householder; his sons grew to manhood with their futures seemingly assured. In the country as in town, young Francis's surroundings were marvelously suited to his nature. Two miles from the ancient Roman town of St. Albans, in Hertfordshire, Sir Nicholas built his favorite mansion. Gorhambury House, it was called, ready for occupancy when Francis was seven years old — a sturdy manor built around a courtyard seventy feet square, with chapel, stables, brewhouse, bakehouse, millhouse, apple and root chambers and all the eminently practical equipment which made a Tudor country house self-sustaining. Each chamber was served with a pipe of water from the ponds, a mile away. And every inch of Gorhambury manor gave token that its owner was a man who loved learning and who belonged to the *togati*, the gownmen. In the hall a noble fire-

[27]

place was ornamented with a picture of Ceres introducing the sowing of grain, beneath it a legend, *Moniti Meliora:* instruction brings improvement. Sir Nicholas was deeply concerned with education, both public and private, endower of grammar schools and giver of books to libraries. *Moniti Meliora:* the motto would one day appear below the frontispiece of Francis Bacon's *Great Instauration.*

In his orchard, Sir Nicholas put up a little banqueting house, "adorned with great curiosity," says an old writer, "having the liberal arts beautifully depicted on the walls; over them the pictures of such learned men as had excelled in each." Music had its place, Rhetoric, Logic, Geometry, Grammar, Astrology — each with its rhymed couplet:

> *The motions of the starry train,*
> *And what these mean, I too explain.*
> *Regiomantus, Haly, Copernicus, Ptolemy.*

In Sir Nicholas's world, astrology was still respectable. Elizabeth herself had consulted the celebrated Dr. Dee as to the day when the planets would be most auspicious for her coronation. Even a skeptical Francis Bacon was to acknowledge that astronomy owed much to the study of planetary influence, as chemistry had its debt to the alchemists. And if Bacon was to write enchantingly of gardens, it was small wonder; Gorhambury gardens were famous.

Lady Bacon, who ruled over this household, was a woman of almost terrifying energy and strength of moral purpose, a Puritan before the word was current, and all her life a hot gospeller. (She would outlive her husband by thirty years.) When she married Sir Nicholas he was already a widower. His first wife, Jane Fernley, had brought him six children, three boys and three girls. By the time the new Gorhambury House was ready for occupancy, the boys were grown and had moved away. Of the girls we know little save that they married well and often, outlived their county knights, their judges and city recorders, and enjoyed tidy connubial inheritances, well entailed for the firstborn males. Lady Bacon gave her husband two sons: Anthony, born 1558, and Francis, younger by three years.

Lady Bacon was one of five remarkable daughters of Sir Anthony Cooke (tutor to King Edward VI). She had made herself fluent in Latin, Greek, Italian and French. When Francis was three years old, his mother translated from the Latin an important ecclesiastical tract. It was accepted by the bishops and published for general use, an extraordinary accomplishment for a woman. Sir Nicholas adored his high-spirited wife, wrote poems to her, and when he composed written prayers, included her in careful legal language. "From the bottom of my heart," he wrote, "praying and beseeching thee, O Lord, so to endue me and *A B uxor* with thy grace and favour . . ."

A B uxor: Ann Bacon, wife. Like any prudent barrister, Sir Nicholas wished to be sure the Party addressed made no mistake of person.

When Francis Bacon was perhaps ten, Sir Nicholas had portrait busts made of his wife, of Francis and of himself. They can be seen today at Gorhambury, composed of terra cotta, brightly colored, and conveying an extraordinary sense of life. Sir Nicholas is heavily bearded, the forehead deeply lined. It is a strong face, a good face, yet careworn. One recalls Sir Nicholas's ill-health, his frequent fevers, his attacks of gout and stone, the asthma that tormented him and which his sons inherited. One recalls, too, that in his last years Sir Nicholas grew extremely fat, so that it was hard for him to mount the judicial dais. In Star Chamber the lawyers would wait, before presenting their briefs, until Sir Nicholas, his chest heaving from the steps, tapped with his staff upon the floor. The Queen was fond of her Lord Keeper: when he died after twenty years in her service, Elizabeth wept. She liked to twit him about his girth. "Sir Nicholas's soul lodges well," she said.

By Sir Nicholas's side in terra cotta, his wife is bolt upright, blue eyes wide and fearless. There is a little flare to her nostrils. She is buttoned into her stiff bodice as though she thought that womankind was born buttoned up against temptation — though her mouth betrays her. Young Francis has his mother's even brows and soft mouth with upward curl of lip. There is a noticeable likeness between the two, though the son is not shown with his mother's open glance. He looks down and sideways.

But it is the boy's skull that is remarkable, the shape of the head. No other portrait will tell us half so much about Francis Bacon. In later representations the Lord Chancellor's robes, the steeple hat and grandeur obscure the face, the head, the spirit. Let us look well, then, upon this boy's wide forehead, jutting above the eyebrows. Observe the startling width from back of head to forehead; there is room for brains inside this skull case. The boy is not so much handsome as strangely attractive. Small wonder that Queen Elizabeth early took note of Francis Bacon. She was a connoisseur of males, and this was a noticeable boy. Forward to learn, they said of him; "endued with that pregnancy and towardness of wit . . . which caused him to be taken notice of by several persons of worth and place, and especially by the Queen; who delighted much then to confer with him, and to prove him with questions; unto whom he delivered himself with that gravity and maturity above his years, that her Majesty would often term him, *The Young Lord-keeper*. Being asked by the Queen *how old he was,* he answered with much discretion, being then but a boy, *That he was two years younger than her Majesty's happy reign;* with which answer the Queen was much taken."

It seemed indeed as if his father were grooming young Francis to follow in his footsteps. Gorhambury manor was situated conveniently to London, about eighteen miles to the northwest. The Queen on summer progress came four times to visit, bringing her train of courtiers, ladies in waiting, grooms, archers and the rest. To Sir Nicholas his house seemed large enough, seeing that it was taxed for "forty-one hearths." But the rooms were low, and the first time Elizabeth came she inquired at once why her Lord Keeper's house was so little. "Madam," said Sir Nicholas, "my house is not too little for me, but you have made me too big for my house." Before the Queen came again, her Lord Keeper had built a wing to Gorhambury, 128 feet long, two-storied, adorned with cloisters and statues in the Tuscan fashion, the walls and windows painted delightfully in scenes and legends from the classics.

Young Francis learned early what was due to royalty. A man might bankrupt himself to honor this Queen, yet if he pleased her there would be reward beyond the risk. The boy came to know the court at close quarters, heard the court gossip under his father's roof, knew of the corruption, the cutthroat jealousies of palace life. "There is little friendship in the world," he was to write, "and least of all between equals." A bitter lesson and no doubt learned early; this was a precocious boy. For men who won and kept Elizabeth's favor and goodwill the benefits were infinite. The youth must have been early aware that this goodwill came down to him in two-fold inheritance: from his father and from his even more influential uncle, William Cecil, Lord Burghley, with his square beard, his gout, his immense wealth and his private corps of foreign intelligencers. Burghley's great houses contained a hundred rooms or three hundred; his wife was Lady Bacon's sister, Mildred. So powerful indeed was Burghley that on the Continent they spoke of England as Cecil's Commonwealth, though the surmise was mistaken. Elizabeth ruled England, and no one knew it better than Burghley.

There was enchantment to this country scene, enchantment in Lord Burghley's house at Theobalds, fifteen miles away, so beautiful that a king would one day covet it. The knights and squires and country noblemen who in another two centuries would rule England — these were developing now a life which for pleasure, grandeur and pure delight would not be surpassed. Educated men of Bacon's day took pride that England was not founded on a society of serfs; they boasted of their "sturdy yeomen" as opposed to the starved peasantry of France. Yet beyond the orchards and garden pleasances of Gorhambury lay poverty and brutish ignorance. Toward spring the poor man's cattle died or grew gaunt until grass came again on the common pasture. Beggars walked the country roads — young men, often enough, maimed from the wars in Flanders, their cheeks branded with the name of their home parish. By the wayside, gibbets dangled their awful fruit; the traveler at night heard chains clank, and forgetting the new church dispensation, crossed himself and muttered the ancient prayers. The English law was cruel. No less than eight hundred men, women and children were hanged each year, perhaps for picking a pocket or stealing a sheep. Within the cottages that nestled against the hills, children died in droves, in dozens — of fevers, of the bloody flux, of a swelling or an infected wound. Charitable gentlemen like Sir Nicholas Bacon did what they could to feed the parish in a bad harvest year. Yet what they could do was brief, its scope narrow and personal.

To the boy Francis, however, these dark matters were remote, glimpsed but not experienced. Gorhambury was Eden; it was home, and to a boy it was surely eternal, a natural state of being which would have no end. Forever the hawks' bells would tinkle as they left the falconer's wrist. Dogs in their kennel would be forever friendly as one approached, friendly even the fierce swans on the pond that snatched bread from one's outstretched hand. Everywhere, greetings for the master's son — welcome from stablemen and grooms, from the maltster in the brewhouse, the blacksmith at the forge. Surely, this welcome was a birthright, to last forever in the world?

Boys went early to the university in those days. Francis was in his thirteenth year when his father sent him to Trinity College. But even Cambridge in its damp fens was no true departure from Eden. Bacon's position remained secure, with a father — a Cambridge graduate — who was Lord Keeper of the Seal, and an uncle, Lord Burghley, who served as Chancellor of the University. Moreover, Francis was not alone. His brother Anthony came with him, fifteen years old, lame, held back in his studies by ill-health; Anthony was asthmatic, always ill. His parents had feared he would lose his eyesight, at two Anthony had nearly died "of a fever." He was a sensitive boy, quick, generous. The two were very close; at Trinity College they roomed together. Cambridge lay only a few hours' journey from Gorhambury; the boys rode home if it was permitted. When plague came to the colleges, the brothers stayed away for six months.

There is nothing to show that Francis Bacon was outstanding at Trinity College, though the Master's records note the brothers as good students, note also frequent monies spent "for Anthony beeing sicke." What Francis gained at Cambridge would seem to have been mostly negative — and yet, as is the case with original minds, no small gain at that. Cambridge was the stronghold of the English Protestant Reformation. The Queen favored it over Oxford. Erasmus had taught there, and Elizabeth's tutor, the gentle Roger Ascham; also John Cheke, who introduced the new pronunciation of Greek. These were great men, inspired teachers. Students who came under their tutelage went away convinced, exalted with the New Learning.

But in 1573, when Francis Bacon came to the University, the old great days were past. Religious inspiration had been replaced by theological quarreling, noisy battles in the colleges over the stricter points of Calvinism. Dispute boiled between the apostles of Geneva and of Canterbury — between the followers of Calvin and adherents of the Anglican Church which Elizabeth and her Parliaments were at such pains to establish. Cambridge students were fined or whipped for coming to chapel without a surplice; tutors were spied on in their rooms, to see if a pyx or Romish symbol might be hidden. The Master of Trinity was no less a person than that preeminent divine, John Whitgift, later to be Archbishop of Canterbury.

These religious disputes were a living issue, they invaded every department of contemporary life. But Francis Bacon's interests lay elsewhere. Early and late he was impatient with theological quarreling. Here at Cambridge he found nowhere to turn his mind except to equally fruitless dispute over the words of Aristotle, as fashioned into dogma by medieval churchmen. We have Bacon's own evidence for his impatience. It was at Cambridge, he said, that he "first fell into the dislike of the philosophy of Aristotle . . . being a philosophy only strong for disputations and contentions, but barren of the production of works for the benefit of the life of man." The early church fathers, expounding Aristotle, had indicated that as a guide to truth, faith was preferable to knowledge. Hardly the motto for a Francis Bacon, to whom knowledge was three parts of faith.

This scholastic aridity, this stultified repetition of classical authority, was offered to young minds at a time when the entire western world, let alone England, was opening to discovery and fresh knowledge of heaven and earth. Not long before the brothers Bacon rode to Cambridge, a new star had appeared in Cassiopeia, shining big and bright. All over Europe, men watched each night for its appearance, an awful question mark in the sky. . . . Whence did it come and what presage? For two thousand years, the heavens had remained the same. Since the first century, old Ptolemy's ten spheres, the epicycles and eccentrics, had wheeled outward to the pure empyrean, where dwelt God with his holy hierarchy, the cherubim and seraphim.

Were God's heavens then no longer immutable? And not only heaven but earth was shifting its geography. Francis Drake sailed home, having seen the limitless Pacific. Frobisher fitted out his brave small barques, the *Gabriel* and the *Michael* — no lesser names would do. People spoke of America as today we speak of the moon, yet far more fruitfully. *"That great wind blowing from the west . . . the breath of life which blows on us from that New Continent."* The words are Francis Bacon's. Columbus, he said, had made hope reasonable.

Yet Cambridge ignored this new-found world of land as if it had no existence. In Sir Nicholas Bacon's new gallery at Gorhambury House were windows of colored glass, depicting flowers and birds and beasts from this new India: the tobacco plant, strange fishes, a savage with a baby slung in a furred hood upon her back. To young Bacon it must have been obvious that the humble artisan who painted Gorhambury windows knew more of plants and people, of their anatomies and properties, than did any Cambridge don. Maps, charts, the sextant, the magnetic needle — these, to Cambridge, were instruments for meaner men, for the mariners of Devon, or artisans who worked with their hands. So also the findings of surgeons at the London College of Physicians: this dissection of corpses was disgusting, impious, beneath the attention of gentlemen and scholars.

"It was esteemed a kind of dishonour unto learning," wrote Bacon, "to descend to inquiry or meditation upon matters mechanical." Thirty years earlier, in 1543, Copernicus had published his great work, the *De revolutionibus orbium coelestium.* Yet, a century and more would pass before plain men could believe that the earth revolved about the sun. Such notions savored of magic or conjuration, of the devil's bargain with man. Was not curiosity the sin by which Adam fell? Dr. Dee the mathematician — Queen Elizabeth's astrologer — had acquired an evil reputation at Cambridge because, in staging a Greek play, he had caused a great scarab to rise and fly across the boards, carrying a man with a basket of victuals on his back. Moreover, a maid saw a cloud of bees swarm downstairs from Dee's chambers — plainly his familiars. All his life, Dee had to defend himself from these early slanders; he wrote Mercator that he had published a book to show that he had done nothing by the help of demons, but all by methods "lawful to Xtian men."

Never to examine, never to question: thus youth was taught at Cambridge. Many in the universities, wrote Bacon, "learn nothing there but to believe." From the sea of knowledge rose the classic Pillars of Hercules, boundary beyond which man durst not venture. To those with ambition to pass the Pillars — in Bacon's phrase to sail *plus ultra* — the University offered no compass. The one tutor who might have helped young Francis on his journey was Everard Digby, who wrote treatises attempting to classify the sciences. But Digby was noisy. He told rude jokes on the master of his college, "blew an horn and halloed disrespectfully," besides which he did not always pay his bills. The University expelled him.

In March of 1576, Francis and Anthony Bacon left Cambridge without waiting to take their degrees. Next autumn the brothers were for the first time parted; Francis went abroad in the household of Sir Amias Paulet. "I was three of my young years bred with an ambassador in France," Bacon reported, later in life. And he was but fifteen, he said further, when on departing England he "first kissed her Majesty's hands as her servant." The incident held high significance; already, this youth thought himself bound to the Queen's service. Elizabeth was accustomed, Francis later wrote, to send with her ambassadors "some towardly young noblemen or gentlemen . . . as assistants or else attendants, according to the quality of the persons, who might be thereby prepared and fitted by this means for the like employment another time."

Sir Amias Paulet, the Ambassador, was a most fervent Puritan. As Lieutenant Governor of Jersey, he had been a great disposer of church bells and putter-down of *obits* — those comfortable yearly masses, commissioned by friends for the beloved dead. Moreover, Paulet had offered what was called "ostentatious" help to Huguenot refugees. Small wonder that Elizabeth was later to name Sir Amias as Mary Stuart's jailer in Scotland, and small wonder also that Mary protested the Ambassador's hostility to her agents while he was in Paris.

There is no doubt that Lady Bacon and Sir Nicholas were reassured to have their youngest son in such convinced Puritan company. Europe not seldom lured young men away to Romish practices. "Suffer not your sons to cross the Alps," Lord Burghley had written, "for they shall learn nothing there save pride, blasphemy and atheism." Nevertheless, the English gentry liked to send their sons abroad in some distinguished household; Sir Nicholas Bacon himself had lived in Paris after leaving Cambridge. England was still looked on as a country barely redeemed from barbarism, her native tongue rude, her food and wines execrable. (In Spain they said the English sucked tallow candles against the cold.)

For two and a half years, young Bacon followed the French court from Paris to Blois, Tours, Poitiers, learning the language, shedding forever any lingering provincialisms of manner, and above all, observing the ways of foreign courts, the subtleties of dealing with foreign princes. Unlike his brother Anthony, Bacon never fell in love with Europe. After this visit, he was not to cross the Channel again for the rest of his

[38]

life. Yet the mature Bacon was to be distinguished by an eclecticism, a cosmopolitanism; his philosophy, like his manner, notably far from insular.

Bacon has left few recollections of this French sojourn, and all of them anecdotal, bearing upon some observation in medicine or natural philosophy. . . . The Ambassador's wife cured him of warts on his hands — by sympathetic magic, says Bacon, something not to be scorned. Lady Paulet hung a piece of lard, skin outward, against her chamber window sill. As the fat dripped in the sun the warts went away — even that wart, wrote Bacon, which he had "so long endured, for company." In the third chapter of his *Natural History,* discussing the reflection of sound, Bacon remembers the multiple echo in a ruined chapel at Port Charenton — how, when he called out, his voice returned "thirteen several times," and how an old Parisian took it to be the work of good spirits. "For (said he) call *Satan* and the echo will not deliver back the devil's name, but will say *va t'en* [get thee hence]."

There is to these recollections a cheerful, congenial note. Young Francis was among friends, still in his Eden, affectionately cared for, moving in court and diplomatic circles, his sole responsibility to observe, to learn from books and from people. During this sojourn he was even trusted so far as to be sent home with a message for Queen Elizabeth, though he has left no details of this brief embassy.

But in the winter of 1579, fate took a turn which put a stop abruptly to this state of happy dependence upon the distinguished friends of a distinguished father. In February, when Francis was just turned eighteen, he had a dream, which he said afterwards he "told to divers English gentlemen." He thought he saw his father's house at Gorhambury "plastered all over with black mortar." Soon afterward came news that Sir Nicholas was dead. Francis crossed the Channel, going to the Queen with a dispatch from the Ambassador, then home to York House on the Thames. His father, he learned, had gone quickly, with no time to revise his will as he had planned. In his extremity Sir Nicholas had dictated a few affectionate words: "I desire my wife for all the loves that have been between us to see to the well-being of my two sons, Anthony and Francis, that are now left orphans without a father."

The three stepsons had long ago been provided for. The eldest, Nicholas, became a rich man by his father's death, with manor holdings which, together with a wife well propertied, were to make him premier baron of Suffolk County, worth £6000 a year. Nathaniel and Edward were well taken care of, Nathaniel already handsomely married to an heiress. Gorhambury manor, the Lord Keeper had left to Lady Bacon for her lifetime, with remainder to Anthony, who fell heir to other properties in Hertfordshire and Middlesex.

Only Francis was ill served. All that he inherited was a doubtful property called Woolwich Marsh, the modest manor of Marks and some leases which together brought him perhaps £300 a year. Much later, Francis said that his father had laid by a considerable sum to buy him an estate, but sudden death prevented. A man could exist modestly on £300, though hardly in the state to which Francis was accustomed. Sir Nicholas had been a prudent man; it is hard to understand this apparent slighting of his youngest and it would seem, his best-loved child. Perhaps it was due to some temporary accident of business, some looked-for occasion of bargain or sale. As we have said, cash was scarce among the landed gentry.

If Francis felt bitterness or hurt, it has not come down to

us, beyond one brief remark in middle age: "For my father, though I think I had greatest part in his love of all his children, yet in his wisdom served me as last comer." It had long been planned that on his return from Europe, Francis would attend Gray's Inn, where his father had studied law and where his stepbrothers had kept brief token residence. If Francis had possessed even a modicum of common sense, his three hundred pounds would have served him adequately. Perhaps it was not common sense he lacked but something else, that sixth sense which tells a man about money — how much he has, how much he will have next month, how much he may spend and give away.

Carefulness about money is not an endearing trait. Yet the lack of it in public men is not tolerated; with Bacon this was to prove a fatal defect — and his ruin. From first to last this man was a spender, a giver, a patron and spreader of largesse. And he assumed the position as if by right, showing helpless indignation when his creditors confronted him. . . . Why were the moneylenders impatient, and must a gentleman be thus harassed? Let the base souls wait! Money would be forthcoming, as it had been forthcoming to one's father and one's uncle, Lord Burghley. Great men, high in the Queen's service, could count on the possession of money, coaches, fine clothes, servants, country manors. . . .

Francis Bacon looked to follow in his father's footsteps, and rapidly. Had not the Queen herself expressed hopes of him? Young Francis was accustomed to men's high opinion, to their close, amused attention when he talked. Even Hilliard, the fashionable miniaturist who took Francis's likeness at eighteen, after the final sitting wrote around the frame, in Latin, "Oh, that I had a canvas to paint his mind!" Bacon moreover had already been in the Queen's employ, had delivered dispatches from her Ambassador and kissed her royal hand as her servant. To Elizabeth, Sir Amias Paulet had recommended Francis in high terms, as one "fit to do your Majesty good service."

On March 9, 1579, Sir Nicholas Bacon, Lord Keeper of the Seal, was buried grandly in Saint Paul's Church. With the throng, Francis followed the hearse from York House to the Strand, then up Fleet Street and Ludgate Hill. He said a sad farewell to his father, whom he had loved, and to York House, where he was born and which would go now to the Queen's new Lord Keeper, Sir Thomas Bromley. Anthony Bacon, with money in his pocket, sailed for Calais. Francis was alone, he had been told that he was poor. His father's chambers at Gray's Inn were an honorable refuge, worthy a gentleman's condition. This was a sanguine nature; on the whole the stars seemed propitious, the way clear.

It was well that young Bacon could not know what lay ahead. All the circumstances of his birth and upbringing, so pleasant and assured, were to avail him little. He was to find himself humiliated by poverty, slighted by men of lesser birth and lesser brains who rose above him. He was to know the ignominy of asking and being refused. "The rising unto place," he would one day write, "is laborious, and by pains men come to greater pains; and it is sometimes base, and by indignities men come to dignities. The standing is slippery, and the regress is either a downfall or at least an eclipse, which is a melancholy thing."

Eden was gone and all the joys of Eden. Like any newcomer, any alien novice, Bacon must climb the heavy stairs alone.

[42]

cৡৡe II ৡৡৡ

The Struggle to Rise
1579–1613

1

Two Conflicting Ambitions

"THERE IS IN MEN an ambition of the understanding, no less than of the will, especially in high and lofty spirits."

Bacon was nearly sixty when he wrote the words. Characteristically, the observation came from his own experience: in this man two ambitions were forever active and often at war. The ambition of the will pointed to a place in government, to power, riches, worldly reputation. Over against it the ambition of the understanding beckoned to a life of study, contemplation and intellectual discovery of the natural world. This was not the Faustian struggle of flesh against spirit, the devil against man's better nature, but a contest between entirely respectable aims, either of which Bacon felt equipped to achieve. The problem was: Should a man devote his talents to his Queen, to the government and laws of England, as Bacon's father — that eminently practical statesman — had done before him? Or should a man serve his own mind, that ambition of the understanding which Bacon early recognized as his genius — "knowing myself," he wrote, "by inward calling to be fitter to hold a book than to play a part."

Few men are presented with such a choice, because few are

[45]

thus doubly endowed. Bacon actually did follow both roads, in an almost hearbreaking alternation. When pressure of business crowded out the life of contemplation, Bacon rebuked himself. "This incessant and sabbathless pursuit of a man's fortune," he said, "leaveth not tribute which we owe to God of our time." Yet we cannot wish that Bacon had renounced the world; indeed, we cannot conceive of his renouncing it. His life was in the world. Plot, contrivance, intrigue, seeking: this was the life he knew. Without the risks taken, without the crushing delays and humiliations from those above him, without indeed the final agony of disgrace, how could this man have written *Of Adversity, Of Envy, Of Cunning, Of Revenge, Of Vicissitude of Things?*

"There is rarely any rising," said Francis Bacon, "but by a commixture of good and evil arts."

Turn back, then, to the year 1579. Francis Bacon, aged eighteen, settled into his father's old chambers at Gray's Inn, began to read law and, after the fashion of bright young men, looked for the world to move in his direction. There is no doubt that Bacon knew his capacity. This favorite son of a Lord Keeper already had been affectionately marked for notice by the Queen; he looked for a career more exalted than that of working barrister in the courts.

The chambers which young Bacon inherited were in Coney's Court, a name long since vanished with the rabbits which must have burrowed beside the walls. Gray's Inn, then as now, was situated high up in Holborn. In Bacon's time there lay behind it bare fields and hills, where a man could hunt small game or set up the butts for archery on a summer's day. The greater part of Bacon's life was to be spent in these surroundings; they were to be his home, his base for action. Star Chamber reports for years would identify him, quite simply, as "Mr. Bacon, of Gray's Inn." Here Bacon was to enlarge his chambers to a four-storied brick house and in the garden set out walks, raise a summer pavilion in memory of a fellow barrister. And from here, Bacon would at the end embark upon the coach ride that was to cause his last, fatal illness.

The four great Inns of Court stood, as they stand today, at the western limits of the City, above the Thames: Lincoln's Inn, Gray's Inn, the Middle Temple and the Inner Temple. Even in Bacon's time they were centuries old — a venerable guild to which a man, once initiated, belonged for the rest of his life. They did not teach the Roman law; that could be had at the two universities. The Inns of Court were highly practical, concerned with the common law as it was used in professional practice — the native, island law which had never been codified but which had grown, like England's unwritten constitution, from custom and long acceptance, from statute law as found in the Parliament rolls, from records of proceedings in the courts as written in the old *Year Books* or such individual case reports as existed in manuscript, and from maxim and rule as interpreted in the treatises of former judges: Glanville, Bracton, Fortescue, Fitzherbert, Sir Thomas Littleton.

In his pleasant chambers, young Bacon wore for a little time the aura of his father's reputation. But Sir Nicholas was dead, a new Lord Keeper sat in Westminster Hall, and men's memories are short. Francis, at eighteen, found himself with very little money, a mother at Gorhambury who cared more for her son's Christian piety than for his worldly advancement, an uncle who could be counted on to help, but who as Elizabeth's first minister occupied a place so exalted that to approach him was almost like approaching royalty. To be poor, young Bacon discovered, was to enter an alien, unfriendly country where one sued for favor rather than was sued. The road of the common law loomed interminable: at least eight years of study before one could plead in Westminster Hall as a barrister, perhaps sixteen years before one was named serjeant-at-law and could become a judge. True, in this England of Elizabeth, practice of the common law was by no means synonymous with the highest legal office. Until Sir Thomas More's day, the lord chancellor had usually been a churchman. Of Elizabeth's chancellors, one at least (Sir Christopher Hatton) possessed little legal training, and in Bacon's time was to acquit himself well enough.

Whether Francis Bacon expected one day to follow his father as head of Chancery, he never openly confessed. Yet he made it plain that the degree of barrister would be a means to a larger end. "I am purposed not to follow the practice of the law," he said, early in his career. "It drinketh too much time, which I have dedicated to better purpose." He would study the common law. He would master it indeed; that was a necessity. Yet he did not look on the road thereto with the loving eye of — for instance — an Edward Coke.

To a man like Edward Coke of Norfolk, life at the Inns of Court was Ultima Thule, the end of dream. Coke could not have enough of Plowden's *Reports,* of the archaism of Littleton's *Tenures,* of the old charters and *Year Books.* The common law was to be Coke's life; for himself he early set the limits of a deep and narrow channel. Coke, moreover, was a born advocate who loved to feel the courtroom floor beneath his feet; he stood before judge and jury with the light of battle

in his eye. Francis Bacon on the other hand was to prove far
less interested in the practice of law than in its theory and
philosophy, together with the problems of legal restatement
and reform. He was, in short, one of those men — they are
rare in the law — whose function it is to examine and to re-
create.

There were in England two great streams of law, pointing
toward two philosophies of government. By inclination or by
rearing a man turned to one or the other. First, the common
law, which bore the Gothic signature, claiming as its inheritance trial by jury and the "freedoms" of Anglo-Saxon parliaments (perhaps more myth than truth). The Tudor philosophy on the other hand magnified the sovereign, relied on a
strong central authority and believed in it. It was to this newer
side that Francis Bacon belonged, both by inheritance from
his father and by his own disposition. "No man can say," he
was to write, "but I am a perfect and peremptory royalist."
From first to last, Bacon showed what seemed an inborn reverence for authority and paternalism in government — the Continental idea — which contrasted strikingly with his intellectual originality and impatience where science and education
were concerned. To Bacon the sovereign's will was supreme
over law as over every department of government. "Let the
judges be lions," he was to say, "but lions under the throne."
Chancery was part of this authoritative tradition, as were the
ecclesiastical courts, which used the Roman law, and whose
practitioners or professors were called civilians, after the
Corpus Juris Civilis.

That Bacon studied the Roman law we know. And what he
learned of Roman law was to give him a broader outlook on
the English common law. To Edward Coke, the common law

was the perfection of reason; Bacon saw it as limited by medieval technicalities and accretions, rigid and slow, urgently needing the relief of equity. Of his actual studies at Gray's Inn, Bacon has left no record. We know he was impatient, that he wrote to his uncle, Lord Burghley, for help in securing some kind of governmental position which would bring him a living while he pursued his studies. For the first five years we have indeed little to go on but these letters to Burghley, sometimes setting forth Bacon's eagerness for a place, sometimes apologizing because his manner has been reported as arrogant. "I find that such persons as are of nature bashful, as myself is . . . are often to be mistaken for proud."

These youthful, suing letters do not make altogether pleasant reading. True, in Elizabeth's government there was no way for a gentleman to advance, short of influence. Yet one is impatient with the brilliant young man, waiting and watching to be carried forward by his uncle or by his uncle's son, Robert Cecil. Bacon was early admitted as barrister — before his time indeed, thereby causing grumbling and jealousy among his colleagues. The Queen's intervention had been sought in this matter; later she was to refer to it angrily: "Did I not pull him over the bar?" By the year 1584, Bacon was seen about the City in his barrister's robe, though he did not seek cases to argue and seems to have lived secluded in his chambers, refusing visitors peremptorily, reading widely in philosophy as well as in law.

It was at this time that Bacon set down notes which contained the nut and kernel of his system of philosophy — not the first immense idea to spring early from an author's brain. Later, Bacon was to refer to these notes as a "juvenile work, which with greatest confidence and a magnificent title I named

'The Greatest Birth of Time.' " . . . Time, said Francis Bacon, aged twenty-four, was not born with the Greeks and Romans, as the knowledgeable world averred. Nor had time stopped with the ending of Greece's Golden Age. It was now, today, that time had its greatest birth. The limits of man's dominion over the universe could expand now, in this most glorious reign of her Majesty, if men would but overthrow those dark idols which infest their minds, keeping out the natural light.

What Bacon envisioned was nothing less than an English Golden Age of learning, the building of a new educational and intellectual empire, founded not upon scholasticism or classical learning, not upon the interpretation and reinterpretation of old books and old philosophies, but upon a study of *things,* of the observable facts of earth and sky. It was a scientific vision which Bacon would never lose sight of, and for which he was to fight all his life. He called it an instauration of learning — a word which has become identified with him, deriving from the Latin *instaurare,* to renew, begin afresh. The over-all title of Bacon's philosophical works was to be *Instauratio Magna,* the Great Instauration.

Whenever Bacon wrote about his great instauration — and apparently when he talked of it — his mind leaped, racing ahead. In a kind of outrageous confidence he simply let his ideas flow out — an exercise which, while it delighted his intellectual friends, did not make for popularity with his more practical associates and colleagues. There was an exuberance, a flamboyance to this young man's utterances. His face worked as he talked, he flung out his hands. That this youthful confidence would later be justified is beside the point.

One thing, however, became plain: the world did not care to listen. Time was passing. Bacon's father at twenty-seven had already been well advanced in Henry VIII's government and had risen steadily through the hazardous changes of three royal regimes. Lord Burghley would not or could not help his nephew forward. It was necessary to command attention some other way, bring oneself to the public eye, before men would read or hear — and before, it seemed, a place in government would be forthcoming. In 1584, the Queen called a Parliament. With the aid of a maternal uncle (not Burghley, this time), Bacon got himself returned from a borough in Dorset. He did well enough and made himself felt, though he managed to irritate that old Parliament man, William Fleetwood, Recorder of London. Rising to speak briefly, as became a fledgling member, Bacon inadvertently mentioned his father's nearness to the Queen — though, he added hastily, this was beside the point. "Then," wrote Fleetwood crossly, in his notes, "you should have let it alone."

It was not the last time Bacon would make this mistake. Concerning his inheritance he showed a curious naïveté, which was not to fade with his youth. Francis seemed to take it for granted that people would be glad to hear about his father, the Lord Keeper, or about his own acquaintance with her Majesty. In Star Chamber a young law reporter noted in annoyance that "Bacon, of Gray's Inn, made a long oration and to no purpose, of the divine and princely regard of the Queen her sacred Majesty, with whose intent towards him he was so blessed as to be privy, and all not to the purpose."

Plainly, Francis Bacon was too bright for his buttons, too big for his boots. Those who recognized his extraordinary powers were attracted — as that beguiling cleric, Lancelot Andrewes, already Bacon's friend. Those who disliked intellectuality and mental precocity were repelled. Beyond the first

row, the House of Commons was filled with country gentlemen, knights and squires who knew more of hounds, horses
and crops than of Latin and philosophy. Even lawyers like
Coke and Lord Keeper Puckering were bluff fellows, talkers
indeed, as lawyers are, but without Bacon's high-flying specu-
lativeness. It is significant that Bacon, without shifting his
intellectual position or indeed his pride, was to adapt himself
and eventually learn — with occasional slips — how to deal
successfully with his colleagues in the House.

This skill did not come quickly. In his first Parliament,
Bacon was named to only two committees, noted by the reporter as concerning "bills of no great moment." Yet he saw
the great men of the realm at close quarters and hard at work:
Sir Francis Drake, Sir Philip Sidney, Walter Ralegh, Sir
Christopher Hatton. He saw Elizabeth's Privy Councilors, who
sat in the front row by the Speaker: Sir Thomas Knollys, Sir
Francis Hastings and the rest, men experienced and discreet,
placed by the Queen and Burghley where they would do the
Crown most good. He heard his fellow members admonished
"for using too much freedom," which meant speaking for
something the Queen would not approve. Bacon listened while
the bills were read three times, such as the bill for confirmation
of letters patent, granted *"unto Walter Rawleigh Esquire for
the Discovery of Foreign Countries"* — known to the House
more succinctly as "Mr. Rawleigh's bill."

To the ensuing Parliament of 1586, Bacon was again returned; his half-brothers, Sir Nicholas and Nathaniel, sat with
him. This time, Bacon was far busier, gratified to be named
to a committee which included, says the reporter, "all the Privy
Councilors of the House." Once or twice Bacon made committee reports himself, and spoke briefly.

Francis Bacon was twenty-five. For him these Parliaments of the 1580's, meeting briefly and seldom, were rather a school and training place than any real step in wordly advancement. Elizabeth never called a Parliament unless she needed money — the tax or subsidy which the Commons alone could grant. Tudor sovereigns tried to be tactful with their Parliaments. But as Francis Bacon well knew, the actual government of England lay in the hands of the Queen, of Lord Burghley and the twenty or more members of Elizabeth's Privy Council. In Elizabeth's eyes, Parliament's function was merely to take instruction from above, pass such bills as her Council suggested, vote heartily for the subsidies as indicated, receive the sovereign's gracious thanks from the throne — and go home. Elizabeth and Burghley contrived to administer this England of four million inhabitants as they would have administered a vast country estate, carefully, paternally, frugally. Government was still conceived of as a form of property, to be looked after benevolently. "Consent of the governed" was a phrase far in the future.

Yet in these early Parliaments, Bacon learned the problems of his country firsthand, as he could have learned them nowhere else. Free speech as we know it did not exist. Important questions such as the Queen's possible marriage, her eventual successor: these were *magnalia regni,* great matters of state. To broach them openly was to risk royal displeasure. Bacon saw members sent to the Tower for overstepping the mark. Elizabeth would listen to petitions, to letters; she would lend her ear by way of grace and favor, never by way of the people's "rights."

Yet the Commons talked, indoors and out, groping to defend their privileges as they saw them. In the 1580's, problems of religion were uppermost — and as so often in history, religion had become synonymous with politics, both domestic and foreign. Beyond a narrow Channel the Catholic monarchies pressed close, ambitious to place a Catholic sovereign on the throne of England. In Scotland, Mary Stuart plotted, connived with France, with Spain, with the Catholic earls of northern England. The common peril gave the Lower House courage to speak out, make its wishes known. Bacon sat on committees to consider the Queen's safety, heard demands for the death of Mary Stuart, a lady whom the Commons referred to as "this great enemy of our felicity." In 1587, Bacon shared the general Protestant relief when the head of that reckless and passionate queen fell under the executioner's axe at Fotheringay. Two years later, Bacon stood on Fleet Street to watch Queen Elizabeth pass in triumphal procession under Temple Bar, celebrating the defeat of the Spanish Armada.

The great Armada was beaten, yet who knew but Spain might bring a second fleet? King Philip had by no means abandoned his plans for a holy war against Protestant England. *The Enterprise,* he called it. England must raise money for warships and armies. In '89, Elizabeth called another Parliament; Bacon sat as citizen from Liverpool. (This, incidentally, was Edward Coke's first session.) The country was divided in religion, and a country divided is an easy prey for enemies abroad. The Pope's excommunication of Elizabeth in 1570 had caused a tragic division in the loyalties of English Catholics, magnified now by the Spanish threat. Laws must be passed to curb these doubtful subjects. Laws were needed also to control the rising tide of nonconformists, who rebelled against Elizabeth's Established Church — persons "which named themselves Reformers," wrote a Secretary of State, "and we commonly call Puritans."

All during the 1580's, Bacon's pen was busy in these matters. He wrote frequently and well on state policy toward religion, arguing an easing of the tension. When only twenty-four he had addressed to Queen Elizabeth a most sensible letter urging some mitigation in the severity of her Oath of Allegiance, ruinous to Roman Catholics, who could not take the oath without forswearing their religion. On the other hand, the oath *ex officio,* as used in ecclesiastical courts, drove Puritans to despair. "Swearing men to blanks and generalities," wrote Bacon, "is a thing captious and strainable." That pseudonymous clever writer Martin Marprelate, with his followers, conducted a fierce pamphlet war, during which Anglican bishops pursued Puritan pamphleteers even to the gallows' foot. Would it not be wiser, Bacon urged, to show "an indifferent hand? . . . For it ever falleth out that the forbidden writing is thought to be certain sparks of a truth that fly up in the faces of those that seek to choke it and tread it out; whereas a book authorized is thought to be but as *temporis voces,* the language of the time."

To the end, Bacon would hold to this middle way. Elizabeth, too, pursued the middle way in religion. Yet she loathed Puritans. She would not, she told Parliament, "tolerate this new-fangledness." Looking back, we know that Bacon's advice, for all its youthfulness, was wise: Protestant dissension, fanned by royal suppression, was to attain the disastrous proportions of civil war. The Queen, however, would listen to no parliamentary advice concerning religion; it had been reckless of Bacon to attempt it. "Till I think you think otherwise, I am bold to think it," he finished, in a not too successful attempt at sweetening bold words.

Bacon's Puritan mother threw herself heartily into these controversies, writing long letters to her brother-in-law, Lord Burghley, on behalf of nonconformist preachers, or traveling down from Gorhambury to attend sermons at Gray's Inn. Meanwhile, Francis's older brother, Anthony, had fallen in love with Europe and would not come home, though the Queen refused to extend his foreign license. This long absence puzzled Francis, who "marvelled," he wrote, "how those that keep abroad could live to their contentment; home life is to be thought upon as of the end in due season." Anthony, actually, had developed into a skilled intelligencer whose dispatches were valued by Lord Burghley and Secretary of State Walsingham. The Queen herself expressed satisfaction that Lord Burghley had "so good a man to receive letters by." Anthony's care and diligence, she said, "showed whose son he was." Anthony made friends in Europe, knew the Catholic spies, was on close terms with Protestant leaders, visited Henry of Navarre, met Montaigne, and in Geneva became so intimate with the celebrated Protestant theologian Theodore Beza that Beza was moved to dedicate his *Meditations* to Lady Bacon. At Montauban, the redoubtable Madame du Plessis pressed hard for a marriage between Anthony and her daughter; Anthony fled to Bordeaux.

Intelligence work was expensive. A frugal Elizabeth allowed her gentlemen agents to spend their own money in the cause. Anthony was forever in need of funds; he even borrowed money from Henry of Navarre. Yet policy forbade writing home to say for whom these large payments, forwarded from his mother or Francis, were intended. Lady Bacon, apprehensive, was persuaded to sell jewels to supply her son. Francis obtained power of attorney and arranged a sale or lien of his brother's land, informing Anthony that their mother "through passion and grief can scant endure to intermeddle in any [of] your business." Plainly, Lady Bacon feared that Anthony was veering toward Rome.

Anthony had been away a full eleven years before he returned to England in 1592, lamer than ever, plagued with gout, too exhausted by his journey to pay his respects to the Queen (an oversight which later may have cost him dear), and bringing with him foreign secretaries and followers, whose presence drove his mother frantic. "French cattle," Lady Bacon called them; nothing agitated her like a papist. At Gorhambury, she turned violently on one of Anthony's messengers and sent him packing back to London.

The brothers Bacon, now in their thirties, set up housekeeping together at Gray's Inn, Anthony continuing his foreign correspondence, laborious and difficult, proof of which may be seen in the sixteen large folios of manuscript letters preserved at Lambeth Library. All this news and intelligence went to Lord Burghley, who quietly appropriated it and got credit from the Queen — later a source of bitterness to Anthony, who complained that his uncle "hath inned my whole harvest into his barn." To her sons, Lady Bacon sent messengers from Gorhambury, bearing admonitory letters, anxious, shrewd, most of them addressed to Anthony. Lambeth Library has some eighty-seven of these, written every which way on the page, full of life, earthy, plain-spoken and tumbled all through with Latin and Greek phrases.*

* I have here condensed several of Lady Bacon's letters, though regretfully. They are worthy of full inclusion.

[58]

"Gratia et salus!" Lady Bacon begins. . . . "Procure rest in convenient time. It helpeth much to digestion. I verily think your brother's [Francis's] weak stomach to digest hath been much caused and confirmed by untimely going to bed and then musing *nescio quid* [I know not what] when he should sleep, and then in consequence by late rising and long lying in bed, whereby his men are made slothful and himself continueth sickly. The Lord our heavenly father heal and bless you both as his sons in Christ Jesu."

Lady Bacon fired off her heavy guns, followed by admonitions that the brothers keep her letters in confidence. She wished, she said, that Francis's cook were more Christian in behavior. "Let not your men drink wine this hot weather. My sons haste not to hearken to their mother's good counsel in time to prevent. Be not speedy of speech nor talk suddenly, but where discretion requireth, and that soberly then. Courtesy is necessary, but too common familiarity in talking and words is very unprofitable and not without hurt-taking, *ut nunc sunt tempora* [the times being as they are]. Remember you have no father. Use prayer twice in a day. Your brother [Francis] is too negligent therein. Be not overruled still by subtle and hurtful hangers-on."

Lady Bacon was no fool. But she sent her words upwind. As well advise these sons to turn parson as to caution them against impulsive speech. As for the quality of their friends, the brothers did not suffer fools gladly. Anthony's associates in Europe had been persons of brains and reputation. Francis would always choose as friends men of intellect, yet who wore their learning lightly, and who, as companions, were entertaining, diverting. In his *Apophthegms* he treasured the bright sayings of such colleagues as the attorney "Mr. Bettenham"

— of whom we know next to nothing save it was to his memory that Bacon erected the little summer house in Gray's Inn gardens.

There is no doubt the brothers liked to laugh. Bacon's *Apophthegms* have a story about Anthony, who one morning rebuked his man Prentise for not waking him sooner. But it was very early day, protested Prentise. "Nay," said Anthony; "the rooks have been up these two hours." "Sir," replied Prentise, "the rooks are but new up. That was some sick rook that could not sleep."

The stories are slight, but they bring the brothers before us. Lady Bacon, however, was unhappy. In their friendships, in their choice of gentlemen servants and secretaries, her sons did not make the proper distinction between piety and suspected papacy. At these chambers was too much merriment and too little prayer. Also the brothers were extravagant, forever seeking ways to raise loans or sell off bits of property. Lady Bacon laid this to their friends and followers. "Filthy wasteful knaves!" she stormed. "Welshmen who swarm ill-favouredly, sinful proud villains, cormorant seducers and instruments of Satan!" Her anger was directed particularly at one Henry Percy. "That bloody Percy," she wrote, "whom [Francis] keepeth, yea as a coach companion and bed companion, a proud profane fellow whose being about him I verily fear the Lord doth mislike."

Elizabethans were rough talkers; the Queen herself swore, on occasion, like a guardsman. As for beds, they were luxuries scarcely anyone had to himself. The sixteenth century took its family, its servants, friends or even strangers to bed for warmth or convenience. What upset that staunch Puritan, Lady Bacon, I think, was not so much her son's taking somebody to bed with him as the fact that his bedfellow was a papist. Anyone with the prestigious surname of Percy was almost certain to be Roman Catholic.

It has become the fashion among historians to declare outright that Bacon was a homosexual. Proof is scanty. There exists no damning letter from Bacon to a man or from a man to Bacon, though among his papers one finds documents both indiscreet and self-revelatory. The written evidence consists of sly hints in the letters of contemporary gossip writers, or such broad talkers as the wonderful John Aubrey and that angry Puritan diarist, Simonds D'Ewes, who hated everything that Bacon stood for and declared him guilty of vices stupendous and great — a phrase that Puritan pens enjoyed.

Aristocratic society was lenient toward homosexuality, perhaps it always has been. One's sexual *mores* were not questioned so long as one did not trouble the peace with a scandal. Bacon's friends were men, and though he married he had little to say of women. A wife and children were the hostages one gave to fortune; women interfered with study, contemplation and the serious business of life. Quite obviously, Bacon could get along without women and preferred other company. It is tempting to interpret his character in terms of homosexuality, yet in such matters there can be no valid generalization. Bacon's nervous sensibility, his tendency to yield under pressure, his instability and about-turns, his naïve expectation that the milk would forever flow, the money be forthcoming and himself be cared for by some intervening hand — all this as much characterizes early parental indulgence as homosexuality. Bacon was thoroughly sophisticated and showed himself careless, even reckless in his friendships, as with that professed Roman Catholic, the beguiling and witty Tobie Matthew. Some of these early friends, Bacon retained through life. His last will and testament gives a hundred pounds to "Mr. Henry Percy" — surely the man to whom Bacon's mother so strongly objected.

My own view is that by the time Bacon was in his middle thirties he had become almost as indifferent to sex as he was passionate about natural philosophy and his personal ambition to get ahead in the world. "A man is but what he knoweth," he wrote at thirty-one. "Are not the pleasures of the intellect greater than the pleasures of the affections? Is not knowledge a true and only natural pleasure, whereof there is no satiety?"

Sometime in the year 1592, Francis Bacon introduced his brother Anthony to Robert Devereux, second Earl of Essex, Queen Elizabeth's handsome young favorite. We do not know the occasion. But we know the three were instantly congenial, and that with all three it was to be a fateful friendship. Here was a nobleman destined to die for treason on the headsman's block, a man whose ambition outran the possible, and who in the end would try to force the Queen herself to his bidding. The story has been often told: How, in 1599, Elizabeth sent the Earl to Ireland as general of her forces to subdue the rebel Tyrone. How Essex, jealous of courtiers who rose to power in his absence, rushed home without permission, leaving his army in the field — in itself an offense worthy of court-martial. How Elizabeth at first forgave and then punished Essex, taking away the principal sources of his income and keeping him in confinement until the Earl became almost deranged in his fury and self-pity. . . . And how at the end, with three hundred followers Essex stormed through London, trying to raise the City to his banner—was captured, imprisoned, tried in Westminster Hall and executed.

All this was to take eight years in the doing. But in 1592, when Francis Bacon first knew him, the Earl at twenty-six appeared as a dashing, openhanded, friendly young nobleman. Essex moreover possessed strong intellectual leanings and was therefore well equipped to appreciate the brothers Bacon, and to use them in his service should they be so inclined. The position of royal favorite consumed a man's full time; it was a business, a career. To combat the intrigues and jealousies of court life, a favorite needed friends, followers, adherents—what amounted to a faction. In the 1590's, it was to be the Essex faction against the Cecils: the young martial Earl against Lord Burghley and his son, Robert Cecil the clever hunchback, already chosen by Elizabeth as her Secretary of State. Cautious men and balanced, these Cecils, desiring peace for England where Essex desired war. Around the Cecils' shield a motto read, *Prudens qui patiens*.

It was now that the brothers Bacon were presented with a most serious choice. To make a career in government without a patron, without belonging to one group or the other, was out of the question. It must be the Cecils or Essex. It could not be both, though now in the early 1590's the factions were not yet openly aligned. Francis's parliamentary activity had made his name known, had brought him prestige in certain circles. But it had earned him no money. Nor had Bacon's writings been of financial help. Like Pantagruel, he "was naturally subject to a kind of disease which at that time they called lack of money." For some twelve years, Francis had applied in vain to his uncle Burghley to help him forward.

Anthony too had a grudge in Lord Burghley's assuming credit for Anthony's work in foreign intelligence. When opportunity came, therefore, Anthony did not hesitate but became Essex's man for better or for worse, never to leave him. Anthony's European correspondence and all his carefully gleaned news henceforward flowed to the Earl's advantage, not to Burghley's.

But Francis Bacon was not content to attach himself thus to any man. With Anthony the case was simpler; it sufficed to be known as "the Earl's under-secretary for state affairs." Francis's ambition was more complex; he looked upon the Earl's service as a step on the way, a means to an end. Francis moreover was cautious. From the beginning he saw shallows, weaknesses in this young nobleman's character. Beautiful, spoiled, impulsive, Essex might rise very high. But was he not in equal danger of failing, through impatience, recklessness, a strong tendency to sulk when thwarted even in trifles? Bacon took note of these signs and portents. Before committing himself altogether he made a last effort to gain Lord Burghley's help and patronage, not only toward his worldly career but toward the philosophical schemes that he had cherished for so long.

In the year 1592, therefore, Bacon wrote his uncle a letter, extraordinary in its naïve expectation that Burghley would be persuaded, and in the lighthearted arrogance of its grand intellectual plans. Yet Bacon's words bear the stamp of sincerity. Moreover he knew his uncle too well to attempt blandishment.

"My Lord," the letter begins. . . . "I wax now somewhat ancient; one and thirty years is a great deal of sand in the hour-glass. I ever bare in mind to serve her Majesty, not as a man born under Sol, that loveth honour, nor under Jupiter, that loveth business (for the contemplative planet carrieth me away wholly). I confess that I have as vast contemplative ends as I have moderate civil ends, for I have taken all knowledge to be my province."

All knowledge to be his province. Ironically, time has proven that Bacon was not boasting but spoke the simple truth. His letter carries inference that these matters had already been discussed, and that Lord Burghley was familiar with his nephew's interest in natural philosophy. In the past eight years, Bacon's ideas had crystallized concerning the "great instauration," that new intellectual empire which he had early envisioned. What Bacon desired now — and the ambition would never leave him — was to found a school or university, altogether different in aim and execution from any university in the world. Here the things of earth would not be despised but cultivated. Here would be workshops, equipped with engines and contrivances. Here would be collections of stones, plants, animals for dissection. Here men would use their hands to find out and interpret the mysteries of nature. Medicine would be studied, astronomy, the motions of the tides; heat and cold in all their properties. Students here would not look backward to Aristotle and the church fathers for authority. They would not concern themselves with the intricacies of formal logic but with flesh, blood, stone, grass; with fishes, beasts, soil, bones. And they would pursue these studies without fear or shame — shame lest a gentleman dirty his hands with delving into earth, fear lest God punish the proud mind that dared inquire into his mysteries of creation.

It was, actually, a scheme essentially practical. And it stemmed from a man whose intellectual speculations bore always the stamp of the scientific mind, revolving round the possible, the feasible, around things that could be proven, verified by experiment. Francis Bacon was no esthete or exquisite, though it is true he had not the common touch. It is to be remembered that he was country bred. He knew crops, cattle, falconry, game, when to plant a field and when to leave it fallow. . . . His plan and *schema,* he wrote Lord Burghley now, was already so fixed in his mind that it could not be removed. Its fulfillment would require "the commandment of more wits than of a man's own." It needed funds, the authority and patronage of someone high in office. "And if your lordship will not carry me on," finished Bacon, frankly, then the only course would be to sell what remained of a small inheritance and retire to the country, to solitary study and the writing of a book.

Nothing came of this letter, and small wonder. To Queen Elizabeth's careworn, prudent minister of state, his nephew's plans must have seemed speculative altogether, the high-flown illusions of a feverish intellect. (Their practicality would await two generations before being proven.) Bacon's letter did not so much as mention the law, though he had now been thirteen years at the Inns of Court. Why would the Queen desire to give Francis Bacon a place, and if so, what place? Her Majesty had no sympathy with speculative schemes. She was interested in the Established Church, the established learning, the maintenance, defense and enrichment of her commonwealth. To Lord Burghley's experienced eye, Francis Bacon possessed neither the face and figure of a palace favorite — a courtier — nor the legal skills necessary for a judgeship, nor the financial acumen and responsibility requisite to an administrative position. Bacon at thirty-one was spare, quick, of middle height and decently proportioned figure. But he lacked the courtier's dash and style; his forehead already bore the scholar's marks. His manners were marred by overeagerness and, if his notebooks are to be believed, a tendency to stutter when excited. The hazel eye, neither green nor brown, had a darting quality. People noted that in conversation Bacon looked upward, away from the person addressed — the habit of one to whom ideas are more interesting than persons. None could deny his brilliance. Yet this was hardly a man to whom Lord Burghley would be drawn in understanding and unqualified acceptance.

2

Bacon and Essex

I T WAS NOW, when his uncle again refused him, that Bacon
turned in earnest to the Earl of Essex's service — not with
his affection and first loyalty, as Anthony did, but with the
power of his mind and all his restless energy. The Earl's business, Bacon said later, was "in a sort my vocation. I did nothing
but devise and ruminate with myself . . . of any thing that
might concern his Lordship's honour, fortune or service."
Bacon lent a hand at anything and everything — wrote letters
of advice to the Earl's young cousins at the University, signed
in Essex's name. Let these youths take care to read original
works, not be content with abridgments and epitomes! "They
that only study abridgments, like men that would visit all
places, pass through every place in such post as they have no
time to observe as they go or make profit of their travel. The
epitome of every book is but a short narrative of that which
the book itself doth discourse at large." For the Queen's entertainment, Essex staged pageants at vast expense; Bacon composed speeches and discourses to be recited by the various allegorical figures. "Mr. Bacon in Praise of Knowledge," one of
them is endorsed.

Essex was named a member of the Queen's Privy Council and turned quickly to Bacon for advice. "Send me your conceit as soon as you can," the Earl wrote. Bacon knew Parliament: the Lords, the Commons, the Bishops, the factions. He knew policy at home and abroad. And though concerning his own affairs Bacon frequently showed himself quite blind to expediency and his own best interests, he had the faculty of standing off to give brilliant, sound advice to others. Essex, genuinely grateful, desired to do something in return. Early in 1593, the office of Queen's Attorney fell vacant. The Earl determined to have the place for Bacon, though everybody knew the obvious candidate was Edward Coke, already Solicitor General, forty-one years old to Bacon's thirty-two, with a record of fifteen years' practical experience in the courts — a man who had come up through the ranks, after the nature of attorneys general. Yet such was the young Earl's confidence in the Queen's fondness and in his own powers of persuasion that he launched his campaign with high-hearted confidence, staking his reputation as well as Bacon's on the outcome.

For Francis Bacon it was an alluring prospect. The place of Attorney General was an honorable one and powerful, besides which it was lucrative, not so much in salary as in fees and what the age called "perquisites." Yet at the outset Bacon did something to mar if not to ruin his chances. In the Parliament of 1593, Bacon had been returned from the key county of Middlesex, which included Westminster and the law courts. Anthony Bacon, too, sat in this Parliament; Edward Coke was Speaker of the House. Francis Bacon's name appeared on the most important committees, he was chosen delegate when the Commons wished to confer with the Lords — always a delicate business. But when the matter of the tax vote came up,

Bacon rose to his feet and challenged the triple subsidy which Lord Treasurer Burghley had asked in the Queen's name. The sum was too large, said Bacon, and the collection period too short. "The poor man's rent is such as they are not able to yield it. The gentlemen must sell their plate and the farmers their brass pots ere this will be paid. As for us, we are here to search the wounds of the realm and not to skin them over; wherefore we are not to persuade ourselves of their wealth more than it is. The danger is . . . other princes hereafter will look for the like; so we shall put an ill precedent upon ourselves and to our posterity."

It was rash, a gesture as impolitic as it was honest. Bacon had spoken out, said what he thought. Others were of like mind. "The House well approving Mr. Bacon's opinion," wrote the reporter. Yet others had not expressed themselves so freely, nor were others in line for an appointment from the Queen. Francis Bacon, all unbeknownst, had given a mortal wound to his chances. Edward Coke, far more independent by nature, would never have made so blatant a mistake. Sir Nicholas Bacon's son, Lord Treasurer Burghley's nephew, had stood up and opposed her Majesty's plans and the plans of her Lord Treasurer. Already, in this Parliament, three members had gone to the Tower for defying the royal will.

Elizabeth was outraged. In the King her father's time, she said, "a less offense than that would have made a man be banished his presence forever." Bacon, who since boyhood had enjoyed the precious privilege of access to the Queen, now was forbidden her presence. He was surprised, bewildered. Later, it was generally agreed that had Bacon apologized, had he prostrated himself and acknowledged his fault, he might quickly have recovered her Majesty's favor. But he did not apologize. "I spake simply and only to satisfy my conscience," he wrote to Burghley: and to Essex, "I am not so simple but I know the common beaten way to please . . . it may be her Majesty hath discouraged as good a heart as ever looked towards her service."

The common beaten way to please this Queen was total obedience, combined with superior intelligence and preferably — but not inevitably — a pleasing physical presence. From now on, Bacon would study the way to please. If he failed to achieve it under one monarch, under another he was to master it. And if, observing him, we could wish that his eventual rise had come by some nobler, less circuitous route, let us remember that a man's actions cannot be judged by the circumstances of any century but his own. "There is no rising," Bacon wrote, "save by a commixture of good and evil."

The Earl of Essex, however, was troubled by no such subtleties, nor daunted by this first catastrophe. Characteristically, he belittled the Queen's displeasure and went ahead with his suit: not Edward Coke but Francis Bacon must be Attorney General. There was an element of fantasy in the Earl's persistence, in his arrogant self-confidence. As the story progresses we see him on his knees, suing the Queen on Bacon's behalf. We see the Queen's irritation at this insistence, her coy permission for further interviews. Essex on his knees was no unappealing sight. The matter became public gossip; bets were laid on the winner. Bacon was too young for the post, Elizabeth protested, upon which Essex declared that between Bacon and Coke "was such a difference in the worthiness of the persons as, if Mr. Coke's head and beard were grown grey with age it would not counterpoise his other disadvantages." The Queen in reply acknowledged that Bacon had "a great wit and an excellent gift of speech and much other good learning. But in law she rather thought that he could make show to the uttermost of his knowledge than that he was deep."

Actually, the most serious count against Bacon was that he had never had a legal client nor argued a case in court; "never yet entered into the place of battle," his opponents said. That this was a matter of Bacon's own choice did not help the situation. In January of 1594, Bacon made a move to overcome the obstacle, arguing his first case with an éclat which caused his uncle Burghley to send congratulations and ask for notes of his pleading to show the Queen. On the fifth of February, Bacon argued another case in King's Bench. Four days later he appeared again, this time before a whole bevy of judges, including the Barons of the Exchequer. A barrister of Gray's Inn wrote to Anthony Bacon about it, declaring that Francis had won extraordinary attention from his audience, and that his argument had been a *bataille serrée*, as hard to lay open as to conquer. Some of his sentences, it was true, were difficult to grasp; he had "spangled his speech with unusual words. . . . All is as well as words can make it," finished the young reporter. "And if it please her Majesty to add deeds, the *Bacon* may be too hard for the *Cook*."

Two months later, Elizabeth granted the Attorneyship to Edward Coke. Bacon had waited sixteen months for the place. When news of his defeat came, he fell ill with the dyspepsia which was always to visit him in adversity — or for that matter, in sudden prosperity. "No man ever received a more exquisite disgrace," he said. But he rallied, and some time in Easter term — before June of 1594 — appeared in a celebrated lawsuit known as *Chudleigh's Case*. Coke, who argued on the same side, gives the pleadings and the judges' arguments in the first volume of his *Reports*. The case concerned inheritance and that famous, much disputed enactment of Henry VIII's reign: the *Statute of Uses*. Bacon was fluent, and this time wholly the professional attorney, citing the *Year Books* with as much ease as Coke, and, it seems, with more accuracy. Meanwhile, Coke's promotion to Attorney General had left open the second place of Solicitor General. Essex, undaunted by his first defeat, now went hotfoot after the position for Bacon. The Queen showed herself more favorably inclined. Bacon, she said, "began to frame very well." She saw "an amends in certain little supposed errors."

Again the months went by, and a second year of waiting. Creditors who had lent money on expectation of Bacon's acquiring a post, began to press and threaten. The Queen told Essex that if he did not cease his importunity, she would search the whole realm for a Solicitor, rather than take Francis Bacon. "Though the Earl showed great affection," wrote Lady Bacon, "he marred all with violent courses. God help my poor sons. Francis hath been tossed *inter spem curamque* [between hope and anxiety] to oppose another manner of man, and he reviling. My sons feel the want of a father now in their ripe age."

Francis lost his head, wrote angrily to his cousin, Mr. Secretary Cecil, and accused him of having been bought by another candidate "for two thousand angels." He wrote angrily also to Lord Keeper Puckering, who filed his letter under the endorsement, *"Mr. Bacon wronging me."* Anthony Bacon laid his brother's failure at Lord Burghley's door. "The old fox crouches and whines," said Anthony. To his friend Fulke Greville, Francis wrote, "I have a hard condition. . . . Her Majesty had by set speech more than once assured me of her intention to call me to her service. Whatsoever service I do to her Majesty, it shall be thought but . . . lime-twigs and fetches to place myself, and so I shall have envy, not thanks. This is a course to quench all good spirits and to corrupt man's nature; which will, I fear, much hurt her Majesty's service in the end. I have been like a piece of stuff bespoken in the shop, like a child following a bird, which when he is nearest flieth away, and lighteth a little before, and then the child after it again, and so *in infinitum,* I am weary of it, and also of wearying my good friends."

For some twenty-eight months, Bacon had been kept dangling. In October of 1595, the matter was decided. Elizabeth passed over Bacon and named as her Solicitor General one Serjeant Fleming, slow, reliable, the perfect second in command. Never, under the patronage of Essex, would Francis Bacon win place or position. Yet he continued the Earl's friend and counselor, and a few years later, ill-advisedly and quite lightheartedly made a third effort to rise by Essex's influence — this time with a rich wife in view. Having failed to win a fortune *in genere politico,* he would attempt one, Bacon wrote, *in genere oeconomico.* Young Lady Hatton, née Cecil, was Burghley's granddaughter, Sir Robert Cecil's niece — rich, beautiful and much courted. Bacon asked Essex to intervene with the lady's parents on his behalf, as suitor for her hand.

The Earl complied. His appeals to the lady's parents were charming and genuine in praise of his friend. But a rival loomed, no less a man than, again, Edward Coke, whose manner was countrified but whose fortune was established and on the rise. Lady Hatton (or her parents) chose Coke. She was twenty, Coke forty-six, a widower with eight children. So surprised were Londonders at the match that one of them exclaimed, "The world will not believe that it was without a mystery." The wedding was hasty, so hasty that Coke was called to account for it by the Archbishop. From a scurrilous joke that went the rounds, the "mystery" hinted that the bride was already with child.

It was at about this time that Essex conceived the ambition to go to Ireland as Deputy General of forces to subdue the rebel Tyrone. Bacon urged strongly against it. Let the Earl not compete with his rivals at court for this dubious martial glory. Nobody could conquer the wild Irish in their bogs and woods. Did not his lordship recall how it had been with the Romans, when they tried to subdue the ancient Britons and the Germans? Her Majesty was already irked at the Earl's popularity, and the increasing numbers of his followers. His absence in Ireland, said Bacon, would "exulcerate the Queen's mind." But Essex, avid for glory, though temperamentally unfit to be the commander of large forces, made a triumphant departure from London with eighteen thousand men, cheered and admired by the people. Even Shakespeare acclaimed him, this conqueror who was expected to "bring rebellion broachèd on his sword."

Six months later, after an entirely futile campaign, the Earl made a sudden return home — against the Queen's command — then sulked ostentatiously under the royal anger. Bacon pleaded with him to yield, swallow his pride. Give in, give in! — said Bacon, in effect: has any man gained aught by defiance of her Majesty? But Essex was beyond heeding. He had turned away; he would follow no advice that led to moderation. "I remember," wrote Bacon, later, "my lord was willing to hear me, but spake very few words and shaked his head sometimes, as if he thought I was in the wrong — but sure I am he did just contrary. . . ."

At some time in these proceedings, Elizabeth took Francis Bacon back into favor. It is to be doubted if her Majesty forgave his part in the Parliament of 1593; this was not a forgiving Queen. Bacon was never to receive from her any position beyond the nominal one of Queen's Counsel Extraordinary. Elizabeth knew of Bacon's intimacy with Essex, knew that for some six years Bacon had been the Earl's close adviser. Grieved as she was and angered over Essex's behavior, the Queen talked with Bacon; he has left on record conversations where he pleaded for Essex. Let her Majesty take the Earl back, put a white staff in his hand to be her Majesty's companion in the palace, "if she meant not to employ his lordship again in Ireland. . . . Her Majesty," Bacon recorded, "interrupted me with great passion: Essex! (said she); whenever I send Essex back again into Ireland I will marry you. Claim it of me!"

It was typical of Elizabeth; the bluntness of it and the intimacy of expression no doubt bedazzled Francis Bacon. Glorious, to enjoy again the privilege of old friendship — for a man her Majesty had known since childhood and whose father had been her faithful servant! Elizabeth gave Bacon the reversion of an office in Star Chamber, worth £2000 a year. (It would be twelve years before he could claim it.) She accepted his New Year's gifts with grace and even had herself rowed across the Thames at Twickenham to take dinner in Bacon's little villa, which had been a present from Essex.

The Queen's favor was very sweet. The Thames at Twickenham is narrow; Richmond Palace with its red turrets and high windows rose enchantingly on the far bank. All of Bacon's conversations with Elizabeth seem to have concerned the Earl. By argument and by art, Bacon endeavored to soften the royal anger and mistrust, even addressing to the Queen a sonnet "tending and alluding," he said, "to draw on her Majesty's reconcilement to my Lord . . . though I profess not to be a poet . . . and this was but a toy." But the Queen's anger grew. She determined to summon Essex before the court of Star Chamber — a severe and ruinous procedure against any man. Bacon dissuaded her, arguing that the Earl's popularity was great; the people might be swayed by sight of him to discredit the truth. Elizabeth compromised with the more lenient proceeding of a hearing at York House (Bacon's old home), before Lord Chancellor Ellesmere and various of the Privy Council. She commanded Bacon to take part — but a small part, concerning nothing more than a "seditious pamphlet," which had lately been dedicated to Essex. Every state trial made much of so-called treasonable books; this one concerned the deposing of Richard II. The Queen had already mentioned the volume in irritation, asking Bacon if he saw treason in it? "Madam," Bacon had replied, "punish the author not for treason but for felony. He hath stolen most of his sentences from Tacitus."

At York House the Earl played a moving role, falling on his knees and weeping contrite tears until half the room wept with him. London saw its darling as the victim of court intrigue. Among the intrigants Bacon (with Robert Cecil) received first mention. Threatening letters came; Bacon's friends feared violence. The Queen, torn between love and prudence, let Essex go free, but denied him access to her presence.

The Earl, distraught and moody, turned to his close followers, the men who lived in his house. From now on it would seem that Bacon saw little of the Earl. On a disastrous February Sunday, Essex staged his crazy, futile rebellion in the streets of London. Whatever he did or did not intend on his ill-timed venture, it was treason. The Earl's "last fatal impatience," Bacon called it. Does a nobleman try to force his way, armed, into the royal presence merely, as Essex declared, to plead humbly what he had earlier pled in vain? In the trial at Westminster Hall, Attorney General Coke led the prosecution, blustering, powerful, and according to some accounts, confused as to both evidence and presentation.

With the rest of the Queen's Counsel, Bacon sat on a bench, listening — then got suddenly to his feet and addressed the Earl direct, as he stood in the prisoner's box. Whether Bacon had planned the move, we do not know. Criminal trials at best were haphazard in procedure. (Chief Justice Popham rose from his place to testify that Essex had locked him in the library before starting his run into London.) It is possible that Bacon stood up simply on impulse. To his marrow he believed Essex guilty, a threat to the Queen and to England. The Earl's attempt, the Earl's ambitions violated Bacon's deep-seated conviction of the loyalty due to monarchy and to the person of the sovereign.

How, Bacon demanded now, could his lordship stand here in self-defense, who should be standing in confession? The Earl had sworn that his Sunday foray was attempted solely "against private enemies." Lived there in history, Bacon asked, an evildoer who had not a reason for what he did? Cain, that first murderer, had had his excuse, as also Pisistratus, who gashed himself and ran through Athens, calling on the citizens to defend him. My lord protested that he came unarmed into the City, in doublet and hose. . . . And how came the Duke of Guise to the barricadoes, but in doublet and hose, with only eight gentlemen to keep him company. *Yet what had Guise intended?* The end and aim was treason.

The Earl stood restless under this barrage. Mr. Bacon, he said in reply, had pretended to be his friend and to grieve at his misfortunes. A strange alteration! Essex spoke from the box. "I call forth," he said, "Mr. Bacon against Mr. Bacon."

For his part in the Essex affair, Francis Bacon has been both damned and defended. If it be true that love alters not when it alteration finds, then Bacon was guilty as a false friend, when he rose in court against the Earl. Yet in the nine years Bacon had known him, Essex had indeed altered. From an appealing, spirited youth he had become an embittered courtier, dangerous in defeat, seeking restitution where he could find it. It is hard to know if Bacon had ever felt deeply for Essex, as his brother Anthony indubitably felt. My own judgment is that Francis had entered into this relationship with practiced calculation and stayed in it long after the cause was hopeless. "I never meant," he said, "to enthral myself to my Lord of Essex nor to any other man, more than stood with the public good."

Before the Earl died, he made public confession — declared his punishment to be just and himself the "vilest unthankfullest traitor." One by one he named friends and accomplices, not excluding his sister, the beautiful Penelope Rich, who he said had urged him on. One cannot love the Earl, one feels indeed small sympathy with him. Yet we could wish that Bacon had not appeared in court that day, against his former benefactor. Had the Queen commanded it? Bacon has not told us. Essex never understood the greatness of Elizabeth, as did Bacon, who four years after her death was to write in her praise the eloquent tribute called *In Felicem Memoriam Elizabethae.* "I do yet bear an extreme zeal to the memory of my old mistress Elizabeth," Bacon wrote elsewhere, "to whom I was rather bound for her trust than for her favour." Essex thought to put fear into Elizabeth's heart, make her give in, give up, yield to his superior masculine force and charm. In his folly the Earl looked to use this Queen for his ends, as Bacon in his turn had hoped to use Essex. That both men were mistaken does not diminish the drama of the long occasion.

So sober a judge as Bacon's contemporary Thomas Fuller the historian had this to say: Sir Francis was "favorite to a favorite, I mean the Earl of Essex, and more true to him than the Earl was to himself; for, finding him to prefer destructive before displeasing counsel, Sir Francis fairly forsook not his person (whom his pity attended to the grave) but practices; and herein was not the worse friend for being the better subject."

As the years passed, Bacon would say and publish much in his own defense concerning this affair. Yet whatever the case, whatever Bacon told himself and others, there must have lingered in his breast that cry from the prisoner's box — the voice of a onetime friend who thought himself betrayed:

"I call forth Mr. Bacon against Mr. Bacon."

3

Bacon Begins to Write

G REAT WRITERS ARE NOT BORN, like Aphrodite from the sea, rising full-splendored to daylight. Invariably there is the period of apprenticeship, if one cares to trace it out. By the time Bacon was thirty-five, he had exercised his pen in political pamphlets, reports of state treasons composed at the Queen's request, arguments concerning church controversies, and masks or pageants composed for Elizabeth's entertainment.

But, like many a writer before or since, Bacon began his serious authorship with a notebook. The world is fortunate to have it; certainly Bacon did not intend it for print. The first page is dated December 5, 1594, at the start of the Christmas vacation, when Bacon, with place and preferment slipping from his grasp, had told his friends he was neither "much in appetite or much in hope." Francis lived alone now, in his chambers at Gray's Inn; his brother Anthony had moved to lodgings eastward in the City, at Bishopsgate. (Lady Bacon protested angrily because a theater was nearby.) With his penchant for elaborate titles, Bacon called his notebook *Promus of Formularies and Elegancies* — formulary being the current fancy version of the word formula, and *promus* the slave who in Roman times dispensed supplies from the household storeroom.

In this *Promus of Elegancies,* Bacon set down phrases, words, tricks of speech — whatever might prove useful not only in writing but in conversation. It is wonderful to read these exercises, with their simplicity, their workaday air. One page is filled with morning and evening salutations: "Good night, good soir, good matins. . . . Good day to me and good morrow to you. . . . I pray God your early rising does you no hurt. . . . Up early and never the nearer. . . . There is a law against liers-abed." A second sheet has phrases to help speed an argument: "Now you say somewhat. . . . Answer me shortly. . . . The matter goeth so slowly forward that I have almost forgotten it myself, so as I marvel not if my friends forget."

The phrases and quips are not remarkable for brilliance, though occasionally they make us smile. "I have known the time, and it was not half an hour ago. . . . Hear me out, for you never were in," writes Bacon. The marvel is the pains the man took, the plainness of his notations and experiments, his meticulous care of words.

"Believe it," he writes, and underneath:

"Believe it not."

"Value me not the less because I am yours."

"As I did not seek to win your thanks, so your courteous acceptation deserveth mine."

One imagines the accompanying bow, easy, elegant, learned perhaps in France. Did Bacon practice these phrases, alone in his room? It is not too fanciful to think that he did. In the *Promus,* no phrase is too brief for Bacon's attention. He rings changes, tries out the words. The exercises are interspersed with phrases descriptive of character, perhaps of lawyers in

court, or Parliament men in the House of Commons. Mixed
with all this are quotations from Bacon's reading, stirred in
his memory and thrown down at random, correctly, incor-
rectly, with no authors given. (Most of the quotations will be
met later, in the *Advancement of Learning* or the *Novum Organum*.) It is hard to tell what is Bacon's and what belongs
to Ovid, Seneca, Horace, Virgil. There is much from Erasmus,
from the Gospels, the Psalms and Proverbs. A group of lines
from the Latin poets speak for themselves, and eloquently for
Bacon:

"Here Phaeton lies buried, who drove his father's chariot.
Though he failed, he fell in deeds of great daring."

"It is good to advance some distance, even though it is not
granted a man to go farther."

"Though I am slight, yet I attempt great themes."

"The poet's prayer: 'Grant me a smooth course, give assent
to my bold undertaking.' "

It is easy to see why Bacon included these; no man has em-
braced vaster projects nor been more often rebuffed. Suddenly,
in the midst of Latin excerpts, we come upon brief, homely
observations in English, jotted perhaps while Bacon walked
through the woods at Gorhambury: "Wild thyme in the
ground hath a scent like a cypress chest. . . . Where harts
cast their horns . . . Few dead birds are found."

It was a custom of the day for readers to copy out, in their
commonplace books, whatever pleased them in other men's
works. Often enough these diligent copyists neglected to cite
the author's name and ended by simply appropriating what
they found. One cannot look on it as plagiarism with Bacon,
because somehow he transformed the material; he called this
the hatching out of other men's creations. "I am glad to do the

[83]

part of a good househen," he wrote, "which without any strangeness will sit upon pheasants' eggs." In the *Promus of Elegancies,* certain lines, whether they come from Herodotus or Aesop, have become pure Francis Bacon:

"Why hath not God sent you my mind, or me your means?"
"Better be envied than pitied."
"Many kiss the child for the nurse's sake."
"The cat knows whose lips she licks."
"Always let losers have their words."

Some of Bacon's phrases are hard to understand. Did other Elizabethans use words like *assentatorily?* If they did, I have not seen it. Did they speak of "the ways and ambages of God"? Had Bacon's confreres his habit of "making words sequacious," as he put it; that is, "teaching words to follow ideas, instead of making ideas wait upon words"? To indicate that a man wrote obliquely, cunningly, would anyone but Francis Bacon describe "the more subtile forms of sophisms with their illaqueations and redargutions"? Lady Bacon at times was irritated by her son's high-flown language. Writing to Anthony, she once enclosed a letter of Francis's, with the comment, "Construe the interpretation. I do not understand his enigmatical folded writing."

Very likely, Bacon did not want his mother to understand; he could be a master of innuendo when he chose. Several phrases of the *Promus* recall sharply the personal ordeal that Bacon had gone through in his suit for Attorney General. "He that never clomb never fell," he says. We wonder also if Bacon was thinking of Lord Essex when he wrote elsewhere, "Certainly it is the nature of extreme self-lovers, as they will set an house on fire, and it were but to roast their eggs." In the

Promus, Bacon set down many self-warnings: "Speech may now and then breed smart in the flesh but keeping it in goeth to the bone." Only the indiscreet find it necessary to excuse or discipline their discretion. "In all kinds of speech," wrote Bacon, "either pleasant, grave, severe or ordinary, it is convenient to speak leisurely, and rather drawingly than hastily, because hasty speech . . . drives a man either to a non-plus or to un-seemly stammering." Making faces, moving the head and hand while speaking — this, said Bacon, "sheweth a fantastical, light and fickle operation of the spirit."

In 1586, Bacon had written out the first of his projects — and there were to be many — for reforming the laws of England. He had seen delay and even miscarriage of justice, due to a con-fusion of laws. He had served on parliamentary committees to compose new statutes, he knew the dangers of unskillful draft-ing. In the Parliament of 1593, Bacon announced his desire to see the entire body of English law recast. The native law was in a state of chaos. What Maitland has called the heroic age of English legal scholarship would soon begin, launched by the great antiquaries, the collectors and expositors of manuscripts — Cotton, Bodley, Camden, Spelman, Selden, D'Ewes and the rest. Now in the 1590's, however, lawyers must depend upon old classic treatises written half a century ago and more: Stam-ford's *Pleas of the Crown,* Fitzherbert and Rastell on *Terms of the Law.* The ancient *Year Books* had ceased in 1535; reports of current cases were scarce and unreliable. Edward Coke's *Reports* were not yet in print, his *Institutes* were a full genera-tion in the future. Richard Tottell the printer had done yeo-man service in putting out new editions of old law dictionaries,

Novae Narrationes and *Pleas of the Crown:* in the counties, a new justice of the peace could find handy treatises on procedure.

Yet the body of legal literature was shockingly limited. A man must dig eternally for what he wanted, and when he found it he was not sure if it were still authoritative. Bacon's first attempt at a restatement was modest enough — a little book called *Maxims of the Law,* dedicated to Elizabeth, who in private and in Parliament had expressed approval of some kind of legal reform. Bacon set out twenty-five legal maxims in Latin, with a commentary on each, written in the hideous jargon known as law French, obligatory in Tudor courtrooms. A legal maxim is not a specific dictate but, rather, a helpful generalization, almost a legal proverb. The best known of Bacon's twenty-five is Number 5: "*Necessitas inducit privilegium quoad jura privata.* Necessity gives a privilege with reference to private rights." This is usually illustrated in the classic case of shipwrecked men on a raft, who refuse to take a third man aboard or push him off, because his weight will sink them. As late as 1884 the maxim was cited in court by Lord Coleridge.

Bacon in his reading had collected three hundred of these maxims. But he thought it better, his preface said, to begin by publishing only a few, that readers might give him the benefit of advice for future ventures. "For it is great reason that that which is intended to the profit of others should be guided by the conceits of others." It was very characteristic. Late and early, Bacon liked to put up trial balloons, looking for approbation and correction before proceeding further. It was his wish, he here declared, to abate somewhat that uncertainty for which the English law was justly challenged. Therefore he had

[86]

broken down these rules and maxims into "a clear and per-
spicuous exposition," illustrated by actual cases which "open
their sense and use and limit them with distinctions . . . sometimes showing the reasons above whereupon they depend, and
the affinity they have with other rules. . . . So that," finished
Bacon, "you have here a work without any glory of affected
novelty, or of method, or of language, or of quotations and au-
thorities, dedicated only to use, and submitted only to the censure of the learned, and chiefly of time."

The little book of maxims, later translated by Bacon from
law French to English, was not published until after his death.
But in manuscript it circulated widely and at once among
lawyers, its influence plain in the works of such contemporary
writers as Attorney General Noye and the Judges Doddridge
and Finch. *Maxims of the Law* can be seen today on the shelves
of research libraries, a thin volume that fits pleasantly to the
hand and invites the layman, its margins scribbled by the pens
of busy barrister owners, long ago. The preface and dedicatory
letter set out larger plans for law reform — a project with a
range as wide as Bacon's instauration of philosophy, and one
which he would work at and urge for the rest of his life.

Early in the year 1597, there appeared on a bookstall in
Chancery Lane — at the sign of the Black Bear — a very small
volume entitled *Essays,* which sold for twenty pence. "Essays"
was a new word. Montaigne had used it in France. Bacon's
book was so slight that he stuffed it out with a piece called
"Sacred Meditations," and another called "Colours of Good
and Evil," both of which are now deservedly forgotten. But
the *Essays* are not forgotten. The first, entitled "Of Studies,"
among reading people today is a household word. "Reading

maketh a full man," wrote Bacon; "conference a ready man, and writing an exact man. Some books are to be tasted, others to be swallowed, and some few to be chewed and digested."

Bacon wrote his essays in aphorisms — each separate thought expressed in a few brief sentences, set off by a printer's mark. It is a form difficult to achieve, requiring, as Bacon used it, almost unbounded imagination, cruelly disciplined by precision of utterance. The aphorism lends itself to sententious moralizing; in Bacon's day the form was popular and, if surviving Elizabethan endeavors are a criterion, usually a disaster. In his *Maxims of the Law,* Bacon had already tried his hand; he said he liked the form. "This delivering of knowledge in distinct and disjointed aphorisms," he wrote, "doth leave the wit of man more free to turn and toss."

Bacon's first essays were to be followed by a second, enlarged edition in 1612, and a third edition in 1625, containing fifty-eight pieces. The early essays have not the magnificence and beauty of the later essays on death, on truth, on revenge, on gardens. But the 1597 *Essays* are sharp with a wit that shocks and wakens. They caught the fancy of Bacon's contemporaries. "They come home to men's business and bosums," Bacon said later. The little book was dedicated to Anthony, in words affectionate and simple, with no trace of the hard cynicism of the text.

> LOVING AND BELOVED BROTHER [Bacon wrote], I do now like some that have an orchard ill neighbored, that gather their fruit before it is ripe, to prevent stealing. These fragments of my conceits . . . will be like the new half-pence, which though the silver were good, yet the pieces were small. . . . I have preferred them to you that are next myself, Dedicating them, such as they are, to our love, in the depth

whereof (I assure you) I sometimes wish your infirmities translated upon myself, that her Majesty mought have the service of so active and able a mind, and I mought be with excuse confined to these contemplations and studies for which I am fittest. . . .

From my chamber at Gray's Inn, this 30. of January. 1597.

Your entire Loving brother,

FRANCIS BACON

The little book did nothing, unfortunately, to ease its author's finances. In the autumn of 1598, Bacon was arrested in the street for debt. Mr. Simpson the goldsmith laid a hand on Bacon's shoulder and demanded three hundred pounds, with interest accrued at the customary ten per cent. Bacon sent frantic calls to his relatives and friends in high places. This Simpson, he said indignantly, would have had him in prison, had not Sheriff More (with whom Bacon had lately dined) "gently recommended me to an handsome house in Coleman Street, where I am." In financial crises, Bacon invariably looked upon himself as guiltless and on his creditors as vultures, persons lacking the finer feelings due to a gentleman and a son of a Lord Keeper of the Seal. It is wonderful to see the self-deception of this mighty mind where money was concerned. Financial embarrassment was never, never Bacon's fault. Rather, he laid it to the crude manners of a Mr. Simpson, or attributed his misfortune to "the strange slipping and incertain or cunning dealing of a man in the City." Bacon screamed for help and was rescued. Always, somebody came forward, oftenest it was Robert Cecil.

As the sixteenth century drew to a close, the rivalry between Bacon and Edward Coke flared up anew. It had been evident in the Essex trial, when Bacon did not hesitate to impugn the legal methods and procedure of the Attorney General. Coke, roaring ahead with his usual ferocity, had permitted his own handsome rhetoric to lead him astray from the point at issue. "I have never yet seen . . . so many digressions," Bacon told the court, "and such delivering of evidence by fractions. . . ." It was not the first time Bacon had criticized the Attorney General's methods. There was about this blunt strong Norfolkman something Francis Bacon could not endure. And the feeling was mutual. Whether the two met as rivals for place and position or whether they competed for a lady's hand in marriage — always, Edward Coke emerged the winner. His star shone forever on the rise, in his lap the prizes showered.

In the year 1601, Coke married off his daughter Anne to a rich and distinguished knight. The ceremony took place at Burghley House in Covent Garden, the mansion of Sir Robert Cecil's older brother, the Earl of Exeter. The Queen herself planned a visit to Coke's country house at Stoke Poges in Buckinghamshire. To honor the occasion, Mr. Attorney was prepared to present her Majesty with jewels "to the value of over £1000." At New Year's, Bacon had given the Queen a handsome petticoat of white satin, "fair embroidered," says the official listing, "with feathers and billets, snakes and fruitage." (Bacon's father, too, had given the Queen a satin embroidered petticoat.) But petticoats are one thing and jewels another. This Edward Coke, plain son of a plain country squire, had climbed to wealth and high position while Francis Bacon, son of a Lord Keeper, remained a mere Queen's Counsel, holding his place by courtesy. "Unsworn," the word was.

It was scarcely to be endured. In the eyes of Francis Bacon, Coke's success was as sand and salt, a perpetual irritation. One morning the two came to open conflict in Exchequer Court. Just what they quarreled about is hard to determine, but their words were loud and the bar was crowded. "Mr. Bacon!" said Coke. "If you have any tooth against me, pluck it out, for it will do you more hurt than all the teeth in your head will do you good."

"Mr. Attorney!" retorted Bacon. "I respect you, I fear you not, and the less you speak of your greatness, the more I will think of it."

The spectators must have been enthralled. "I think scorn," Coke went on, "to stand upon terms of greatness towards you, who are less than little, less than the least."

"Mr. Attorney!" said Bacon. "Do not depress me so far. For I have been your better and may be so again, when it please the Queen."

There was more, after which Bacon went home and wrote Sir Robert Cecil a detailed report, word for word. Mr. Attorney, reported Bacon, spoke "as if he had been born Attorney General. In the end he bade me not meddle with the Queen's business but with mine own, and that I was unsworn, &c. Then he said it were good to clap a *capias utlagatum* upon my back. To which I only said he could not, and that he was at fault, for he hunted upon an old scent."

By the *capias utlagatum* (writ of outlawry), Coke no doubt referred to Bacon's arrest for debt three years ago. In rage and humiliation, Bacon sent off his letter to Cecil, then wrote to Coke direct. What he said was inadvisable from start to finish — the kind of letter a man should keep overnight and throw in the wastebasket. The words fell helter-skelter on the page, revealing bitter, naked humiliation:

[91]

Mr. Attorney,

I thought best, once for all, to let you know in plainness
what I find of you, and what you shall find of me. You take
to yourself a liberty to disgrace and disable my law, my experience, my discretion. . . . You are great and therefore
have the more enviers, which would be glad to have you paid
at another's cost. Since the time I missed the Solicitor's place
(the rather I think by your means) I cannot expect that you
and I shall ever serve as Attorney and Solicitor together. . . .
And if you had not been shortsighted in your own fortune
(as I think) you might have had more use of me.

But that tide is passed. I write not this to show my friends
what a brave letter I have written to Mr. Attorney; I have
none of those humours. But that I have written is to a
good end, that is to the more decent carriage of my mistress' service, and to our particular better understanding one
of another. This letter, if it shall be answered by you in deed
and not in word, I suppose it will not be worse for us both.
Else it is but a few lines lost, which for a much smaller matter I would have adventured. So this being but to yourself, I
for myself rest.

If Coke replied, the letter is lost. He seems to have taken a
pose of lofty indifference. Firmly entrenched with the Cecils
and Elizabeth, Coke had no need for self-assertion. Up and
down the corridors of Westminster Hall strode Mr. Attorney
General, winning cases, buying up land and manors until he
would soon be so rich a king would envy him. Bacon, at about
this time, was called to be Double Reader at Gray's Inn — a
necessary preliminary to higher rank in the law. It is significant
that for his six lectures Bacon chose the same subject Edward
Coke had used when Double Reader at the Inner Temple:

namely, the *Statute of Uses.* Upon this famous law of 1535, *Chudleigh's Case* had depended, in which, incidentally, Bacon had criticized Coke's interpretation of the statute, openly before the judges. Now, at Gray's Inn, Bacon had his chance again. Of the six lectures, about fifty printed pages remain; they leave no doubt that Bacon had mastered his subject. We read of legal history and current usage, problems of dower and courtesy, of discontinuance, contingent remainders and all the complexities of inheritance at the common law.

Yet amid this jungle of legality and ancient lore, the style of Francis Bacon is unmistakable. He refuses to be sententious. One hears the light voice and quick delivery, one sees the hands move, the shoulders raised; one waits for solemnity and it does not come. "I have chosen," Bacon begins, "to read upon the Statute of Uses, made 27 Henry VIII, Chapter 10, a law whereupon the inheritances of this realm are tossed at this day as upon a sea, in such sort that it is hard to say which bark will sink and which will get to the haven: that is to say, what assurances will stand good and what will not."

In these lectures it would seem that Bacon's simplicity of utterance was intentional. He confessed his plan to revive the ancient manner of reading, which was, he says, "of less ostentation and more fruit than the manner lately accustomed." There is not much doubt this particular shaft was aimed at Edward Coke, whose manner in the law was inevitably ostentatious, and it may be said, enormously successful. People liked Coke's rolling Latin, his ponderous repetitions and authoritative air. To aim at Coke was hazardous. "When you shoot at a king you must kill him" — and Coke had a talent for survival.

Yet in these lectures, Bacon acquitted himself brilliantly. In our own time that encyclopedic authority, Professor W. S. Holdsworth, has said these readings earned for Francis Bacon a place "beside those few great teachers who have appeared at infrequent intervals in the history of English law — beside men like Blackstone and Maitland."

The century was ended, the reign of Elizabeth was nearly done. When she died in 1603 she would have ruled England for nearly forty-five years. Her great minister, Lord Burghley, died before her; Francis Bacon walked in his uncle's funeral. Anthony Bacon died, at forty-two. Strangely, we have no record, no word even, of Bacon's grief at his brother's death. We know the event only through a gentleman's casual correspondence, which with businesslike brevity gives out that Anthony had died "so far in debt I think his brother is little the better by him." We do not know where Anthony is buried. We know only that in the spring of 1601, Anthony Bacon took his departure, with his lameness, his loyalty and some quality that won men's love.

1603, and Francis Bacon was forty-two years old. Since 1579 he had waited for preferment at the Queen's hands, had looked for it, sued for it, heard his name on men's lips as candidate and as loser. He had aged; in his face the lines were noticeable above and below the darting brilliant eyes. There had been enough, surely, to age him. He had lost his brother, he had been part of great political events. He had seen his patron, Essex, condemned to the scaffold and had heard what men said of Francis Bacon's part in that condemnation. Old Lady Bacon, his mother, still lived, frantic with age, pious as ever, viewing with alarm, keeping up the estate of Gorhambury as best she could — with, we gather, lucid intervals and dark lapsed times when she remembered only the far past and did not know her son. Seven years of life remained to Lady Bacon, but we shall hear no more of her.

Francis was frequently ill with colds, "rheums," light fevers, dyspepsia. He had the temperament for slight bodily ailments and quick recovery, together with a steady cheerfulness concerning his indispositions. (Perhaps illness gave him privacy to read, to study and fill out his notes.) He lived much at Twickenham. His half-brother's estate lay next to his, eighty-seven acres of woodland, field and riverbank. Elizabeth had granted the lease of it to Edward Bacon in 1574, no doubt from gratitude to Edward's father, Sir Nicholas; the reversion of the lease she had given to Francis. The records are vague concerning the house at Twickenham. They tell us it lay near a small lake and that it was sufficiently large, with a central portico and wings of red brick, faced with stone. Bacon had his herb garden, where he could experiment with seeding and growth; along the river he planted alders to strengthen the bank. "Twitnam Park," he spelled it when he wrote.

In his career to date, Bacon had had little but disappointment, except in Parliament. He possessed a scholar's knowledge of the law, and some small practice in the courts. His name was known in government circles — not, as formerly, on his father's account but on his own. His personal ambition still burned hot, but it did not consume and waste him, though it well might have. When ambition of the will failed, Bacon turned to study, contemplation, natural philosophy, the "ambition of the understanding," wherefrom he derived fresh fuel to his fire and to his torch a brighter light.

Elizabeth the Queen had only a few weeks to live. Francis Bacon's long struggle was nearly ended. With the advent of a new monarch, before too long Bacon's star, like Edward Coke's, would be on the rise.

The Ambition of the Understanding

O N MARCH 24, 1603, Queen Elizabeth died. Sir Robert Cecil rode through London with his heralds, proclaiming the new ruler: "James the First, King of England, Scotland, France and Ireland, Defender of the Faith. . . ." Early in April, James left Holyrood, riding south in triumphal progress to claim his kingdom. England looked for nothing but felicity from this new reign. Few saw the true signs and portents. Here was a king pious, good-natured, who loved hunting and hawking, who grieved more for the death of a hound than of a man. Here was a king who shuddered at the sight of a naked sword. There would be peace in England while James I reigned — peace and a growing corruption under this talkative ruler, so helpless in the face of advancing circumstance and whom, as time advanced, Europe would learn to speak of as *La Reine Jacquette,* successor to *Le Roi Elizabeth.*

James rode southward in the pleasant fitful weather. Bells pealed, songs were sung, presents showered. In crowds, Elizabeth's courtiers rushed northward to meet the monarch. It was a kind of springtime sport, wrote Bacon — "this continual posting by men of good quality towards the King." The prospect was radiant. After forty-five years, to have a king upon the throne of England, and in the very prime of life! So great was the general hope and pleasure that men overlooked the unkingly appearance, a tongue too large, lips that slobbered, the strong, almost comic Scotch accent, the rolling walk and weak legs. Even Roman Catholics were hopeful. Was not this King born of Catholic parents? And his young wife, the blond Danish princess, had she not shown a leaning toward Rome? Surely, James would sanction a toleration in religion! It was said he had already promised it to the Catholic family of Howard, which had suffered much for the sake of the royal mother, Queen Mary Stuart.

To Francis Bacon it seemed the royal advent would soon mend his fortunes. "With what wonderful still and calm this wheel is turned round!" he wrote. King James was bookish, even learned, a sovereign who might well wish to support a grand instauration of knowledge, a college of experiment in natural philosophy and the mechanic arts — and who might well appreciate the mind that had envisioned it. Among the courtiers who rode north to meet the King was Bacon's close friend Tobie Matthew, son of an Archbishop. In joy and confidence for the future, Bacon wrote to Tobie: "The canvassing world is gone and the deserving world is come. And withal I find myself as one awaked out of sleep, which I have not been this long time."

Bacon spoke too soon. James's policy, his choice of state advisers had already been suggested by knowledgeable English minds, long before he set out from Holyrood. Robert Cecil, as well as the powerful Catholic Earl of Northampton — and the Earl of Essex — had begun their campaign while Elizabeth was still alive. It had been clever, successful, accomplished by secret correspondence with James in Scotland. Now in this hopeful springtime Essex was dead but his name was still evocative; among the rival factions it counted heavily. James believed that Essex had desired nothing so much as to help him to the English throne. To James, Essex remained "the unfortunate Earl, my martyr."

Sir Walter Ralegh had been no friend to Essex. Because of it, Ralegh was already doomed. Francis Bacon too had not been Essex's friend; Bacon moreover had appeared against the Earl in court. And Bacon must have suspected that though his defection from Essex had won him a Queen's favor, there was a possibility it might lose him a King's. His brother Anthony, however, had been one of the Earl's most faithful followers, loyal to the end; there were those who said that Anthony died of grief because of Essex's execution. Anthony moreover had been vitally useful in the secret correspondence between Essex and James.

Approaching his Majesty now in 1603, Francis Bacon did not hesitate to use his brother's name. The Earl of Northumberland had been Anthony's friend; so had two of James's Scottish emissaries, by name Foulis and Bruce. All three were in the King's train, riding down from Scotland. Bacon asked their good offices with James, reminded them of Anthony's services and of their mutual friendships. "My good brother deceased . . . the constant amity and mutual good offices which passed between your Lordship and my good brother deceased." To the King direct, Bacon recommended himself in like terms. "There might perhaps have come [to your Majesty] some small breath of the good memory of my father . . . but also of

the infinite devotion and incessant endeavours (beyond the
strength of his body and the nature of the times) which appeared in my good brother towards your Majesty's service."

It was indeed a springtime sport, this trying what luck a man
might make for himself with the new monarch. Bacon even
went so far as to write an open letter to Essex's old friend and
adherent, Lord Mountjoy, newly created Earl of Devonshire
and Lord Lieutenant of Ireland. The letter was entitled *Apology in certain imputations concerning the Earl of Essex:* it
was published in book form and set out for sale in St. Paul's
Churchyard. Though we have no record of what men thought
of it, we know the little book was bought and read, because
next year it was reissued.

King James made knights by the dozen, to celebrate his English homecoming — eleven dozen on that May day when first
he entered London. Lord Keeper Sir Thomas Egerton, Bacon's friend, became Lord Chancellor Baron Ellesmere. Sir
Robert Cecil was created Baron Cecil of Essendon and left the
House of Commons forever. (Soon Cecil would be made a viscount, then an earl.) Bacon wrote Cecil that he could be content
to have "this almost prostituted title of knighthood," and have
it without charge. Others had to pay. Bacon's funds as usual
were low, he had been arrested a second time for debt. He
desired knighthood, said Bacon, both because of "the late disgrace" and because he had three new knights in his mess at
Gray's Inn commons. Also, he had thoughts of marrying. "I
have found out an Alderman's daughter, an handsome maiden
to my liking." He could wish the honor of knighthood to come
with some privacy and particularity, "not merely gregarious in
a troop," he said. "I desire to meddle as little as I can in the

King's causes. . . . For as for any ambition I do assure your Honour mine is quenched. . . . In the Queen's my excellent Mistress's time the *quorum* was small. Her service was a kind of freehold, and it was a more solemn time. . . . My ambition now I shall only put upon my pen."

On July 23, Bacon received his title at the palace of Whitehall, lost in a crowd of three hundred claimants. His rival, Attorney General Coke, had been knighted three months earlier as one of only six, and, it was said, "graced by the King with much favor." Like Bacon, Coke had begged the honor from Mr. Secretary Cecil, and like Bacon, Coke had declared himself to be without ambition. "I thank God," he wrote, "I am not ambitious. . . . P.S. When you read this letter it is fit for the fire."

Behold, then, the two most ambitious men in England, marching toward their destiny at this outset of a new century and a new reign: Mr. Attorney General resolute, strong, arrogant; Sir Francis with a mind brilliant but as yet essentially unproved, at forty-two without place or position in the government and lacking the money to maintain an independently respectable position. Along with the knighthood, James had granted to Bacon a pension of sixty pounds a year; it was understood this was in Anthony's honor. With the pension came a patent as King's Counsel Extraordinary — a very small sop to a man's pride, yet Bacon's first step forward. He had served Elizabeth without patent, a source of real chagrin. (Edward Coke had taunted him about it openly in Exchequer Court.) The egregious Mr. Mill, whose Clerkship in Star Chamber was worth £2000 a year, must die eventually. Long ago, Elizabeth had promised the place to Bacon.

Yet while Coke remained Attorney General, Bacon knew that he could never serve as Solicitor; as well harness two leopards in a team. Should the King call on him for any state service Bacon would be ready; moreover there would doubtless be a place for him in James's Parliament. Yet the moment revealed no prospect of rising in the law courts. Once more the ambition of the will must be kept reined, kept under; once again Francis Bacon must curb himself to wait. Beyond the will's ambition, men of lofty spirit, he had said, possessed a second ambition — of the understanding. Bacon turned to it and gave it free rein, set himself down to work on his philosophy, that scheme for men's education which had been in his mind so long. Planning now in earnest and committing his plans to paper, Bacon called this first book the *Advancement of Learning*. It would be politic to dedicate the volume to King James, in hope of that learned monarch's help and patronage.

Bacon wrote out a preliminary brief statement, which bore a characteristically grandiose title: "The Interpretation of Nature, or the Kingdom of Man." (Sir Francis was never one to underrate his theme.) Nature, to Bacon, was man's true kingdom, neglected for centuries by churchmen who looked for a kingdom in heaven, or by scholiasts who despised the world about them and the evidence of their senses. Yet in order to attain this new kingdom of nature, men must draw fresh maps of exploration. "Those who aspire not to guess and divine," wrote Bacon, "but to discover and to know . . . who propose to examine and dissect the nature of this very world itself, to go to facts themselves for everything."

In the twentieth century, this is no revolutionary thought. We are used to dissecting nature; our technological age is ruled by such activities, some think to extreme degree. But in the year 1604, men were far from used to it. True, there had been scientists at work, technicians far more skillful than Bacon: in

Italy, Galileo and Clavius; Tycho Brahe in Denmark, Kepler in Germany, Vieta in Paris, Stevinus in the Netherlands. In London, Thomas Gresham had founded his college of the mechanic arts; William Gilbert already had published his work on the magnet; Dr. Harvey was beginning his investigation of the properties and motions of the blood. In some countries men risked prison or death for their discoveries; even in England they were discredited. (When Dr. Harvey announced that the heart was a pump which caused blood to flow and ebb, he was derided and his physician's practice fell off to nothing.)

The very word *innovation* was suspect; it smacked of vainglory, of overboldness in scholarship, of bad taste. Yet what Francis Bacon called for was the apogee of newness and boldness. Break free from the universities! he cried. Break free even from the fetters of religion! The earth is God's creation; to examine it is not impious. Must man then pretend to ignorance, pretend to an innocence long since forfeited? Bacon asked Job's question: "Will you lie to God as one man will do for another, to gratify him?"

The *Advancement of Learning* was to be a call and summons to this new feast of knowledge. Later, a plan of practice could be laid out, which Bacon saw in two parts: the first, to be called *Experientia Literata,* would proceed methodically from one experiment to another — experiments of heat, of light and motion, study of the winds, tides and stars, of man's physical and emotional properties and their effect one upon the other. The second part, the *Interpretation of Nature,* would arrive, by experiment, at axioms or general principles, and thence to new experiments.

As a working program it was far too vast. Even had Bacon commanded the help of a college or three colleges, a lifetime would have not been enough. Yet Bacon's genius lay in the proposition itself, and in his supreme felicity of expression. For the most part he recognized this, though at times he lost himself in detail and nearly despaired. "If any one call on me for *works,* and that presently," he wrote, "I tell him frankly, without any imposture at all, that for me — a man not old, of weak health, my hands full of civil business, entering without guide or light upon an argument of all others the most obscure — I hold it enough to have constructed the machine, though I may not succeed in setting it on work. . . . If again, any one ask me . . . for definite promises and forecasts of the works that are to be, I would have him know that the knowledge which we now possess will not teach a man even what to *wish.*"

Is it surprising that Bacon for thirty years would urge in vain his program, and that for comprehension it would need time and a new generation? We cannot blame Bacon's contemporaries for their indifference. But we see also why Bacon cherished a most passionate ambition to hold some position that would command attention and let him realize his plans and his ideas. Bacon was aware that what he offered was unique, revelatory and his own. "There is no thought to be taken about precedents," he wrote; "for there is no precedent." To urge such notions upon his countrymen would need the prestige of a chief justice, a lord chancellor. For his own person, Bacon had no doubts of his ability to set forth this program. In a Proem to the *Advancement of Learning* he tells why he considers himself suited for the undertaking — the only time in his life when Bacon will make such open confession. In the confidence of full maturity he speaks simply, without apology:

"For myself," he says, "I found that I was fitted for nothing so well as for the study of Truth; as having a mind nimble and versatile enough to catch the resemblances of things (which is the chief point), and at the same time steady enough to fix and distinguish their subtler differences; as being gifted by nature with desire to seek, patience to doubt, fondness to meditate, slowness to assert, readiness to reconsider, carefulness to dispose and set in order; and as being a man that neither affects what is new nor admires what is old, and that hates every kind of imposture. So I thought my nature had a kind of familiarity and relationship with Truth.

"Nevertheless, because my birth and education had seasoned me in business of state, and because opinions (so young as I was) would sometimes stagger me; and because I thought that a man's own country has some special claims upon him more than the rest of the world; and because I hoped that, if I rose to any place of honour in the state, I should have a larger command of industry and ability to help me in my work — for these reasons I both applied myself to acquire the arts of civil life, and commended my service, so far as in modesty and honesty I might, to the favours of such friends as had any influence."

It was true; one cannot doubt the sincerity of the statement. Bacon continues: "When I found however that my zeal was mistaken for ambition, and my life had already reached the turning point, and my breaking health reminded me how ill I could afford to be so slow, and I reflected moreover that in leaving undone the good that I could do by myself alone, and applying myself to that which could not be done without the help and consent of others, I was by no means discharging the duty that lay upon me — I put all those thoughts aside, and (in pursuance of my old determination) betook myself wholly to this work. . . . I am not hunting for fame. I have no desire to found a sect, after the fashion of heresiarchs; and to look for any private gain from such an undertaking as this, I count both ridiculous and base."

One asks indeed, what private gain could any man have looked for in such an undertaking? On the contrary, unless Bacon found a patron, he risked loss of prestige with the practical men in Parliament and government, risked assuming the reputation of a dreamer and a merely speculative man. Bacon was aware of the danger. "For the injuries therefore which should proceed from the times," he goes on, "I am not afraid of them, and for the injuries which proceed from men I am not concerned. For if any one charge me with seeking to be wise overmuch, I answer simply that modesty and civil respect are for civil matters; in contemplation nothing is to be respected but Truth."

During the rest of his life, Bacon would enlarge and refine upon the ideas presented in his first "Interpretation of Nature, or the Kingdom of Man." And though he would never again digress into particulars about himself and his qualifications, always he would feel the need to sound in some measure the personal note. Nor was this due to egotism but rather, I think, to an essential modesty — as though, in presenting ideas so vast and novel, some word were needed to bring the matter within mortal scope. A later treatise opens with the words, *"Francis Bacon thought in this manner.* . . . He thought that knowledge is uttered to men, in a form as if every thing were finished. . . . He thought also, how great opposition and prejudice natural philosophy hath received by superstition and the immoderate and blind zeal of religion. . . ."

Bacon's greatest work strikes the same resounding note, direct, magnificently arrogant yet in essence humble. Below the title, *Novum Organum*, Bacon had the printer set out certain words in short lines, one under the other, like a poem:

FRANCIS OF VERULAM
REASONED THUS WITH HIMSELF
AND JUDGED IT TO BE FOR THE INTEREST OF THE PRESENT AND FUTURE
GENERATIONS THAT THEY SHOULD BE MADE ACQUAINTED
WITH HIS THOUGHTS.

There is something solemn yet charming about it, first and last. One thinks of Christian in the *Pilgrim's Progress*, or of Christian's friend Mr. Great-Heart, with sword and shield setting out for Jordan and the Promised Land.

In the autumn of 1605, Bacon's *Advancement of Learning* was published. We learn of the event in a letter of John Chamberlain's, that peerless correspondent, the historian's friend. Chamberlain spells Francis Bacon with the F-r-a-u-n which reveals current pronunciation: "Sir Frauncis Bacon hath set foorth a new worke of the proficience and advancement of learning."

Bacon's treatise was divided in two parts or books, dedicated separately to King James, and in terms of the most egregious flattery. Since Christ's time, said Bacon, there had not been a temporal monarch so learned in all literature and erudition, divine and human. Like Hermes of old, his Majesty could claim that venerable triplicity — "the power and fortune of a King, the knowledge and illumination of a Priest, and the learning and universality of a Philosopher."

The amount of sugary eulogy which James and Elizabeth could absorb was marvelous. Everyone expected it; there was no other way to address a great prince. Bacon moreover seemed fairly to believe what he said. Certainly he never complained concerning this very odd figure of a monarch, with his amusing, homely eloquence, his masculine favorites, his stubbornness with Parliament and his fatal conviction of the divinity of Kings. It was natural that Bacon should share the common acceptance. Kings, after all, were acts of God. They came along in their proper succession; men thought themselves lucky it was no worse. "Princes are like to heavenly bodies," wrote Bacon, "which cause good or evil times." Some planets are auspicious, some are threatening. And might not King James yet prove himself an intellectual savior of the commonwealth? It was an illusion which for Bacon would persist until the end.

Flattery disposed of, however, Bacon sets to in earnest and writes his treatise very simply. Indeed, though he never again addressed the King by name or title, the *Advancement of Learning* reads like a plea for understanding, man to man. It is hard to see how James withstood it. . . . Nothing, says Bacon, that is part of the world is denied to man's inquiry and invention. Ordinary citizens have a dislike of scholars, and "seek to disable learned men by the name of Pedantes." In this connection Bacon was fond of quoting Demosthenes, on an occasion when Demosthenes' adversary, a man of pleasure, told the orator sneeringly that his speeches smelled of the lamp. "Indeed," said Demosthenes, "there is a great deal of difference between that that you and I do by lamplight."

King James liked to laugh. But he was theologically minded, an eager disputer with learned divines in England and on the Continent. It would be difficult, perhaps impossible, to shake the royal conviction of already established learning, that same conviction and inertia which in general were to prove a stumbling block to the new philosophy. Cast away certainty! said Bacon. Cherish the quality of doubt! "The sinews of wisdom are slowness of belief and distrust. . . . The entry of doubts are as so many suckers or sponges to draw use of knowledge. . . . If a man will begin with certainties he shall end in doubts, but if he will be content to begin with doubts, he shall end in certainties." Doctrines, moreover, "should be such as should make men in love with the lesson, and not with the teacher."

What Bacon wrote applies today as it did three centuries ago. "A faculty of wise interrogating," he says, "is half a knowledge. . . . And therefore the larger your Anticipation is, the more direct and compendious is your search." It was Bacon's forte to ask questions; the largeness of his anticipation was his genius. There is little he does not touch upon. The *Advancement of Learning* carries hints on how to write history: natural history, civil history, ecclesiastical or literary history. The biographer can learn from Bacon's remarks upon what he calls Ruminated History, where the author's thoughts, says Bacon, are mixed with fact and event. When Bacon is being practical he is always interesting. But when he soars off into his empyrean he is fascinating; there is an irresistible seduction to this prose. Let us stay a little longer, says Bacon, "upon the inquiry concerning the roots of good and evil, and the strings of those roots." And again: "The mind of man is far from the nature of a clear and equal glass, wherein the beams of things should reflect according to their true incidence. Nay rather, it is like an enchanted glass, full of superstition and imposture, if it be not delivered and reduced." And elsewhere, urging men not to fear passion in their intellectuality: "Icarus, being in the pride of youthful alacrity, naturally fell a victim to excess." Yet "in excess there is something of magnanimity — something, like the flight of a bird, that holds kindred with heaven."

Reading, one thinks of another line of Bacon's, which applies so aptly to himself: "Some interpretations, yea and some writings, have more of the Eagle than others."

5

The Ambition of the Will

IN WHAT SPIRIT King James received the *Advancement of Learning,* we do not know. Certainly, it brought its author neither money nor improved position in the state. Bacon indulged now in that very proper pleasure of authors: the sending of copies to his friends — to Tobie Matthew and Lancelot Andrewes, who had helped by reading the manuscript; to Sir Thomas Bodley, the great bookman, whose collection, under the royal letters patent, had already become the Bodleian Library at Oxford. A copy of Bacon's book went to his cousin, Robert Cecil, Lord Salisbury, premier statesman of the realm. Bacon had confidence in his thesis, but he could not be sure that he had done it justice. Therefore, he wrote Cecil, "I shall content myself to awake better spirits, like a bellringer, which is first up to call others to church." To Sir Thomas Bodley, Bacon spoke more intimately. "I do confess, since I was of any understanding, my mind hath in effect been absent from that I have done. . . . Knowing myself by inward calling to be fitter to hold a book than to play a part, I have led my life in civil causes, for which I was not very fit by nature, and more unfit by the preoccupation of my mind. Therefore

[111]

calling myself home, I have now for a time enjoyed myself, whereof likewise I desire to make the world partaker."

Francis Bacon was forty-four, a time of life when to most men their situation is settled. "Calling myself home," he had written symbolically. Yet where, for this man, was "home"? Fiercely ambitious, he found himself scarcely farther advanced in the world than he had been at eighteen, when with his father's death he came to live in London. Only the royal patent as King's Counsel Extraordinary set Sir Francis above his fellow barristers at Gray's Inn — and very slightly above. All well enough for him to speak of the preoccupation of his mind, and to dedicate his book in flowery terms to the King of England. Yet no matter how gracefully Sir Francis deprecated his "life in civil causes," there is no doubt he knew his capacity for both sides of experience — the intellectual and the active, the world and philosophy. There is no doubt also that his nature craved both sides; from time to time he justified this dual position. "In this theatre of man's life," he wrote, "it is reserved only for God and angels to be lookers on." And again, "The most ancient and reverend philosophers and philosophical men did retire too easily from civil business, for avoiding of indignities and perturbations; whereas the resolution of men truly moral ought to be of a stouter web, and not so fine as that everything should catch in it and endanger it."

In the three years since King James's coming, Bacon's life had been far from the private and retired program which he had protested to Robert Cecil that he craved. Actually, the *Advancement of Learning* had been written during intervals between the most demanding kind of public business. In James's first Parliament of 1604, Bacon had sat for Ipswich and St. Albans. Both Houses had chosen him as Commissioner in the King's great cause of a proposed union between Scotland and England — a complex matter which was to take a century for its accomplishment. The Commons were stubbornly jealous lest a wild and barren country encroach upon a prosperous one; they hated every Scottish courtier that James brought to England. The politics of religion was still uppermost, and here Bacon again had been useful to both Parliament and the Crown. At the time of the Hampton Court Conference he had summed up his ideas in an eloquent and practical treatise, addressed to James and entitled "The Pacification and Edification of the Church."

The Union, the Established Church, the better regulating of affairs in Ireland, improvement in the relations between Crown and Commons — with these urgent matters Bacon concerned himself, believing they should be settled now, while the tide ran strong in a new reign. In the House of Commons Bacon was at his best. When he rose to speak, the crowded benches were quiet. We have Ben Jonson's testimony: "The fear of every man that heard him was, lest he should make an end." The light quick voice was no longer hurried; a speaker can learn the tricks of good delivery. The lines were deep, now, in Bacon's forehead and around his mouth. As always his clothes were rich, with a touch of the dandy. But there was a suavity, an ease of bearing, almost a weariness. Bacon meant what he said and men recognized it. "I have spoken out of the fountain of my heart," he told the Commons one morning. Reading his speeches, one knows that it is true.

There were shifts in the judiciary, a rumor that Edward Coke was to be promoted from Attorney General to a judgeship. Bacon heard it and asked Robert Cecil for the lower place of Solicitor General, which for his services he now patently deserved. The position would make him, he said, more happy than he had been, which would make him also more wise. Yet for some reason the entire shift was postponed and Bacon remained, as he put it, "still next the door."

In the spring of 1606, Sir Francis made a move to correct his financial status. To the general surprise he married, though no one found it odd that the bride was only fourteen to Bacon's forty-five. Alice Barnham was that same Alderman's daughter, whom three years earlier Bacon had noted as "an handsome maiden to my liking." Her father and grandfather had been rich drapers to Queen Elizabeth. Alderman Barnham was dead, his widow had married a goodnatured courtier and sporting knight named Sir John Pakington. *Lusty Pakington,* they called him. Lusty Pakington suffered much harassment from his wife. Alice's mother proved one of those quick-witted, attractive women who are devils in their household; Bacon was to have much trouble with her.

We know of Bacon's marriage quite casually from a gentleman's letter, dated May 11, 1606. "Sir Francis Bacon," it says, "was married yesterday to his young wench in Marylebone Chapel. He was clad from top to toe in purple, and hath made himself and his wife such store of fine raiments of cloth of silver and gold that it draws deep into her portion. The dinner was kept at his father-in-law Sir John Pakington's lodging over against the Savoy."

To say this was a marriage of convenience is merely to say that it followed the accepted pattern of good Elizabethan society. Anything less or more than an arranged match was frowned upon. How should young people recognize a suitable partner? The penalties for an unauthorized love match were severe, especially in court circles. Sir Walter Ralegh had married secretly and found himself in the Tower for it, his wife Bess with him. John Donne at twenty-seven fell in love with Lord Chancellor Ellesmere's niece of sixteen and ran away with her. (She was dressed charmingly as a page, the standard costume of young women embarking on such adventures.) Society found this behavior vexatious in the extreme. Good county families looked upon land as more important than persons, and certainly more important than love. One married off one's daughter, one's son, to neighbors with adjoining estates, thus multiplying the tribal pastures; or one set them up handsomely in a neighboring shire. Bacon's three half-brothers had done very well in this regard; the eldest, Sir Nicholas, was an important man in his county and so was Nathaniel. Bacon's half-sisters too had married profitably.

Francis Bacon at forty-five had arranged his own marriage; apparently he had asked Alice Barnham's parents for her hand when the girl was no more than eleven. City money was desirable at any age; and to Alice's parents, Sir Francis Bacon's birth and breeding were not to be despised. What, after all, is a better mixture than good blood and good money? Bacon's world was amused at the match. Sir Francis had taken to himself a young wife at an age when his friends had begun to boast of grandchildren. Actually, the surprising thing about Bacon's marriage was that it went along so smoothly through the years. There were no children, but for two decades no breath of scandal touched the pair. The gossips were silent — a matter of no small significance. This was a tight little society; everyone knew everyone else. Connubial difficulties often reached the ears of royalty and the Privy Council — as with Sir Edward Coke, whose marital battles before long would be London's premier scandal.

All the same, Francis Bacon was not the stuff of which satisfactory husbands are made. Surely he was not an unkind husband; in his household Bacon was notoriously undemanding. One thinks of him rather as an indifferent husband; likely enough he was no husband at all.

Unfortunately we know little of Alice Bacon as a young wife. But at Gorhambury there is a portrait, done in her thirties. It shows a handsome oval face with strong, high-bridged nose, bold eyes heavy-lidded, a firm mouth and dark hair smooth above the forehead. Alice is richly dressed and wears her clothes with style; the face and carriage are those of a woman who could hold her own, even against a Francis Bacon. One small hint we have, from a writer who remarked that Alice Bacon's wit "lay forward, viz. in her tongue." In short, Alice was a great talker, like her mother, that "little violent lady," who wedded four husbands before she was done and ended up a countess.

Bacon married into a turbulent family. His mother-in-law, perennially contentious, caused her second husband, Lusty Pakington, to be haled before the courts for spending her money. Bacon was legally concerned with the case; he made Lady Pakington yield and withdraw her charges. A letter exists from Bacon to his mother-in-law, letting her know in strong terms that if she does not cease to sow dissension in his household she will be no longer welcome. Alice's sisters married into the highest society — one of them being the first wife of Lord Castlehaven, who eventually was involved in the nastiest scandal, short of murder, ever to absorb the fascinated attention of London society.

Beyond these facts we know nothing of Francis Bacon and his Alice until, at the very end, discord is revealed and Bacon cuts his wife summarily out of his will — "for just and great causes," he writes. In the year 1606, however, Bacon no doubt was able to control his spirited young wife; at any rate we hear of no friction. It seems as if Bacon, not young Alice, was the one to find difficulty in adapting. A month after his marriage, the bridegroom had occasion to write to his friend, Lord Chancellor Ellesmere. A married man, Bacon said ruefully, "is seven years elder in his thoughts the first day." In the *Essays* of 1612, Bacon's remarks on marriage are little less than scorching — like his remarks on love — a passion "which hath its floods in the very times of weakness. . . . They do best who, if they cannot but admit love, yet make it keep quarter."

"He that hath wife and children," wrote Bacon, "hath given hostages to fortune; for they are impediments to great enterprises, either of virtue or mischief. Unmarried men are best friends, best masters and best servants. Wives are young men's mistresses, companions for middle age, and old men's nurses. . . . He was reputed one of the wise men that made answer to the question, when a man should marry? *A young man not yet, an elder man not at all.*"

In June of 1606, Justice Gawdy died. Sir Edward Coke succeeded him as Chief Justice of Common Pleas, Sir Henry Hobart became Attorney General in Coke's place, and it looked surely as if Bacon would at last be Solicitor General. But he was kept waiting another full year. "What a discomfortable thing is it for me," he wrote, "to be unsettled still . . . and to have that little reputation which by my industry I gather, to be scattered and taken away by continual disgraces, every new man coming above me."

Bacon's situation seemed unendurable. One marvels that his spirit did not fail and that he did not abandon hope and retire into the country to nurse disillusionment and genteel poverty forever. What made it the more bitter was that Sir Robert Cecil had given definite promise of advancement, once Coke should be promoted. "Time groweth precious with me," Bacon wrote. "I am now *vergentibus annis* [in my declining years]." No man of his ability had served the state for so long without reward, nor had any man of ability been so often promised and disappointed. It is impossible not to lay this at Robert Cecil's door. Whether Bacon's grandiose philosophic plans seemed to Cecil disturbingly impractical, indicative of an unsettled mind, whether Cecil mistrusted his cousin's easy propensity to get into debt, whether he disliked the range of Bacon's friendships — from a Bishop Lancelot Andrewes and a Ben Jonson to a Tobie Matthew, a Button Bushell — we do not know. Between two such natures there must have been antipathy, very likely there was jealousy. For myself I feel sure that Bacon never would have attained the Chancellorship if he had not outlived his cousin, Robert Cecil.

In June, 1607, at long last Bacon was named Solicitor General. His salary was only a hundred pounds a year. Yet the place was worth, in fees and perquisites, about a thousand pounds annually. Added to this, Mr. Mill, the long-lived Clerk of Star Chamber, at last was gathered to his fathers. Bacon inherited his place, as promised by Queen Elizabeth; it brought no less than £2000 a year. Bacon moved suddenly from a man embarrassed financially to a gentleman of substance. If he had known how to manage his money he would have been safe, fixed securely for life.

A place in government, a pension from Star Chamber, a rich wife . . . Francis Bacon's foot was on the ladder. It is odd —

SIR NICHOLAS AND ANN, LADY BACON
From busts in terra cotta at Gorhambury House.
Circa 1571. Artist unknown

FRANCIS BACON AT THE AGE OF TEN

From the bust in terra cotta at Gorhambury House. Artist unknown

ELIZABETH I

Entrance front from the South

Clock tower and portico, painted in 1842. The portico stands
today and is being restored

GORHAMBURY HOUSE

WILLIAM CECIL, LORD BURGHLEY
Attributed to M. Geerarts

ROBERT DEVEREUX, EARL OF ESSEX
1597. Artist unknown

JAMES I

Sir Robert Cecil
Attributed to J. de Critz. 1602

and very human — that something in Bacon's nature would not let him glory over the rise. At home in Gorhambury he found himself uneasy, half sick. This was not the first man of brilliant intellect and sensitive nerves to react adversely to success. "I have found," wrote Bacon, "now twice upon amendment of my fortune, disposition to melancholy and distaste, especially the same happening against the long vacation when company failed and business both. For upon my Solicitor's place I grew indisposed and inclined to superstition. Now upon Mill's place [the Clerkship in Star Chamber] I find a relapse unto my old symptom as I was wont to have it many years ago, as after sleeps; strife at meats, strangeness, clouds, etc. . . . Strangeness in beholding," he noted again, "darksomeness, offer to groan and sigh." In the afternoon especially, these fears came upon him. "Some comforting drink," Bacon wrote, "at four o'clock which is the hour of my languishing, were proper for me. When I was last at Gorhambury I was taken much with my symptom of melancholy and doubt of present peril."

Doubt of present peril. The phrase is extraordinarily suggestive of that distress known to the twentieth century by the name of anxiety. There are men who cannot bear success, who feel guilty under it and who move, though unconsciously, to destroy what they have gained. Always, Francis Bacon strove to emulate his father, to follow in the paternal footsteps. And always, as each step was attained, he paused and looked back, shaken. Was it fear of falling or of rising? For all his valetudinarianism, Bacon was essentially healthy-minded. His fears did not master him. He never retreated — unless the tragic, crazy debacle at the end was in essence a retreat. Always, however, Bacon expressed his fears, and their expression is wonderfully revealing. One never finds an Edward Coke, for instance, glancing back over his shoulder, or downward toward the pit.

The year after he attained the Solicitorship, Bacon compiled a notebook, which he called his *Commentarius Solutus* [Free Commentary]. It is seldom quoted, perhaps because its frankness is shocking — until one stops to consider that every ambitious man is apt to think in like manner, though few are indiscreet enough to say so. Bacon's notes are thrown down carelessly, written apparently on the run as he passed by his writing table. Some are in Latin, some in a kind of shorthand. They cover such matters as the King's revenue, problems of the Established Church and the desirability of annexing the Low Countries. They touch on Bacon's business in the law courts and suggest future books to be written: a *History of Marvels,* a *History of the Mechanic Arts.* They suggest the foundation of an ideal "College for Inventors," and list the names of men who might be useful in scientific experiment — the Earl of Northumberland for instance, of imaginative and inquiring mind, at the moment prisoner in the Tower for his suspected part in the Gunpowder Plot of 1605. Ralegh too was a prisoner. With Thomas Hariot the mathematician, the three made a venturesome trio. "The setting on work," wrote Bacon, "my Lord of Northumberland and Ralegh, and therefore Hariot, themselves being already inclined to experiments."

Never was mortal man so busy. If one of Bacon's rivals had seen the *Commentarius,* I think he would have been awestruck, so complete are the plans and so implacable, so wide the range and so painstaking the detail. Bacon jots down ways to increase his law practice in Chancery and Star Chamber, also maneuvers by which King James might control the Puritan common lawyers, especially when Parliament is in session. "Keep the lawyers in awe," writes Bacon; "point of reforming the laws and disprizing mere lawyers."

Bacon's immediate superior, Attorney General Hobart, seems to annoy his Solicitor General merely by existing. "A solemn goose," notes Bacon. "The coldest examiner, weak in Gunter's case, weak with the judges, too full of cases and distinctions. Nibbling solemnly he distinguisheth, but he apprehends not." Bacon itches to have his own abilities seen and appreciated; he has been too long in shadow. "To win credit comparate to the Attorney," he writes, "by being more short, round and resolute." Aware that his reputation is rather for abstruse scholarship than for practical procedure in the courts, Bacon makes a memorandum touching what he calls "Vulgaria in Jure: being the ordinary matters, rules and cases admitted for law." He must not give appearance of being "unperfect or unready in common matters." Also it would be well to abridge and memorize certain cases and to prepare in other points "for show and credit of readiness and reading."

Wherever Francis Bacon will henceforth stand in life, the man next above will have hazardous footing. The *Commentarius Solutus* is filled with implacable suggestions for self-improvement; Bacon is no more sparing of himself than of others. "To suppress at once," he writes, "my speaking with panting and labor of breath and voice. Not to fall upon the main [topic] too sudden, but to induce and intermingle speech of good fashion. To compose and draw in myself. To free myself at once from payment of formality and compliment, though with some show of carelessness, pride and rudeness." These were needed cautions for a man who was impulsive beyond the bounds of common caution, who wrote reckless letters to enemies in great place and who entered all too fully into the moment, to his own hurt.

Long ago, in his *Promus of Formularies and Elegancies,* Bacon had noted that it was better to be envied than pitied. Now he intends to act upon it. He lays his plans, makes assessment of his friends and his enemies. Yet nothing can be effected, in this year of 1608, without the goodwill and good offices of Robert Cecil, once known as plain Master Secretary, now Earl of Salisbury and Lord Treasurer of England. "To furnish my Lord of Salisbury with ornaments for public speeches," notes Bacon. (Plainly, ghost-writing was useful in the seventeenth century.) Bacon did not love his cousin. Yet it was his cousin who could bring him forward, make him Attorney General or judge. It would be well to let Cecil know that Francis Bacon, if Chief Justice, would show respect beyond the cousinly. "To make my L. of S.," wrote Bacon, "think how he should be reverenced by a Lord Chief Justice if I were [named]. Princelike."

For six years, Bacon held his place of Solicitor General, acquitting himself brilliantly. No dramatic political trials came up, such as the Essex case, the Ralegh case, the Gunpowder trials which had made Edward Coke's reputation as Attorney General. (The Earl of Somerset's spectacular trial for murder was not until 1615.) Solicitor General Bacon found himself concerned not with courtroom drama but with larger issues such as the jurisdiction of courts, a proposed code of Scottish and English law in preparation for a union of the countries; the much-debated legal status of persons born of Scottish parentage after James's coming to England — the Post-nati, they were called. Children similarly born before the accession were aliens. These were constitutional questions, significant to the history of English law, to policy and the spread of the empire.

The most celebrated of Solicitor Bacon's suits was *Calvin's Case,* concerning the Postnati. King James was vitally interested, the union of Scotland and England being very dear to his heart. Bacon from the first had been a champion of the plan. His *Discourse touching the Happy Union,* published in 1603, his speeches in Parliament on the subject were well known. His views of empire were large. "All states," he said, "that are liberal of naturalization towards strangers are fit for empire." Actually, *Calvin's Case* was brought to court largely at James's instigation — a test case. Parliament had defeated the royal plan of union with Scotland; James hoped to salvage at least the rights of citizenship for his onetime countrymen. Bacon's argument, when his turn came, concerned the nature of allegiance — whether due first to the law, to the Crown, to the kingdom, or to the person of the King. Yet at bottom Bacon knew that it was a question rather of policy than of legality, and that Parliament was jealous of every Scotsman who settled below the border. What of the Indies? — the Commons had asked, during debate. Surely, the Indies would one day come up as a similar problem? "If we like not their consort," Bacon told the court, "we can make an act of Parliament for separation." * What of Ireland, too, and of Normandy, Gascoigne and Guienne? And if a Scotsman invade England with an army, is he an alien enemy or a rebel? Where, in short, does the King's writ run?

The case was decided as James had hoped. Calvin, born in

* What would Bacon have said of the Notting Hill (London) riots against Jamaicans in 1962, and of England's first act to limit immigration, passed the same year?

Edinburgh in 1605, was declared a natural subject of King James and thus could hold land in England. Yet Bacon continued to do battle for the cause, and to advise King James also concerning his plantations in Virginia and Ireland, dispatching to the palace *Discourses* and *Advices,* suggesting the best crops to sow and the most suitable craftsmen to send as settlers.

There seemed indeed no end to the range of Bacon's activity as Solicitor General. For the King he prepared reports on abuses practiced by officers of the inferior courts, or outlines of suggested reform in the penal laws. ("It is ever a rule that any over-great penalty deads the execution of the law.") In the Parliament of 1610, Bacon was ranking spokesman for the crown — Robert Cecil being now in the Upper Chamber. Bacon was in fact a workhorse in this Parliament, busy with every question that came up. In debate he showed an unflagging good humor that was perhaps his best weapon. "Many a man's strength is in opposition," he had written. "And when that faileth, he groweth out of use. . . . It is often seen that a few that are stiff do tire out a greater number that are more moderate."

The House chose Bacon as their messenger to carry to the King a most serious Petition of Grievances. It was summer, and the King at Whitehall. Bacon knew the Petition would infuriate James because it went against the royal plans and wishes; moreover the very word *grievance,* as the Commons used it, was an incitement. Bacon knew also that one way to conciliate this strange stubborn monarch was to make him laugh. Standing before the throne, Bacon unrolled the Petition, a parchment nearly four feet square. James watched him and laughed aloud, calling out that it was big enough "to serve as a piece of tapestry."

[124]

"Excellent sovereign!" Bacon began. "Let not the sound of grievances, though it be sad, seem harsh to your princely ears. It is but *gemitus columbae,* the mourning of a dove, with that patience and humility of heart which appertaineth to loving and loyal subjects. . . ."

Although the King relied on Francis Bacon, in terms of a man's ambition it was no triumph to be Solicitor General. Bacon's great rival was still far beyond him and above. Lord Coke, men called Sir Edward now. Robed in scarlet broadcloth or lilac silk, the judge's coif snug upon his head, the heavy gold chain of SS about his shoulders, Lord Coke sat in his corner of Westminster Hall, presiding over the great Court of Common Pleas. Here came suitors in private property. Here were adjudged quarrels of *meum* and *tuum,* mine and thine. And here the fees were high, the judicial perquisites delicious. There was no hint of peculation or that Coke had abused his position. But during his judgeship Coke's wealth increased enormously. In London it was said that no one in the law was by way of amassing so large a fortune.

In the year 1612, an event occurred which for Bacon was to be decisive. Robert Cecil died — the tiny hunchback whom James had called his little beagle, and Elizabeth her pygmy. . . . First Secretary of State, Lord Treasurer of England, the clever, patient son of Elizabeth's great minister, Lord Burghley. Robert Cecil died one of the richest men in England and perhaps the most hated. No man is loved whose business it is to stand in the middle and play both sides. In the streets, ballads passed from hand to hand:

> *Here lies, thrown for the worms to eat,*
> *Little bossive Robin that was so great:*

Owning a mind for dismal ends,
As traps for foes and tricks for friends.

Here was a depth of malice from which Cecil's father had
not suffered. Francis Bacon walked in his cousin's funeral
procession. Six earls walked with him, clad in black. In the
coffin, enclosed from air, lay a near kinsman; as boys the two
had been in and out of their parents' houses together. Yet the
family of Cecil — what had it done for Francis Bacon but to
cause him suffering? Always the Cecils, father and son, had
given fair words, their speech "all kindly outward." How
many times Bacon had sued them for intercession with a
Queen, a King! They had failed him. He had been refused,
passed over for another candidate, left forever "next the door."

While Robert Cecil lived, Bacon had been, he said, "as a
hawk tied to another's fist, that mought sometimes bait and
proffer but could never fly." Now the Cecils both were dead,
powerless, while Francis Bacon at fifty-one survived. Must a
Christian grieve then for the death of an enemy? The little
crooked body of his cousin came to mind, and the pale intelli-
gent face, blond and secretive. . . . Had any other, so deformed in person, achieved in England a station as high? Before the year was out, Bacon would answer the question, and
in print, for all to read. "Of Deformity," the essay was called —
"Wherein," wrote a gentleman, "the world takes notice that Sir
Francis Bacon points out his late little cousin to the life."

"In a great wit," wrote Bacon, "deformity is an advantage to
rising. . . . Whosoever hath any thing fixed in his person that
doth induce contempt, hath also a perpetual spur in himself to
rescue and deliver himself from scorn. Therefore all deformed
persons are extreme bold: first, as in their own defence, as being exposed to scorn; but in process of time by a general habit.

[126]

Also, it stirreth in them industry . . . to watch and observe the weakness of others, that they may have somewhat to repay. Again, in their superiors, it quencheth jealousy towards them, as persons that they think they may at pleasure despise; and it layeth their competitors and emulators asleep, as never believing they should be in possibility of advancement, till they see them in possession."

Suave, bitter as acid, Bacon drew his portrait. Now at last he dared speak out; the hawk that had been tied might fly. To the King, Bacon drafted three letters, planning to send one of them. "Your Majesty," began the second draft, "hath lost [in Cecil] a great subject and a great servant. But if I should praise him in propriety, I should say that he was a fit man to keep things from growing worse but no very fit man to reduce things to be much better. . . . And though he had fine passages of action, yet the real conclusions came slowly on."

It was a valid estimate; Cecil's great quality had been caution. His death would occasion a general shift of place. For Bacon the situation was crucial. Should he miss this opportunity, should he again be passed over, it would be the end. There was no time to waste, the hungry mouths were open. London gossips laid bets on who would win Cecil's vacant positions, with Bacon in the lead as Secretary of State. Bacon's third letter to the King carried neither censure of the dead nor flattery of the living, but an almost desperate plea.

"Your Majesty may have heard somewhat that my father was an honest man. . . . My offering is care and observance: and as my good old mistress [Queen Elizabeth] was wont to call me her watch-candle, because it pleased her to say I did continually burn (and yet she suffered me to waste almost to nothing), so I must much more owe the like duty to your

Majesty, by whom my fortunes have been settled and raised. . . ."

When Bacon said that his offering was care and observance, it was true. For thirty-three years, in despite of plot and suing, of intrigue and the *Commentarius Solutus* — what Bacon had actually asked for was a way to serve the state. A man, he had often said, owes somewhat to his country and somewhat to his profession. The positions Bacon aimed at had not been the highly lucrative ones, nor any easy sinecure about the palace and person of the monarch. Bacon loved pomp, fine clothes, resounding titles, the opportunity to spread largesse and cut a figure. But what he craved far more was the chance to use his capacities to the full; of this none can doubt who studies the record. Ambition, sleepless and merciless, was directed not only toward the world but toward himself. Bacon was his own severest rival; he must prove himself or perish. Looking about him after Cecil's death, Bacon saw blatantly dishonest and self-seeking ministers and councilors of state, not one of whom Elizabeth would have tolerated in her service. There was Henry Howard, Earl of Northampton, crooked as a forked stick. There was James's royal favorite, the handsome Robert Carr, whom James had created Viscount Rochester and on whom he lavished money and favors past counting. There would be others, weak and dangerous; James was wholly lacking in discrimination. He dared not name Bacon, and thus offend the men about him whom he had raised. James hesitated, declaring he would be his own Secretary. In late spring of 1613, Chief Justice Fleming of King's Bench died. King's Bench was looked on as one step higher than Common Pleas, its Chief Justice sometimes was called Chief Justice of England.

Bacon saw his chance. Should Edward Coke be moved upward to King's Bench, then Attorney General Hobart could take Coke's place in Common Pleas — and Francis Bacon be named Attorney General at last. It was a beautiful plan, if his Majesty could be induced to see it in all its guileful simplicity of effect. As Attorney General, Sir Henry Hobart had been, in Bacon's eyes, soft, ineffectual — "a solemn goose." In Common Pleas, Hobart would be malleable to the King's wish. Whereas Lord Coke had been obstreperous from the first, defying Lord Chancellor Ellesmere, sending out prohibitions and *premunires* until King, Chancellor and Solicitor General Bacon had been baffled how to proceed. The court of King's Bench was traditionally closer to his Majesty than was Common Pleas; Coke would not dare to proceed in his old course. Moreover, should Coke be offered a seat in Privy Council (dear to every ambitious man), he would surely be checkmated, especially with Francis Bacon as Attorney General.

All this, Bacon wrote to King James, going carefully over each facet of the scheme. The King's Attorney must be of metal to prod the judges onward. "For what," asked Bacon, "is a back without an edge?" Edward Coke got wind of these machinations and made vehement outcry. He had no ambition to be Chief Justice of England; he was being kicked upstairs and he knew it. Common Pleas was where he belonged — besides which, the court was extremely profitable. "The Lord Coke," wrote a London gentleman, "doth so stickle and fence by all the means and friends he can make, not to remove. . . . And all to make way for Sir Francis Bacon to be Attorney, whom the King hath promised to advance."

Bacon waited eagerly; this time there existed no Cecil to gainsay him. In October, 1613, he saw his plans fulfilled. Sir Edward Coke was named Chief Justice of King's Bench, the tractable Henry Hobart stepped into Common Pleas — and Francis Bacon was sworn Attorney General. No one whose business lay in Westminster Hall missed the implications of the shift. In the courtroom, Attorney General and Chief Justice met face to face. "Mr. Attorney!" Coke said angrily. "This is all your doing. It is you who have made this great stir."

Bacon's reply must instantly have gone the rounds. "Ah! my Lord," he said. "Your Lordship all this while hath grown in breadth. You must needs now grow in height, or else you would be a monster."

The smile, the bow ironic: Bacon was master of these arts. For this moment he had waited twenty years. Sir Edward Coke, Chief Justice of King's Bench and of England, was not defeated. But surely, most assuredly he was discomfited.

꧁꧂ III ꧁꧂

Bacon Ascending. A Time of Glory
1613–1620

Lord Coke's Defeat

IN WESTMINSTER PALACE, where lay the law courts, the legal lines were drawn plain. On one side stood the King's supporters, the prerogative men, led in Chancery by Lord Chancellor Ellesmere and on the floor of the arena by the King's Attorney General, Sir Francis Bacon. Strongly on the prerogative side also were the courts of Star Chamber and the ecclesiastical High Commission, where cases were tried according to Roman law, by inquisition rather than by inquest. Over against these stood the common-law courts of King's Bench, Common Pleas and Exchequer. The House of Commons, with its barristers and Puritan members, when it met was vocally and irrevocably on the common-law side.

And now began in earnest the great struggle that would culminate in rebellion, civil war and a king's execution at the hands of Parliament. Nothing was as yet in the open, nor was the word *rebellion* considered. With the people at large, James was not unpopular, being easygoing and strongly inclined to peace. To the populace it is a convenient king who loathes the sight of a naked sword. James called few Parliaments; since 1610 only one had sat, and briefly. Parliament men however were restless, impatient for power. Above all they were impatient with the King's handsome male favorites who bled the commonwealth for their own nourishment.

Civil rebellion, early or late, shows itself in a struggle for control of the law courts and the judges. So it was now. Between Lord Chancellor Ellesmere and Chief Justice Coke of King's Bench, the battle ostensibly was one of legal principle. Yet it would be hard to say how much of the quarrel stemmed rather from Coke's fanatical jealousy for his court. To Francis Bacon it was unthinkable that suitors should be stopped in their appeal from the common-law courts to Chancery. Chancery by tradition was the court of the King's conscience. Bacon looked on the King as above the law, *legibus solutus,* with every right to preside in Star Chamber and to consult with any of his judges upon cases pending. "Let the judges be lions," Bacon wrote, "but lions under the throne."

Edward Coke, as Attorney General for Elizabeth and James, had been altogether on the Crown side, ferocious in his role of public prosecutor. Not until he became judge of Common Pleas did he change his aspect. When Lord Chancellor Ellesmere commanded equitable review of common-law cases, Chief Justice Coke countered with prohibitions, *premunires,* which in effect accused Ellesmere of contravening the laws of England. In defense of his court of Common Pleas, Coke defied not only the Chancellor but the King's prerogative power in general. Moreover, to fight his battle Coke was ready to use such weapons as came to hand — lawsuits that were unworthy of the cause.

The struggle had begun in the court of High Commission, whence it moved to *Fuller's Case* and the matter of the oath *ex officio,* so hated by Puritans. In *Calvin's Case,* Lord Chancellor Ellesmere had gone so far as to declare that "the monarch is the law." *Rex est lex loquens.* (The King is the law speaking.) *Bonham's Case* wrung from Coke the pronouncement that the common law controlled even acts of Parliament — a dictum that would prove useful to Massachusetts lawyers at the outset of the Revolution. After *Bonham's Case,* the struggle centered for a time around James's policy of issuing royal proclamations which bore the force of law, with penalties attached. Here Bacon, arguing for the King, quoted Coke's own former decisions against him. In 1615, *Peacham's Case* came up, wherein Bacon advised James to ascertain the judges' opinions before trial. Coke refused. Yet even Coke had no mind to martyrdom, and after much contrived delay, won his point by a legal trick. Whereupon Bacon reported to the King that "in *Peacham's Case,* for as much as in him was, the Lord Coke prevailed." The same principle was soon tested again in the *Case of Commendams,* and in the suit called *De Rege Inconsulto:* namely, the King's right to consult with his judges before the trial. Here, as in *Calvin's Case* during his Solicitorship, Bacon threw aside his character of prerogative champion and argued brilliantly from the law and the facts. "The common law is an old servant of the crown," he said. The case ended in compromise, but Bacon was exultant. "I lost not one auditor that was present in the beginning!" he reported, reported also that even the Lord Coke had declared it to be a famous argument.

To the modern mind, trained in Whig principles, it is abhorrent that a king should ask a judge for his opinion before trial. "Tampering with the judges," we would call it. Yet James was more mistaken than wicked. Before assuming his English throne, he had reigned for thirty-five years in Scotland, where, though the royal career had been tumultuous, a king was freer of constitutional checks. Parliaments, James said ruefully, were a custom he found when he came to England and could not change. James battled still for the divine right of kings, something no English monarch would achieve. Francis Bacon, however, saw the judicial struggle in subtler terms. There was in England a valid tradition of "the King's justice." The country had known times when noblemen were high-handed and ruthless, and when a king's intervention and a king's mercy were the poor man's hope. In the great Court of Star Chamber (not as yet discredited), the central seat was emblazoned with the royal arms. Elizabeth could have sat there had she chosen; in her wisdom she did not so choose. To Bacon, Coke's persistent use of the Statute of Premunire against Chancery was "a strange attempt to make the Chancellor sit under a hatchet instead of the King's arms."

The question was by no means the simple moral issue of a king's tyranny against a persecuted bench. There have been evil kings in history, but there have been evil judges too, who could not be trusted with the supreme judicial power. Even a historian with a possible Whig bias — Samuel Rawson Gardiner — has spoken in defense of Bacon's view. "Although Bacon's wish to bring the judges into subjection to the Crown," says Gardiner, "has not found favour in later times, it must be remembered that his doctrine of the necessity of referring elsewhere than to them for the final decision on all constitutional questions has stood the test of modern experience. The victory of Parliament has, indeed, thrown the supreme political power into other hands than those in which Bacon would have placed it; but it is not one of the least happy results of that victory that it has now become possible to exercise a control over the judges without sacrificing their independence."

Such "victories" take time; reform in the law comes by slow degrees; often it is sparked by trivial causes. In the years between 1612 and 1620, men's personal prejudices entered the struggle, and their individual strivings for power. The common lawyers were jealous of Chancery's encroachment. Remunerative cases slipped away, out of Common Pleas or King's Bench into the prerogative courts of equity and Roman procedure. The common-law judges — notably Edward Coke — attacked Chancery therefore on the high grounds of legal principle and the ancient "freedoms." (When men's pockets are touched, the thrust goes through to the heart.) Coke moreover had a strident, brutal way of moving toward his objective. In a letter to the King, Bacon had a word for it, gorgeous and five-syllabled: *plerophoria.* "The Lord Coke's *plerophoria,* or over-confidence, doth always subject things to a great deal of chance," said Bacon. The autumn term of court (1615) was not ended when Coke threw himself — plerophorically — once more into the battle. Bacon looked on these tactics as the aberrations of a diseased mind. Was Edward Coke trying to do away altogether with Chancery, that indispensable court of equity and of the King's conscience? "A kind of sickness of my Lord Coke's," Bacon said, writing to James. It was in April of 1616 that the celebrated *Case of Commendams* came up. The King once more insisted on his royal right to intervene. The judges, James said, were sworn to consult with their liege lord when occasion demanded. Let proceedings in the common law therefore be halted until after consultation with his royal self.

Bacon drafted a letter to this effect and sent it around to Coke, together with suave, hortatory admonitions of his own concerning the duty of a Chief Justice — enough to drive Edward Coke to madness. In open defiance, Coke heard the *Case of Commendams* next day. All twelve judges then signed a statement to the King which said their judicial oath instructed them to "go forth to do the law notwithstanding any letters [such as the Attorney General's]" that came to them. King James, furious, summoned the judges to Whitehall Palace and with a violent gesture, tore their signed statement to pieces before their eyes. Twelve judges fell on their knees. ("Flat on all fours," the reporter wrote.) James, as if to cinch the matter, then went down to Star Chamber and occupied the royal seat — so long empty — with his coat of arms emblazoned on the back. His coming was announced by trumpets. Addressing the court and the assembled throng — "Judges!" James said. "Keep yourselves within your own benches, not to invade other jurisdictions! Keep you all in your own bounds!"

Within a fortnight, James published his final decree in the matter, written, it is generally thought, by Bacon. *"We do will and command that our Chancellor or Keeper of the Great Seal shall not hereafter desist to give unto our subjects upon their several complaints such relief in Equity (notwithstanding any former proceedings at the common law against them) as shall stand with the true merits and justice of their cases, and with the former ancient and continued practice and precedency of our Chancery."*

Attorney General Bacon had won the battle. From that day forward, Chancery's right to issue injunctions was not questioned. King James's decree was unpopular, yet it held. Decisions in the common-law courts today are still subject to review by higher authority — in England by Parliament, in the United States by the Supreme Court. Chancery would continue under criticism. Yet the major issue was settled, and with it, much time-consuming battle and jurisdictional quarreling. "I do take comfort," Bacon wrote to James, "that I was the first that advised you to come in person to Star Chamber."

For Chief Justice Coke, the King's decree spelled disaster. He was suspended from his place as Privy Councilor and forbidden to ride in the ensuing summer circuit. Coke had become a thorn in the monarch's side. The man was popular and could not be summarily dismissed. Moreover he was useful. He knew Parliament and how to raise money from the Commons; he had friends everywhere. James looked on this stubborn Norfolkman with a mixture of respect and quite frantic frustration. With Coke as Chief Justice, how could prerogative government proceed? For James the time had come to rid himself of this encumbrance.

With such plans, Francis Bacon was easily in accord, though at first he held back and, with Lord Chancellor Ellesmere, urged the King to caution. If a Chief Justice were to be publicly disgraced, the people at large would have to be informed of the reasons. Charges against Coke must be drawn into discernible bounds, such as the prohibitions and premunires sent out from Coke's court, the points of impudence or defiance in the eleven volumes of his law *Reports,* his stubborn carriage and demeanor in the cases *De Rege Inconsulto, Peacham's Case* and others. Concerning the law *Reports,* Coke, after a summer's cogitation (commanded by James), returned his eleven volumes to Bacon with a single sheet on which were noted five small, entirely trivial mistakes of fact or of Latin translation.

Bacon turned this off lightly. "Your Majesty may perceive," he wrote (enclosing Coke's single sheet), "that my Lord [Coke] is an happy man, that there should be no more errors in his five hundred cases than a few cases of Plowden." "To give every man his due," Bacon wrote elsewhere, "had it not been for Sir Edward Coke's *Reports* (which though they may have errors, and some peremptory and extrajudicial resolutions more than are warranted, yet they contain infinite good decisions and rulings of cases), the law by this time had been almost like a ship without ballast."

Coke meanwhile begged for royal audience, saying he had somewhat of importance to impart to his Majesty. James refused to see him. (Embarrassing, to give kingly access one day and disgrace a man the next.) It was now that Bacon took over the whole burden of the campaign. In June of 1616, Bacon was named a member of the King's Privy Council, achieving in his fifty-sixth year a distinction toward which he had yearned and intrigued for more than three decades. The position added incalculably to Bacon's prestige. Moreover it meant that he could in person inform the Privy Council of the course his Majesty proposed to take in removing Coke from the bench. Procedure would be highly important. The scene must be set, the cues prompted from the wings. Queen Anne was fond of Coke; she had interceded for him, which did not make matters easier. Before long, James would be forced to call a Parliament; the royal treasury was low. In the House of Commons, Coke would be as usual powerful, greatly influential. Should his martyrdom be too conspicuous, there was no telling what the Lower House would do in retaliation.

Bacon went about the matter with the zest and swiftness of a seasoned hunter. When we aim at the enemy's heart it is never difficult to persuade ourselves that we act from principle. (No doubt Coke would enjoy a like self-deception five years later, when he moved in Parliament to destroy Francis Bacon.) For James's guidance, in this year of 1616, Bacon wrote out directions in his own hand. Let his Majesty make public declaration that on grounds of deceit, contempt and slander of the government, Lord Coke might well have been dismissed from his place as Chief Justice — or even brought to account in Star Chamber, "which would have been his utter overthrow." Coke's "perpetual turbulent carriage" should be noted, his raising of "troubles and new questions," his flouting the prerogative royal "and the branches thereof." Besides all this, let his Majesty declare that he had made two special observations of Lord Coke. "The one, that he having in his nature not one part of those things which are popular in men, being neither liberal, nor affable, nor magnificent, he hath made himself popular by design only, pulling down government."

Popular by design only, pulling down government. . . . To Francis Bacon it was the cardinal sin. If Bacon's tastes were toward the aristocratic, his view of government was Machiavellian, Continental. Bacon placed his reliance in the strong ruler, the philosopher-king whose reign, efficient and benevolent, would benefit art and education as well as the people.

Yet the House of Commons, though still royalist, had begun to put their faith elsewhere. Led by Coke and the common lawyers, the Commons turned back to the medieval conception of law as the supreme authority, supreme even over the king. Lord Chancellor Ellesmere in *Calvin's Case* had declared, *"Rex est lex loquens"* (The King is the law speaking). But Coke cited Judge Bracton: "The King should not be under man, but under God and the Law." Francis Bacon, aiming at the downfall of Edward Coke, aimed at the Commons' heart, at its very spokesman.

The matter of Coke's dismissal had hung fire seven months, when in the autumn of 1616, James went hunting the red deer and apparently forgot the whole affair. Bacon nudged the royal memory with a new and much fuller statement of Coke's offenses, a memorandum containing seventeen charges, definite, pertinent. Opposite each charge, Bacon set down clarifying comments in his own handwriting.

1. The Ecclesiastical Commission.	In this he prevailed, and the commission was pared. . . .
2. Against the Provincial Councils [These were the Welsh Marches whose jurisdiction Bacon had upheld in 1608].	In this he prevailed in such sort . . . as the jurisdictions grow into contempt, and more would, if the Lord Chancellor did not strengthen them by injunctions. . . .
3. Against the Star-chamber for levying damages.	In this he was overruled by the sentence of the court, but he bent all his strength and wits to have prevailed; and so did the other Judges by long and laborious arguments: and if they had prevailed, the authority of the court had been overthrown. But the plurality of the court took more regard to their own precedents than to the Judges' opinions.
4. Against the Admiralty.	In this he prevaileth, for prohibitions fly continually; and many times are cause of long suits, to the

discontent of foreign ambassadors and to the King's dishonour and trouble by their remonstrances.

5. *Against the Court of the Duchy of Lancaster prohibitions go; and the like may do to the court of wards and exchequer-chamber.*

This is new, and would be forthwith restrained, and the others settled.

6. *Against the Court of Requests.*

In this he prevaileth; and this but lately brought in question.

Down the pages went the King's finger and the King's eye, tracing it out . . . Premunire for suits in Chancery . . . Against the writ *De Rege Inconsulto . . . Peacham's Case . . . Owen's Case* . . . Suits for legacies taken from their proper dioceses. The Lord Coke prevailed . . . prevailed. . . .

On November 13, 1616, Bacon sent to James the note that sealed Coke's fate:

> May it please your excellent Majesty,
> I send your Majesty a form of discharge for my Lord Coke from his place of Chief Justice of your Bench.
> I send also a warrant to the Lord Chancellor for making forth a writ for a new Chief Justice, leaving a blank for the name to be supplied by your Majesty presently.

The scroll was delivered to the Chief Justice in his chambers. He read it, said a news writer, "with dejection and tears." There was no way for Edward Coke, at sixty-five, to know that the final victory would not be in Bacon's hands but in his own. He who now sat defeated would find revenge more thorough than his headiest dreams could contemplate. What

Francis Bacon had done would in a few years rebound upon him, sharp and threefold.

In January, 1617, Lord Chancellor Ellesmere lay mortally ill at York House on the Thames — the mansion in which Bacon had been born and which had been his home until his nineteenth year. Bacon had frequently visited his old friend in his long sickness. "I was with him yesterday almost half an hour," Bacon wrote the King after one of these occasions. "He used me with wonderful tokens of kindness. We both wept, which I do not often." It is the only occasion on which we hear of Francis Bacon weeping. Like Bacon's father, Ellesmere had served as Chancellor for twenty years; to the King he now recommended Bacon as his successor. It was a powerful commendation, Ellesmere had great prestige.

As Attorney General and Solicitor, Bacon had used his legal knowledge in affairs of general policy and indeed of empire. His reputation rested, therefore, not on the daily matters of the law (what Bacon called *vulgaria juris*) but rather on his use of law and legal history in Parliaments and on his expressed plans for the reformation of English law. As early as 1593, Bacon had risen in Parliament to propose this latter undertaking; for some twenty years he had continued to urge it. "To enter into a general amendment of the state of the laws," he said, "and to reduce them to more brevity and certainty." His intention was never codification, which would mean, Bacon said, the casting of English law in a new mold. "Sure I am there are more doubts that rise upon our statutes, which are a text la *w*, than upon the common law, which is no text law." No — he desired rather to prune and graft, not to plow up and plant again. "The entire body and substance of law shall remain," he wrote, "only discharged of idle and un-profitable or hurtful matter, and illustrated by order and other helps, towards the better understanding of it, and judgment thereupon."

In the Parliament of 1614, Bacon had introduced a Bill of Grace to reform the penal laws. The bill failed, as did every-thing in that brief and ineffectual assembly, though the lawyers in Parliament desired such reform. But Bacon persisted. Dur-ing the battle over Coke's dismissal from the bench (1616) Ba-con wrote to James "A Proposition touching the Compiling and Amendment of the Laws of England" stating what ought to be done and how to go about it. "The law is my profession," Bacon begins, "to which I am a debtor. Some little helps I may have of other learning, which may give form to the matter."

Giving form to matter is an exercise that goes beyond the specialist, the legalist and jurisprudent. Bacon's wide culture and shrewd perception of men's motives, the reading he had done in history and philosophy fitted him for the task of re-stating the English law — let alone his Parliamentary experi-ence in drafting new laws, and in the courts his involvement with the difficulties of enforcement. His charges to juries from the bench have a conciseness that carries and projects. Concern-ing manslaughter, or killing upon sudden heat or an affray — "wrath," Bacon told one jury, "is a short madness . . . where-unto the law gives some little favour, because a man in fury is not himself." . . . And again, on the offense of dueling: "Life is grown too cheap in these times. It is set at the price of words, and every petty scorn or disgrace can have no other reparation; nay, so many men's lives are taken away with impunity that the life of the law is almost taken away."

In this "Proposition" to James, Bacon presents first his own arguments, then the arguments against. "There is such an accumulation of statutes concerning one matter," he writes, "and they so cross and intricate, as the certainty of law is lost in the heap. *Objectus:* That is a great innovation, and innovations are dangerous beyond foresight. *Responsus:* All purgings and medicines, either in the civil or natural body, are innovations; so as that argument is a common-place against all noble reformations."

Bacon's suggestions on how to proceed were entirely feasible, yet wonderfully prophetic concerning the future as well as present needs of the law. His letter to James was to be frequently printed in eighteenth-century editions of the legal writings. In 1826, Sir Robert Peel, Home Secretary, used Bacon's letter as preface to a speech in Parliament, urging consolidation of the laws against theft. "The lapse of two hundred and fifty years," said Peel, "has increased the necessity of the measure which Lord Bacon then proposed, but it has produced no argument in favor of the principle, no objection adverse to it, which he did not anticipate."

Perhaps the most brilliant exposition of Bacon's plan is to be found in the ninety-seven legal aphorisms of the *De Augmentis Scientiarum.* Bacon was at his happiest writing aphorisms. To borrow his own phrase, he was felicitous therein; he seemed to have been born with aphorisms on his tongue. No one need be a lawyer to enjoy these pages; even the headings have their charm. "Title One," writes Bacon. *"Of the Primary Dignity of Laws, that they may be certain.* Certainty is so essential to law, that law cannot even be just without it. 'For if the trumpet give an uncertain sound, who shall prepare himself to the battle?' . . . [The law] ought therefore to warn before it strikes."

[146]

There is a largeness and sweep to Bacon's conceptions. The end and scope of laws, he writes, "is no other than the happiness of the citizens." Yet his suggestions were practical, immediate. First and foremost, he said, a digest of the statute laws should be made. Obsolete laws ought to be expunged from the books; what remained should be shorn of contradiction and confusion, remodeled and reduced to a "sound and manageable body. . . . For law is nothing less than a commanding rule." Let the ancient volumes not perish, however, but remain in libraries, that lawyers may examine and consider the successive changes that have taken place. Then let the new body of law be confirmed by Parliament, "lest under pretence of digesting old laws, new laws be secretly imposed." The drafting of new laws should not be occasion for interminable meetings and interminable dispute. Rather, new laws should be written without "locquacity and prolixity, noise and strife of words," nor yet "a too concise and affected brevity." In the matter of preambles, Bacon was precise — and what he said was highly pertinent. Every important bill as proposed in Parliament had its preamble. In towns and boroughs, these preambles were read aloud or posted by Justices of the Peace — in the old days a source of irritation to Queen Elizabeth, who saw no need of these hortatory paragraphs, unless dictated by herself. For Elizabeth it had been enough that her Privy Council suggested a new law. James was of like mind. Why must the Commons justify each bill by sententious and contentious preamble, digressing into matters of "right," "privilege," "grievance"?

Bacon, however, declared that preambles were necessary, both in persuading Parliament to pass new laws, and to satisfy the people. "From preambles," he said, "the lawyers of this realm were wont always to take light. Our preambles are annexed for exposition, and this gives aim to the body of the statute. For the preamble sets up the mark, and the body of the law levels at it." (In the United States today, the preamble to an act of Congress still defines the mark; the courts refer to it in deciding what the legislature actually had in mind.)

Bacon had something to say about the teaching of law and much to say about reporting in the courts. Hitherto this had been a haphazard business, lacking authority and organization. Attorneys, judges, even spectators simply took notes as the cases proceeded; these were circulated in manuscript and occasionally published. Bacon recommended that reporters be chosen from among the most learned counsel and paid a liberal salary by the state. Nor should the judges meddle with reporting, "lest from being too fond of their own opinions they exceed the province of a reporter. . . . Great judges are unfit persons to be reporters, for they have either too little leisure or too much authority." Judge Dyer's Reports, Bacon added, are "but a kind of note book, and those of my Lord Coke hold too much *de proprio* [of himself]."

A subject badly needing regulation was the respective jurisdiction of courts, which tended to decline into rivalry, one court against another and even one judge against another. An intolerable evil, said Bacon, who had lately seen the actual existence of Chancery endangered by Sir Edward Coke's prohibitions and premunires. The way and road to a repeal of judgments, wrote Bacon, should be "narrow, rocky and as it were paved with flint stones."

Like Bacon's grand instauration of science and education, this legal reform and restatement would need for its achievement more than one man and one mind. It should be looked on, said Bacon, as "an heroic work," the authors to "be justly and deservedly reckoned among legislators and reformers of law." (Today, men are still struggling to restate the laws; it is a work that will go on as long as government endures.) Bacon was convinced the undertaking should not be in the hands of mere practicing lawyers, who, addicted to the positive rules of the native or the Roman laws, "have no freedom of opinion, but as it were talk in bonds." Nor should the work be launched by philosophers, "who lay down many precepts fair in argument but not applicable to use." Historians also were lacking proper qualification. "For it is a misfortune even of the best historians, that they do not dwell sufficiently upon the laws and judicial acts; or if by chance they use some diligence therein, yet they differ greatly from the authentic reports."

The consideration of law reform, said Bacon, "belongs properly to statesmen, who best understand the condition of civil society, welfare of the people, natural equity, customs of nations, and different forms of government; and who may therefore determine laws by the rules and principles both of natural equity and policy." Elsewhere, Bacon put it more poetically. The writings of men who have mingled their law with other studies, he said have "perhaps the more depth of reason. For the reasons of municipal laws severed from the grounds of nature, manners and policy are like wall flowers, which, though they grow high upon the crests of states, yet they have no deep roots."

Bacon's suggestions were eventually incorporated in the English legal system, though the doing took centuries; Sir Francis's imagination far outran his times. Hopefully, he rang his bell "to call the wits together" — in Parliament, in letters to the King, in published prefaces and epistles dedicatory to works on other subjects. These explanatory statements, thrown out when opportunity presented, in themselves proved valuable, pregnant with suggestion. They are applicable today, it has been pointed out, "to any body of civilized law."

Bacon's ninety-seven legal aphorisms in the *De Augmentis* end with a charming brief apologia: "This treatise of mine," he writes, "seems to me not unlike those sounds and preludes which musicians make while they are tuning their instruments, and which produce indeed a harsh and unpleasing sound to the ear, but tend to make the music sweeter afterwards. And thus have I intended to employ myself in tuning the harp of the muses and reducing it to perfect harmony, that hereafter the strings may be tended by a better hand or a better quill."

Lord Chancellor

O<small>N THE THIRD OF</small> M<small>ARCH</small>, 1617, old Lord Chancellor Ellesmere, ill and dying, surrendered the Seal to the King.
Four days later it was given to Francis Bacon, with the title of
Lord Keeper. Bacon's speech, on first taking his seat in Chancery, was businesslike yet easy. He said it would be his care to
avoid the delays for which this court had been blamed. "The
subject's pulse beats swift, though the Chancery pace be slow.
Fresh justice is the sweetest." Lately there had been stays and
stoppages, due to quarrels of jurisdiction between the different
courts — wherein has been "a great rattle, and a noise of a
premunire, and I cannot tell what." He had considered the
matter, said Bacon, and in cases of complaint after judgment at
common law he had various remedies to offer. But he would
grant no injunctions merely on priority of suit, as heretofore,
nor "make it a horse-race who shall be first in Westminster
Hall. By the grace of God," Bacon finished, "I will make in-
junction an hard pillow to sleep on."

To clear his court of a heavy arrear of business, the new
Lord Keeper promised that he would sit in the afternoons as
well as the mornings. But the depth and leisure of the three

long vacations he intended to reserve in some measure "for studies, arts, and sciences, to which in my nature I am most inclined." (The *Great Instauration* was still unfinished, and the *Novum Organum* that was part of it. In Francis Bacon the ambition of the understanding still held sway.)

At the end Bacon sounded a personal note, brief, but to him imperative, a necessity of his nature. If their lordships (the Judges and Privy Councilors) would give him leave, he would tell them a fancy, he said. "It falls out that there be three of us the King's servants in a great place, that are lawyers by descent: Mr. Attorney son of a Judge, Mr. Solicitor likewise son of a Judge, and myself, a Chancellor's son."

It was only a word, yet for Francis Bacon a significant word. After nearly forty years of striving he had reached his father's place, had stepped into his father's shoes. Now at last Bacon could refer when he chose to his father's high position and his father's service — and no man could say it was done for self-aggrandizement, as a son who is obscure bespeaks the glory of past forebears.

His investiture completed, Lord Keeper Bacon made his way home through the streets in glory — "waited on," wrote a barrister, "in the bravest manner that ever I saw. All the lawyers and gentlemen of the Inns of Court and Chancery went before him and all the [Privy] Council, the nobility, the judges, knights and gallant gentlemen about the town rode behind him in such a deal of bravery as is almost incredible." The barrister in his description used terms from heraldry. "All the windows from Fleet Conduit to Westminster Hall were filled with ladies and gentlewomen, adorned, equipped and armed at all points for the purpose, and most of them ruffed and cuffed, or faced, gorged and papped *argent*, cheeked, lipped and tipped *gules*. His lordship is daily attended with fifty or sixty as brave gentlemen as any about London."

Lord Bacon, the world called him now. And the world paid court to Lord Bacon, begged his favor; the world doffed its hat and stood upon York House threshold, asking entrance. One of the Lord Keeper's first moves was to request King James for a warrant conferring precedency on his wife. James complied. "We will command and express our royal pleasure to be, that all ladies of what estate or degree soever, under the estate or degree of a Baroness . . . shall hereafter at all times and in all places permit and suffer the Lady Bacon to have, take, and enjoy the place and precedency before them and every one of them. And this shall be your warrant. . . ."

Alice, Lady Bacon, aged twenty-five, lifted her long skirts, stepped into her high place and assumed the honors that were due. At York House stairs the barges thronged; in the stables there was a stamping of horse and across Thames water the rough cheerful voices of grooms and horseboys sounded. Among Bacon's congratulatory visitors was the Spanish Ambassador, Count Gondomar, witty, suave — "well skilled in court holy water," people said. Gondomar and Bacon got on well together; in each other's company they were mutually amused. Compliments passed, to which Bacon replied by thanking God for the honor that had come upon him. Yet in some ways, he added, he would willingly forbear the burden, for he had always harbored a desire to lead a private life.

The Spaniard accepted this modest statement for what it was worth, then asked the Lord Keeper if he would enjoy an allegory, a fable. Upon Bacon's acquiescence — "an old rat," Gondomar proceeded, "would needs leave the world and acquainted the young rats that he would retire into his hole and spend his days solitarily and would enjoy no more comfort; and commanded the young rats upon his high displeasure not to offer to come in unto him. They forbore two or three days. At last one that was more hardy than the rest, incited some of his fellows to go in with him, and he would venture to see how his father did, for he might be dead. They went in, and found the old rat sitting in the midst of a rich Parmesan cheese."

Bacon must have relished the story, because he wrote it down word for word among his *Apophthegms*.

At the upper end of Westminster Hall, some two hundred feet from the high arched door and the courts of common law, Sir Francis Bacon sat in the marble chair where his father had sat before him. Raised three steps from the echoing stone floor, the King's Lord Keeper surveyed as it were the universe of law. Bacon knew that his place now represented the legal center of the English constitution. Every legal action in the courts of law began with a writ issuing under the Great Seal of England. Bacon as a boy had seen it in his father's house. Big as a barrow wheel, in its gold-threaded tapestry purse it was carried ceremoniously before him as he walked to court and when he went hence in the afternoons. In ceremonies and processions, the Lord Keeper had precedence over everyone except the Archbishop of Canterbury. His patronage was impressive. In his hands was the appointment of justices of the peace for every county, as well as the Master of the Rolls and Masters and Clerks of Chancery. In the House of Lords he sat as prolocutor or speaker, not by election as in the Commons but by virtue of his office.

The new Lord Keeper followed Sir Thomas More's example of giving a dinner for the common-law judges. For Bacon it was especially politic; no doubt the twelve still felt the sting of the recent royal decree. After the judges had feasted, Bacon sat down with them and begged them to look upon him "as one of them, but a foreman." The late discords had been matters merely "of flesh and blood," he said — quarrels between persons rather than principles. "Now the men are gone the matter is gone."

It would have been more correct to say, now that Sir Edward Coke was gone from the common-law bench. To the twelve judges, Bacon made his position further plain. He would suffer no diminution of the power of Chancery. Yet should the common bench look on any of his decrees as exorbitant or inordinate, let them come to him and "freely and friendly acquaint him with it, and they should soon agree."

"At which," Bacon reported afterward, "I did see cheer and comfort in their faces, as if it were a new world."

For Chancery, Bacon produced a new set of orders, one hundred and one of them, reforming weaknesses of structure and fixing practice — making rules that would endure until the reforms of the nineteenth century. Bacon had promised that he would do speedy justice in a court notorious for delays. He kept his word. Talkative lawyers were rebuked, sometimes held in contempt, as with one barrister whose argument covered ten skins of parchment, "containing," it was said, "much idle and impertinent matter for the purpose of putting the plaintiff to unnecessary trouble and expense to the derogation of the court."

Did Bacon perhaps recall his father's dislike of long-winded attorneys, and how Sir Nicholas in his latter days had suffered from asthma and shortness of breath? Interrupted repeatedly by a counselor at the bar — "There is a great difference betwixt you and me," said Sir Nicholas. "A pain to me to speak, and a pain to you to hold your peace."

Three months after he became Lord Keeper, Bacon could say the court docket was caught up. To achieve it had been a *tour de force*. "Not one cause unheard," wrote Bacon. "The lawyers drawn dry of all the motions they were to make. Not one petition unanswered. And this I think could not be said in our age before." In this prerogative court, this "court of the King's conscience," the new Lord Keeper was very much at home. He listened to suitors, studied petitions, took his notes home with him in the afternoons to look up precedents or think the matter out. Occasionally he heard cases in chambers at Whitehall Palace, sometimes in the great withdrawing room of York House. The suits varied widely. There was a case in piracy, when Count Gondomar sued to regain the contents of two Spanish caravels captured by British sailors on the coast of Ireland. There were suits left over from Lord Chancellor Ellesmere's day: one friend had obtained a knighthood for another; the knight, safely titled, refused to pay for the service as promised. Bacon rebuked the plaintiff, saying he utterly misliked to see matters of knighthood made venal and mercenary. (Francis Bacon could afford such strictures; he had never paid a penny for title or place.) There was the case of the mariners, hurt and maimed while voyaging with Drake and Hawkins long ago, for whom a fund had been set up. Yet when the chest was opened to pay them, the money was gone. . . . There were cases in bankruptcy, cases of escape from debtors' prison, a case where a witness could not testify because he was too old to ride a horse one hundred and sixty-seven miles to court.

The very insignificance of the suits is reassuring; Chancery

did not disdain the small petitioner. Bacon was one of those
Chancellors before whom the plain man must have been glad
to appear. A judge, Bacon said, should be patient and grave.
"An over-speaking judge is no well-tuned cymbal. It is no
grace to a judge first to find that which he might have heard
in due time from the bar; or to shew quickness of conceit in
cutting off evidence or counsel too short; or to prevent information by questions, though pertinent."

The great matters with which Bacon dealt in these years
were outside his court; they related to his responsibility as
Privy Councilor — as for instance the hot political question of
Prince Charles's proposed marriage to the Infanta of Spain.
For James the marriage was a way of insuring peace with
Spain — his dearest wish, next to the union of Scotland and
England. But to Protestant England, in particular to the lawyers of Coke's faction who would soon meet in Parliament, the
Spanish marriage was anathema, an offense against religion
and patriotism. The King's heart was set on it; Bacon, with his
parliamentary experience, could be useful in persuading the
opposing faction. In Treasury matters also, Bacon was effectual. He and the great London merchant, Lionel Cranfield, between them made large retrenchments and savings in the
royal household and Navy.

There is no doubt that Lord Keeper Bacon enjoyed his position to the full and made the most of it; London gossips said
he made too much of it. Not long after Bacon's investiture,
King James went to Scotland on progress, naming the Lord
Keeper as regent of England during his absence. At the palace,
Sir Francis kept almost royal state, receiving ambassadors in
the banqueting hall as if he were sovereign. As summer ad-

vanced, Bacon, losing caution in his new glory, made an almost fatal mistake of policy. Dramatically enough, it concerned his old enemy and rival, Sir Edward Coke.

After Coke's dismissal from the bench, he had spent some seven months in angry, restless idleness, exiled to a married daughter's estate in Hertfordshire. Desperate to recover the royal favor (without which no man could hold high place), Coke conceived the hopeful stratagem of a marriage between his youngest daughter, Frances, aged fourteen, and Sir John Villiers, elder brother of James's current and very powerful favorite, George Villiers, Earl of Buckingham. Coke's wife, Lady Hatton, threw herself violently against her husband in the matter and even succeeded in kidnapping their daughter and spiriting her off to a castle near Hampton Court. Bacon went so far as to file an information against Coke in Star Chamber, charging riotous behavior.

The affair became public knowledge. London was entranced, the Privy Council disturbed. By some incredible blindness — or perhaps by intrigue of an enemy, Secretary of State Winwood — Bacon mistook both the King's and Buckingham's wishes and sided with Lady Hatton, that same handsome and imperious woman to whom Sir Francis once had proposed marriage. Bacon wrote to the court in Scotland, giving his reasons for obstructing Coke's plans, reasons also why the proposed marriage would be bad policy for the family of Villiers. In no time at all the Lord Keeper discovered his mistake and knew that it was serious enough to peril his career. From Scotland there arrived messengers with cold, peremptory letters. James was irritated, Buckingham angry. Coke, it seems, had offered an enormous dowry with his daughter. And though Sir John Villiers declared the girl's beauty such that he would take her penniless, "in her shift" — to the family of Villiers and hence to the King, Coke's money was not to be despised. The marriage went through. The King kissed the bride and gave her away at the altar. Coke produced a dowry of ten thousand pounds and found himself restored to his place in Privy Council, though not to his judgeship. Lady Hatton retired to nurse her wounds. And Francis Bacon, Lord Keeper of the Seal, bent his head, took pen in hand and wrote lengthy, tormented letters of apology to James and Buckingham.

London watched and listened and laughed. "Lord Coke," it was said, "is tossed up and down like a tennis ball. Lord Bacon is in slippery places, and self-interest prevails." Did Bacon, in this hazardous time, recall the old verse his brother Anthony had liked to quote, concerning the risks and shifts of a career at court and palace?

> *To laugh, to lie, to flatter, to face:*
> *Four ways in court to win men grace.*
> *If thou be thrall to none of these,*
> *Away, good Peek Goose! Hence, John Cheese!*

Bacon's letters in this affair make painful reading. The subtlest mind in England strained to twist upon itself, undo what was done, retreat from a cause in which both retreat and victory were unworthy. In the end, Bacon was forgiven. James was not Elizabeth, whose enmity and displeasure were implacable. Next year, Bacon's title was advanced from Lord Keeper to Lord Chancellor and he was created a peer — Lord Verulam. From now on, Bacon expanded his position recklessly. He dearly loved York House, where he had been born, with its ancient turrets and steep roof. Now he repaired the old house to the tune of "a thousand marks" — more, he said, "than had been laid out by all the tenants that had been in it since his remembrance." He furnished it lavishly, persuaded the Mayor of London to lay on a pipe from the City's mains to supply him with water, and built an aviary which cost three hundred pounds.

None of these domestic expenses were overlooked by London. The Lord Chancellor, it was noted, "exceeds all his predecessors in the bravery and multitude of his servants. It amazes those that look on his beginnings." From an income of three hundred pounds per annum — what, said another, had this gentleman not attained? Bacon kept more than a hundred retainers, including a Gentleman of the Horse, Gentlemen Ushers and various Gentlemen in Waiting, one of whom was his nephew, Nicholas Bacon. Embroidered on his servants' livery, across the back, was his crest, a boar. Talk had it that the Lord Chancellor's servants dared not appear before him unless in Spanish leather boots; the smell of neat's leather offended his lordship. Many "scurril jests are passed on his extravagance," it was said. At the University of Cambridge, Bacon gave great feasts, and for one of James's favorites he presented a masque at Gray's Inn which cost him two thousand pounds.

There was no end to it. Bacon's gentlemen servants kept race horses; his largesse was out of all proportion. "In giving of rewards," men said, "Lord Bacon knew no bounds but the bottom of his own purse. Wherefore, when King James heard that he had given ten pounds to an underkeeper by whom his Majesty had sent a buck, the King said merrily, 'I and he shall both die beggars.'" Bacon's money lay about in chests and boxes, unlocked. A gentleman, calling on him, was left alone for an hour in the Chancellor's study. In came a member of Bacon's retinue, opened a chest of drawers, took money by the handfuls, stuffed it in his pockets and went out without a word.

He was followed by a second man who repeated the perform-
ance. When the Lord Chancellor returned, the astonished visi-
tor told what had occurred. Bacon only shook his head. "Sir,"
he said, "I cannot help myself."

The words are ominous; almost they bear the mark of com-
pulsion. In his reckless spending, Bacon was like a gambler
caught in the toils of a temptation he could neither control nor
comprehend. *"Sir, I cannot help myself."* Bacon knew well
that his resources were limited. In his household accounts one
finds the interest due on large loans. Partial payments on small
bills indicate that in the midst of plenty, cash was scarce.

In fine weather, the Lord Chancellor took coach for St. Albans in Hertfordshire, eighteen miles to the northwest of London. Here were the woods, the park and orchards of his father's manor house, the "sweet airs" which he said revived
him. And here at Gorhambury, Francis Bacon now lived magnificently among oak groves and stately walks of trees, using
his father's mansion for winter and Verulam House, his own
creation, for summer. (A gentleman should have, he wrote,
seats for summer and winter as well as clothes.)

The two houses were a mile apart. Between them, Bacon
built three parallel roads, running straight and wide so that
three coaches could roll abreast. Throngs of noblemen and
knights came up these roads to visit, or to ask for place and
favor. It was said the Chancellor lived so nobly, "it seemed as
if the court were there." On the upper doors of Verulam House,
above the balcony, were painted tall figures of Jupiter and
Apollo, gilded and flashing in the sun. From the roof — "the
leads" — where Bacon loved to walk and meditate, one could
look down upon a prospect of wide artificial ponds, set in the
low ground. If one stood at the brink and looked down into

the water, one saw fish traced in colored stones along the bottom. In the tall doors of Verulam House, Bacon set mirrors. Returning from the ponds, one saw again the water and was charmingly deceived. There was a little contemporary verse about Verulam House:

> *That spatious, spacious precious refectorie,*
> *Which cost a world of wealth (so saith the story)*
> *Those pebble pavèd brooks, empalèd lakes,*
> *Thick clad with countless shoals of ducks and drakes. . . .*

Under his oak trees, Bacon planted peonies and tulips; from the grove a door, painted blue and gold, opened to a coppice where Bacon liked to walk. A secretary followed with inkhorn, quill and paper to take his master's spoken meditations. (Among his secretaries, young Thomas Hobbes, said Bacon, was his best amanuensis. The others set down his words, but without comprehension.) When he meditated indoors, the Chancellor liked to have music played in the next room; lute and viol made a gentle harmony which took away the distraction of care. Bacon was nearly sixty. Now and again he was absent from his courtroom; London ascribed it to "tender health." The Chancellor was cheerful about his infirmities, his gout, his attacks of the stone. "I have been a little unperfect in my foot," he wrote from York House. "But if it be a gout it is a good-natured gout, for I have no rage of it and it goeth away quickly. I have hope it is but an accident of changing from a field-air to a Thames-air."

Bacon's writings are filled with ideas for the conservation of health. Some are wonderfully perceptive; Bacon had a prophetic sense of the vital correspondence between health of the mind and of the body. To attain a long life — "avoid envy," he wrote. Avoid "anxious fears, anger fretting inwards, sadness not communicated. . . . A man's own observation, what he finds good of, and what he finds hurt of, is the best physic to preserve health." Interspersed with such excellent good sense we find medical hints and nostrums which seem to us quite mad, and which serve to place Francis Bacon where he was — not quite at the end of medievalism. Observe, for instance, his numbered list of "New Advices in order to Health and the prolongation of Life." There are thirty-two of these advices. Some are fantastic, some bawdy in the frank Elizabethan manner, some could hardly be bettered today by the experts:

1. Use once during supper time, wine in which gold is quenched.
2. Bathing of the feet once a month with camomile, sweet marjoram, fennel, sage and a little aqua vitae.
3. Provide always an apt breakfast.
4. Macerations in pickles.
5. Heroic desires.
6. To do nothing against a man's genius.

No man knew better than Francis Bacon what it meant to cherish heroic desires, or knew more bitterly the corrosion that comes of their denial. Often he had quoted Plutarch: *"Cor ne edito:* eat not thy heart." Bacon's sensitive body vibrated painfully to sudden change of fortune. Now, in his glory, when all should have been well, he suffered from occasional fainting fits. Dr. Rawley, his chaplain, said this happened only when the moon waned. "It may seem," wrote Rawley, "the moon had some principal place in the figure of [my lord's] nativity; for the moon was never in her passion, or eclipsed, but he was surprised with a sudden fit of fainting; and that though he observed not nor took any previous knowledge of the eclipse thereof; and as soon as the eclipse ceased, he was restored to his former strength again."

In current parlance, the passion of the moon was her darkening, the eclipse her waning. It almost seemed as if, having suffered his own eclipse for so long, Bacon could not endure to see the light fail and darkness descend once more.

In October of 1618, Bacon served as one of six Privy Councilors, named by King James as a commission to examine Sir Walter Ralegh concerning his recently completed — and disastrous — voyage to Guiana in search of gold. Bacon's part in Ralegh's condemnation was small, though often mentioned by historians. The truth is that Ralegh's name has become glorified until he is the very archetype of hero. Every man who had to do with his condemnation, either in 1603 or 1618, partakes of infamy.

Yet the records tell us that Ralegh the poet, Ralegh the sea fighter and colonizer, Ralegh the magnificent adventurer, the martyr who suffered nearly fourteen years' imprisonment — was also a born intriguer who did not hesitate with a lie when lying was expedient. Ralegh, in short, was dangerous. Even Queen Elizabeth had recognized it, who knew his quality. To the men that governed England in 1618, Sir Walter was a nuisance — proud, intransigent, unmanageable. Freed from prison, in 1617 he had voyaged to Guiana with fourteen ships in search of gold, swearing to King and Council that he would attack no Spaniards nor molest any property of Spain. A year later he had returned *sans* gold, *sans* plunder for King or Treasury, his son Walter lost in a fight with the Spaniards, the town of San Tomás burned to the ground by Ralegh's men. (In Venezuela to this day men speak of Sir Walter as "the English thug.") The defiant adventurer had set all James's plans awry: the peace with Spain, the cherished Spanish marriage. Count Gondomar, in the name of his royal master, gave out the angry cry: *Piratas, piratas, piratas!*

There was no question of a court trial. Ralegh had already been convicted of treason; he was civilly dead. Among the six commissioners named for a hearing were Bacon and Edward Coke. A letter to James, in Coke's handwriting, exists today, dated from York House on October 18, 1618; one recognizes Bacon's phraseology. (For once, the rivals must have worked amicably together.) The letter advised a public hearing, where Ralegh should be charged with "acts of hostility, depredation and abuse of his Majesty's commission." Ralegh should be permitted to answer these charges publicly, after which his Majesty's Judges and Lords of Privy Council could advise if "in justice and honor," warrant might be issued for his execution on the old charge of treason.

James refused the public hearing, saying that once before (in 1603), Sir Walter by his wit had "turned the hatred of men into compassion of him." Let the hearings therefore be private, before the Attorney General, the Solicitor and the Lords of Council.

It was done. On October 28, Ralegh appeared for the last time before the commissioners. Most of the testimony is lost, but it is said that Lord Chancellor Bacon was the man who told Sir Walter that he must die. Ralegh was led into Westminster Hall; the Chief Justice of King's Bench pronounced sentence of death. Next morning Ralegh was beheaded in Old Palace Yard, in the presence of a great throng.

The magnificence of that last awful scene, Ralegh's courage and patience in the face of death, has become one of history's great epics. It has made all who participated seem infamous, including Francis Bacon who censured the prisoner, and Edward Coke who in 1603 had prosecuted him in Westminster Hall. Yet Bacon cannot be called to account for Ralegh's death; the Lord Chancellor was a small cog in this wheel. Ralegh had disobeyed. He had put his own judgment and desires above those of the sovereign and the state. Sir Walter's existence was inconvenient and he must go; nothing Bacon might have said or done would have saved him.

"That great wise knight," wrote a contemporary, "being such an anti-Spaniard, was made a sacrifice to advance the matrimonial treaty."

At the time of Ralegh's death, Bacon had held the Great Seal for nearly twenty months. On the day of his investiture he had declared publicly the intention of continuing his philosophic studies, despite great business in a great office. Likely enough, Bacon thought his high position would enable him, now at last, to achieve the ambition of a lifetime — that ambition of the understanding which he had defined so long ago. Since early manhood, almost since youth, Bacon had endeavored to engage men's attention toward a new way of thinking and learning, and toward that knowledge of the natural world which could be thereby discovered. To Bacon these ideas had now their title: they were the *Instauratio Magna,* the Great Instauration of Knowledge. Bacon could boast the highest position in England, next the King. Yet his colleges and workshops were still unbuilt; place and prestige had not been sufficient to set his scheme at work. Among thinking men, only a handful were in sympathy with his ideas. Sir Francis Bacon, said Dr. William Harvey scornfully, wrote philosophy "like a Lord Chancellor."

Forty years must pass, and a civil war, before England would be receptive to Bacon's challenge, ready for the new science and the road to enlightenment. In 1608, after he published the first two books of his *Advancement of Learning,* Bacon almost at once had begun the greatest of his works, to be called the *Novum Organum.* Characteristically, Bacon composed it in bits and pieces, working on practical scientific experiments (the *Natural History*), then developing the theoretical end. Some time before 1618 — we do not know exactly when — Bacon put aside the *Great Instauration* and sat down to try if he might draw men's minds to his scheme by way of a simple tale, a fable, an allegory after the manner of that *Utopia* composed by another, earlier Lord Chancellor, Sir Thomas More. Bacon called his fable the *New Atlantis.*

The *New Atlantis* is one of those rare and happy works which read as if composed at a sitting, almost with a single long flowing stroke of the pen. Bacon left it unfinished, and that again was characteristic; never was such a fragmentary writer. Yet the *New Atlantis* was destined to be one of Bacon's most influential works and to many readers the most appealing of them all.

With the first line, Bacon sweeps us into the narrative: "We sailed from Peru (where we had continued by the space of one whole year), for China and Japan, by the South Sea, taking with us victuals for twelve months; and had good winds from the east, though soft and weak, for five months' space and more." Bacon's voyagers land eventually on the island called Bensalem, where they are housed hospitably and visited by officers and principal statesmen of this hitherto undiscovered community. At last comes a very high official, who declares himself one of the Fathers of *Salomon's House,* or the *College of the Six Days Works.* The Father's clothes are marvelous; Bacon describes them in detail. . . . Shoes of peach-colored velvet, a robe of fine black cloth with wide sleeves and a cape, gloves set with gems, a Spanish hat like a helmet. The Father was "of middle stature and age," writes Bacon, "comely of person, and had an aspect as if he pitied men."

The phrase is wholly Baconian. Clearly, this Father was fashioned upon Sir Francis's ideal of what a gentleman should be. *An aspect as if he pitied men.* Here is no brutal, solemn authority, no tyranny of intellect or person. Rather, here is one in whose presence the mind expands, the spirit grows receptive, and in whose bearing is the quality of compassion. As the narrative proceeds, the people of Bensalem appear as Francis Bacon's spiritual brothers. They are cheerful, merry of speech, with minds quite obviously "pliable to the occasion." Their bearing carries not only dignity but felicity. It was in Bacon's nature to be impatient with pompousness, or with the secretive and stubborn mind . . . "these grave solemn wits," he said, "which must be like themselves and cannot make departures," and whose nature it is "to be somewhat viscous and inwrapped, and not easy to turn."

And now among our voyagers to Bensalem, one is singled out for private audience with the Father of Salomon's House. The two gentlemen meet in a "fair chamber, richly hanged and carpeted under foot." The Father proceeds to explain the true state and function of Salomon's House, or the *College of the Six Days Works, dedicated to the study of the Works and Creatures of God.**

---

* I have condensed the Father's account somewhat.

"The end of our Foundation," says the Father, "is the knowledge of causes and secret motions of things; and the enlarging of the bounds of human empire, to the effecting of all things possible."

This of course was the heart and gist of Bacon's own ambition for an English university, for a system of colleges devoted to the sciences; it was his *Novum Organum,* his *Great Instauration* brought to fulfillment. The Father of Salomon's House continues: "The preparation and instruments are these," he says. "We have large and deep caves . . . for refrigeration and conservations of bodies; great lakes both salt and fresh for fish and fowl . . . also for burials of some natural bodies, to see if things buried in water are differently preserved from those buried in earth or air. . . . We have high towers, the highest about half a mile in height, and some of them likewise set upon high mountains . . . for the view of divers meteors, as winds, rain, snow, hail and some of the fiery meteors also. . . . We have pools of which some do strain salt water out of fresh. . . . We have large and various orchards and gardens wherein we practice all conclusions of grafting and inoculating, whereby we make trees and flowers to come earlier or later than their seasons, and their fruit greater and sweeter and of differing taste, smell, colour, and figure from their nature; and likewise to make one tree or plant turn into another."

The college has parks and enclosures, the Father goes on, for beasts and birds to be viewed alive or killed for dissection, "that thereby we may take light what may be wrought upon the body of man. We try also all poisons and other medicines upon them, as well of chirurgery as physic. By art likewise we can make them more fruitful and bearing than their kind is; and contrariwise barren and not generative. . . . We have brew-houses and bake-houses, dispensatories or shops of medicine . . . furnaces, instruments also which generate heat only by motion. We have also perspective houses, with divers means of seeing objects afar off, as in the heaven and remote places, also glasses and means to see small and minute bodies perfectly and distinctly, as the shapes and colors of small flies and worms, observations in urine and blood, not otherwise to be seen.

"We have also sound-houses, where we practice and demonstrate all sounds, quarter-sounds and lesser slides of sounds, and we have means to convey sounds in trunks and pipes, in strange lines and distances." There is more, and all of it enchanting. The college had perfume-houses, to imitate smells and tastes. It had engine-houses and fireworks; "some degrees of flying in the air," said the Father; "ships and boats for going under water, swimming girdles and supporters, images that imitate the motions of living creatures — men, beasts, birds, fishes and serpents. We have a mathematical house where are represented all instruments, as well of geometry as astronomy, exquisitely made. We have also houses of deceit of the senses; false apparitions, impostures and illusions and their fallacies.

"For our ordinances and rites," finished the Father, "we have two very long and fair galleries. In one of these we place patterns and samples of all manner of the more rare and excellent inventions; in the other we place the statuas of all principal inventors. There we have the statue of your Columbus, that discovered the West Indies: also the inventor of ships, your monk that was the inventor of ordnance and of gunpowder, and the inventors of music, glass, wine, letters, silk, printing, corn and bread and sugars."

At last the traveler kneels to take his leave and to receive the Father's blessing. The sage's farewell gesture is characteristically Baconian. "And so he left me," Bacon writes, "having assigned a value of about two thousand ducats, for a bounty to me and my fellows. For the Fathers of Salomon's House give great largesses where they come upon all occasions."

In October of 1620, Bacon's *Novum Organum* appeared in print. Actually the book contains, in substance, the entire plan of the *New Atlantis,* but set out theoretically, schematically, and in Latin. We do not know exactly when the first page was written. Bacon's chaplain said that he had seen at the least twelve different copies, "revised year by year one after another, and every year altered and amended in the frame thereof." Bacon intended, of course, a much longer work, and wrote out his scheme for the whole. Lofty though the conception is, and brilliantly though its famous aphorisms shine, we can read the *Novum Organum* only in some comparatively modern translation; the originality and charm of Bacon's English prose is lost. Bacon looked on the English language as distinctly limited, a local, provincial tongue. To reach a European audience, to reach the world, a book must be written in Latin, which Bacon referred to as "the general language."

Bacon sent a copy of his *Novum Organum* to the King, who wrote back a friendly letter in his own hand. A copy went also to Sir Edward Coke, bound luxuriously in vellum, goldtooled, with Bacon's crest stamped in gold. I have seen this copy, with its beautiful title page, engraved with a ship in full sail, setting out, between the Pillars of Hercules, toward the boundless sea of knowledge. Above the drawing, Coke has scrawled in inky Latin, "Gift from the author"; under this a scornful couplet, destined to be quoted down the years:

> *It deserveth not to be read in Schooles*
> *But to be freighted in the ship of Fooles.*

Bacon seemed never to remember that his enemies hated him. King James, too, was later overheard to remark that Bacon's book, like the peace of God, passeth all understanding. An Oxford scholar grumbled that a fool could not have written the book and a wise man would not. Yet among the *cognoscenti* of England and Europe the work enhanced Bacon's reputation greatly, though it was a little slow to make its way.

On January 22, 1621, Bacon reached the age of sixty. At York House he gave a feast for his friends. Music played from the balcony, candlelight wavered against dark paneling. Ben Jonson, genial before his host and friend, declaimed verses composed for the occasion:

> *Hail, happy Genius of this ancient pile!*
> *How comes it all things so about thee smile?*
> *The fire, the wine, the men! and in the midst,*
> *Thou stand'st as if some mystery thou didst . . .*
> *Son to the grave, wise Keeper of the Seal,*
> *Fame, and foundation of the English weal.*
> *What then his father was, that since is he,*
> *Now with a title more to the degree;*
> *England's high Chancellor: the destin'd heir*
> *In his soft cradle to his father's chair;*
> *Whose even thread the Fates spin round, and full,*
> *Out of their choicest, and their whitest wool . . .*

Five days later, Bacon was created Viscount St. Alban, a notch higher in the peerage. He chose his title from the old Roman town that lies three miles from Gorhambury House.

To Bacon's pleasure, the creation took place at Theobalds, once his uncle Lord Burghley's great country mansion, now King James's favorite palace.

It was a ceremony of more than usual glitter and show. Bacon's robe was carried before him by Lord Carew; Lord Wentworth bore the coronet. Francis Bacon, Baron Verulam, Viscount St. Alban, Lord Chancellor of England, his cup of joy overflowing, went home and wrote his thanks to the King who had raised him step by step, he said, from nothing to this high honor. "Your Majesty found me of the Learned Counsel Extraordinary, without patent or fee; a kind of *individuum vagum*. You established me, and brought me into Ordinary. Soon after, you placed me Solicitor, where I served seven years. Then your Majesty made me your Attorney or Procurator General. Then Privy Councilor, while I was Attorney, a kind of miracle of your favor, that had not been in many ages. Thence Keeper of your Seal; and because that was a kind of planet and not fixed, Chancellor. And when your Majesty could raise me no higher, it was your grace to illustrate me with beams of honor; first making me Baron Verulam, and now Viscount St. Alban. So this is the eighth rise or reach, a diapason in music, even a good number and accord for a close."

Secure, happy, splendid in place and power, Lord Chancellor St. Alban, once plain Francis Bacon, looked out upon his world and approved the prospect. Within five days, Parliament was to meet. Bacon was busy with plans for the session. He had been strongly influential in persuading James, against the royal will, to summon this Parliament, the first since 1614. No doubt there would be difficulty with the Commons, who were

[173]

violently opposed to the Spanish marriage and becoming almost openly opposed to the King's adored favorite, George Villiers, Marquis of Buckingham. Yet the Commons could be managed. Bacon had done it before, he had confidence he could do it again.

On January 30, 1621, King James came down to open Parliament, and with his Lord Chancellor by his side, performed the ancient pageantry. There were no signs, no portents to hint or tell that this Parliament in a few weeks would encompass Bacon's ruin.

CHAPTER IV

Impeachment
1621

Impeachment

> He knew how the bushes were beaten, and how
> the beagle ranged the field for game. He heard the
> cry of the bloodhounds that nosed the field where
> he trod.
> — JOHN HACKET
> *Life of Bishop Williams*

FEBRUARY, 1621. Lord Chancellor Francis Bacon — Baron
Verulam and Viscount St. Alban — sat on his crimson
woolsack in the House of Lords, by virtue of his office presiding. Beside him the mace glittered, the Great Seal lay in its embroidered bag. Having been elected to the Commons of every
Parliament since 1584, as well as giving legal assistance in the
Upper Chamber, Bacon was probably the most experienced
man present and certainly the most knowledgeable.

In another part of the sprawling palace of Westminster, the
Commons met in their arched and ancient chapel, ranged face
to face along the benches like singers in a church choir.
Among them Sir Edward Coke was known as *pater patriae,*
bellwether of the flock. Old Coke, he was now, at sixty-nine,
without occupation since his dismissal as Chief Justice, bitter
with idleness and happy to be once more in Parliament. Bacon

and Coke: the two greatest lawyers of England; some say the greatest that ever were in England. Patriots both, yet implacably divided in their ideas of government and of essential procedure in the courts of law.

The royal treasury needed money. King James had not called a Parliament in seven years and had not received a subsidy in ten — which was, somebody said, "a very long time to live like a shellfish upon his own moisture." James loathed Parliaments, hated the House of Commons' habit of bargaining "grievances" against subsidies, their stubborn questioning of the royal prerogative. When he was King in Scotland, James said, their Parliament had neither argued nor bargained. To a sovereign who held his throne by divine right, it was not part of the people's business to criticize royal expenditure or the royal privilege of granting commercial monopolies to palace favorites. Nor was it the Commons' business to query great matters and mysteries of state such as the projected alliance with Catholic Spain, or to urge reformation in the court of Star Chamber, where Kings of England had a right to sit. Yet since Bacon's first Parliament nearly thirty years ago, the temper of the Lower House had altered. It was far more self-conscious and mindful of its privileges. Experience had taught the Commons how to bargain for what they wanted. Bacon was well aware of it, and did his best to make the King aware of it. "Nowadays there is no vulgar," Bacon said, "but all statesmen."

Barrister members of the Commons were especially adept at bargaining and maneuvering grievances against subsidy. Around Sir Edward Coke sat a brace of experienced Parliament men like Heneage Finch, Noye, Glanville, Alford, Hakewill — tough quick legalists and speakers who knew when and how to pull the strings, sparked and abetted by fiery young members such as John Pym. So irked was King James by these names and these men that before Parliament met he had sent out a proclamation, warning the towns and counties not to elect "curious and wrangling lawyers, who may seek reputation by stirring needless waters." Francis Bacon begged to delete the words "wrangling lawyers," but James was adamant. Foreseeing trouble, Bacon at Christmas had sent a plan of procedure to the King. "I have broken the main of the Parliament business into questions and parts, which I send," he wrote. "It may be it is an over-diligence, but still methinks there is a middle thing between art and chance: I think they call it providence."

The Commons were more than justified in their dissatisfaction. England was still governed as if it were a vast country estate belonging to the Crown: the nation had dangerously outgrown such administration. Between public funds and private funds no real line was drawn. Customs duties were farmed out by the Crown to private syndicates. Commodities such as tin, wines, playing cards, were granted as monopolies to public servants or palace favorites. Patents for the manufacture of gold lace, for the operation of inns and ale-houses were handed out to be administered as the lucky recipient saw fit. Widespread abuse resulted, squeezing of the poor, with monopolistic spies and pursuivants sent through the country to garner proper tribute. Even in Elizabeth's day the system had flourished. The Queen's last Parliament had demanded fiercely if *bread* would be next on the patent list?

Actually, the Crown was helpless, caught in the same net with the citizens. King James had no funds to pay his public servants. Taxes came in slowly and piecemeal. No credit organization existed large enough to float an adequate loan; when James borrowed of the London Aldermen he borrowed at ten per cent. In this system or lack of system, every man along the line had his cut and share, whether it came as a "gratuity," a "grant," a New Year's gift or something more doubtful. Ministers of state accepted Spanish money in return for news concerning England's intentions; even Robert Cecil had enjoyed a Spanish pension. James knew it — and knew also that whoever gave money to his ministers favored the royal treasury. It was not planned corruption but appalling inefficiency and confusion, ingrown, customary, accepted by society at large. For those involved it presented insoluble problems of ethics and morality. A man had to live. Moreover, a great man had to live greatly, with a score at least of liveried servants to follow him in the streets, and largesse to scatter — else he would be accused of "meanness," of betraying the dignity of his position. The government paid minimal wages. No Chancellor or Chief Justice could maintain a household on his yearly stipend.

There was a hole in the royal cistern, a Commons member had remarked. Monies voted to the Crown leaked down into the pockets of royal favorites. From the beginning, James had lavished money on these men. Now, in 1621, he actually ruled the kingdom through the most celebrated of his favorites. George Villiers, once an untitled country gentleman, stood at the King's right hand as Marquis of Buckingham and Lord Admiral of England, having risen to that high eminence by virtue of magnificently shaped legs, a charming nature and a face so beautiful that the King blasphemed in adoration of it. Buckingham's rise had been spectacular. It had begun when he was twenty-four, and James saw him run and leap in the palace courtyard after dinner with the other gentlemen waiters. Everyone now paid tribute. No suit could be advanced, no place attained without a gift to this courtly strong white hand. (Sir Walter Ralegh had paid Buckingham £1500 for his release from the Tower.) While the favorite was still plain George Villiers, Bacon had befriended him, sending thoughtful, lengthy letters of advice upon his position, as once he had done for the Earl of Essex. It was to Buckingham's influence that Bacon attributed his gaining the Chancellorship.

The House of Commons knew this, knew that Lord Chancellor Bacon, though a friend to Parliament and the Commons, was also a friend to Buckingham. But as Parliament opened in 1621, the Commons evidenced no slightest intention of wishing ill to Francis Bacon. They even accorded him the honor of naming him as the fittest man to present a certain highly important petition to the King. Yet concerning the Marquis of Buckingham the Commons were deeply resentful, and the feeling ranged beyond Buckingham to his entourage, his friends and dependents. In short, the Commons were primed for bear. Yet the weapons at their command were clumsy. As government was then organized, its ministers were not responsible to Parliament but to the Crown — a situation that would require a revolution for its cure.

Restless, the Commons showed their protest by threatening to "reform" one government organization after another; the Court of Wards, the King's purveyors, the Court of Exchequer, the two great courts of common law. In any era, there exists no more efficacious way of embarrassing a public official than a seemingly dignified effort to "reform" his office. In the course of such activity, a parliamentary committee can achieve thorough demoralization wherever they aim their blow. Moreover, when a vital, eager assembly like the House of Commons needs a channel for discontent, inevitably the channel is found. The Lower House of 1621 was dissatisfied first with the Marquis of Buckingham; second with the monopolies, for which they chose to hold Buckingham responsible; and third with the King's foreign policy, which leaned toward permanent peace with Catholic Spain, to be cemented by a marriage between Prince Charles and the Infanta.

The Commons turned their opening guns on two monopolists, Michell and Mompesson by name, who were summarily disposed of, after heated and apparently enjoyable debate, including much difference of opinion as to legal procedure. Michell went to prison. Sir Giles Mompesson, under threat of being condemned to ride his horse to the Tower sitting backwards, with sundry other humiliations too uncomfortable to be borne, jumped out a window and escaped to France. The Commons, growing bolder, aimed next at victims on a higher level — the referees of monopolies, men named earlier by James to study certain patents and pass on their legality, receiving in the process much tribute. Buckingham's two brothers were among the referees. So was Francis Bacon. " 'Twas loudly proclaimed," wrote a contemporary historian, "that there were sucking horse-leeches in great places. Things not to be valued at money were saleable, and what could not gold procure."

On his woolsack, Bacon waited, anxious — but only a little anxious — concerning these events. "I woo nobody," he wrote to Buckingham. "I do but listen, and I have doubt only of Sir Edward Coke, who I wish had some round *caveat* given him from the King; for your Lordship hath no great power with him, but I think a word from the King mates him."

Parliament had opened on the thirtieth of January, 1621. On

March 8, a committee of the Lower House was named to inquire into the conduct of the referees. James, hearing of it, summoned the Commons to appear before him in the Upper House. By what right, the King demanded angrily, did the Commons found their claim to omnipotency? "Before Parliament met," said James, "my subjects, whenever they had any favour to ask, used to come either to me or to Buckingham. But now, as if we had both ceased to exist, they go to the Parliament. All this is most disrespectful." And James told the story of a cow, whose tail in winter was so heavy she had it cut off. But when summer came and the flies annoyed her, Cow asked for her tail back again. "I and Buckingham," said James, "are like the cow's tail, and when the session is over you will be glad to have us back again to defend you from abuses."

Was there ever a king like James Stuart?

Buckingham's name might well be next on the list; in both Houses there was a large party that hated him. And after Buckingham, who next? Bacon was called to the palace. "Those that will strike at your Chancellor," he told James, "it is much to be feared will strike at your Crown. I wish that as I am the first, I may be the last of sacrifices." Buckingham appeared before the House of Lords and with swift change of front apologized for his brother's part in this abuse of monopolies, promising to do all he could to make restitution. The Commons, mollified, went on to business more important — the framing of a bill against monopolies.

For the moment, Bacon had escaped. Yet while all this was stirring, a second committee had been quietly at work. It was called the *Committee for Inquiring into Abuses in the Courts of Justice,* and it opened the door to Bacon's ruin. Behind it was a Commons member and Privy Councilor named Lionel

Cranfield, Master of the Court of Wards, a rich City merchant, shrewd and able, who, with Bacon, had been deeply involved in reforming various departments of the King's administration, with a view to economy. In the course of business in his Court of Wards, Cranfield had fallen foul of Chancery. Moreover Bacon seems to have treated him carelessly, as an aristocrat to a City merchant; Cranfield deeply resented it. This was a quarrelsome man, quick to take affront. Challenged later in the King's presence, Cranfield admitted it was he who had "set this business afoot. I repent it not," he said. (Bacon later declared that Cranfield had been "the trumpet" in this affair.) To the committee, Cranfield complained that Chancery sheltered debtors, making it difficult for merchants to collect — a serious thing in these times of languishing trade. Also, there was peculation. A dismissed Chancery clerk, named Churchill, had confessed to forging orders, pretending they came from barristers. He had taken fees for it. And he would not sink alone, Churchill said, but draw others after him.

On March 14, Sir Robert Phelips, chairman of the committee of inquiry, rose in the House with his report. Following Churchill's complaint, two gentlemen had brought petitions, alleging bribery and corruption on the part of the Lord Chancellor, "who is," added Phelips with troubled courtesy, "a man so endued with all parts both of nature and art as that I will say no more of him because I am not able to say enough." The Chancellor, it evolved, had been offered a hundred pounds to further the suit in Chancery of one Christopher Awbry, who had actually delivered the money to a gentleman of Bacon's household, Sir George Hastings, now sitting as member of the Commons. (Awbry's case in Chancery had eventually been settled against him.) The second complainant, Edward Egerton, embroiled in an endless lawsuit, had presented £400 in gold to one of Bacon's staff, who delivered it duly in the presence of Sir George Hastings, telling the Chancellor it was a "thankful remembrance from a client, designed to buy a new suit of hangings for York House." The Chancellor, having already received plate worth fifty pounds from Egerton, showed surprise. Weighing the purse in his hand he said it was too much, "but presently," said the witness, "put it behind a cushion. 'Mr. Egerton,' said my Lord, 'had not enriched him but laid a tie upon him to do him justice in his right cause.'" In the end, Egerton lost his suit, Bacon's judgment, though in the courts held unassailable, was furiously resented by the complainant.

As the story unfolded, John Finch, member from Oxfordshire, refused to believe the witness. Sir George Hastings, he said, probably kept the money himself. He hoped, Finch continued, that "so great a man should not fall by the testimony of one who had most reason to excuse himself for so foul a fact as the delivery of a bribe." He was "sorry to see a man so noble born, whom he loved, fall under an ungrateful accusation." Moreover, if Edward Egerton had desired to congratulate the new Chancellor and at the same time reward his kindness and pains in former business — "What wrong hath my Lord done," said Finch, "if he hath received a present? We have no sufficient grounds to accuse so great a Lord."

Among the Commons there was not a local justice of the peace but had accepted New Year's gifts, nor among the Lords a judge sitting as assistant who had not taken gratuities from aldermen or town fathers when riding circuit. Edward Alford, an old barrister, greatly respected in the House, rose to say that he had seen a "ledger book of a great baron in Henry VIII's time, wherein ten pounds was entered to be given to the Lord

Chancellor for his pains in hearing a cause, and thirty shillings to his secretary."

No one gainsaid it, though legal memories could have produced instances much nearer home. William Noye, a distinguished barrister from Cornwall, objected that the witnesses were all of them either *participes criminis* (participators in the crime) or single witnesses, whereas two witnesses were customary. Edward Coke quickly set the House right on this last point. Bacon's confidential secretary and friend, Thomas Meautys, Burgess from Cambridge, rose to remind the House that the original informants, Churchill and Keeling, were nothing more than guilty solicitors who thought to win pardon by their confessions. "My Lord sowed justice," said Meautys. "The envious sowed tares."

Chancery had long been hated by the common lawyers (led by Coke) because it took business from King's Bench and Common Pleas. As debate continued, accusation was aimed sometimes at Bacon, sometimes at the Court of Chancery. A member said he would have the Upper House note "the luxuriant authority" of Chancery, "and how it is an inextricable labyrinth, wherein resideth such a Minotaur as gormandizeth the liberty of all subjects whatever." Sir Edward Coke spoke often on this point, but without mentioning Bacon's name. Chancery, said Coke, had no business to "meddle with matters determinable by the common law." Repeating himself in Latin, Coke let the syllabled great words roll out: *"Non traditur extraordinariae quod subiiciatur ordinariae."*

When Coke expanded into Latin he was irresistible; none ventured to argue. Yet in this business Coke showed himself surprisingly gentle. (Two centuries later, Lord Macaulay said this was the only time Sir Edward Coke behaved like a gentleman.) "I speak," Coke said, "not because the Chancellor is in a cloud, but according to the true liberty of the subject." In short, it was the Commons' privilege to air their grievances; no man should dare to stay them. "I had rather speak thus in my Lord's greatness," Coke continued, "than now when he is suppressed." Named on a committee to report the business to the Upper House, Coke mentioned four abuses that had long been prevalent in Chancery — technical matters of presentation and procedure. A fifth abuse, Coke said he would "retain in his heart." This courteous little suppression was enormously effectual. If Edward Coke, righteously indignant, retained anything in his heart, it must be significant. In London it was said that Sir Edward "would die if he could not help to ruin a great man once every seven years."

When the first charges had been brought, on March 14, Bacon sat as usual, presiding in the House of Lords. That evening he sent a letter to Buckingham. "Your Lordship spake of purgatory. I am now in it, but my mind is in a calm. . . . I know I have clean hands and a clean heart; and I hope a clean house for friends or servants. But Job himself, or whosoever was the justest judge, by such hunting matters against him as hath been used against me, may for a time seem foul, specially in a time when greatness is the mark and accusation is the game."

It was true. Small charges can ruin a man in high office, destroy him even when disproved. John Finch of Oxfordshire had told the Commons as much. "If," he said, "we shall but make a presentation of this, we do in a sort accuse him, nay, judge him." Bacon knew it. "If this is to be a Chancellor," he wrote Buckingham, "I think if the Great Seal lay upon Hounslow Heath, nobody would take it up." Above all, Bacon feared his health would break under the strain and it would be thought "feigning or fainting." He hoped in God he would hold out.

The first charges had been heard on Thursday. Friday and Saturday were spent in further investigation by a committee of four: Coke, Noye, Phelips, Digges. The second complainant, Egerton, it now appeared, had promised — should judgment be pronounced in his favor — six thousand pounds to be divided between two of Bacon's retinue. (One of the two, Dr. Field, was an Anglican bishop, a fact which Puritan members used to advantage, though Field's guilt was afterward disproved.) On March 17, the word *bribe* was used for the first time, and by Edward Coke. Hitherto, members had said "gift" or "gratuity." The Chancellor's household, with or without his knowledge, had carried on a thriving trade with suitors in Chancery. Bacon seemed bewildered. By Sunday, March 18, he was prostrate in bed. "It is no feigning nor fainting," he wrote the Lords, "but sickness both of my heart and of my back." He asked time to advise with counsel and make answer to the charges. "I shall not, by the grace of God, trick up an innocency with cavillations; but plainly and ingenuously (as your Lordships know my manner is) declare what I know or remember." A judge that makes two thousand decrees and orders in a year is hard put to it, Bacon added, to recall each case. If more petitions against him should appear, he begged the Lords that he might answer them "according to the rules of justice, severally and respectively."

It was the cry that Essex had made in court, and Sir Walter Ralegh: *Let me have the charges that I may study them and reply to them one by one!* But Edward Coke had already conferred with the Upper House concerning these rules of justice.

"A corrupt judge," he said, "is the grievance of grievances." It was the perfect word — *grievances* — the word of art, a political rallying cry for a Lower House which in the past thirty years had been learning in all seriousness how to treat with grievances. With the Commons as fact-finders and grand jury, the Lords as judges, Parliament now revived the ancient weapon of impeachment, unused these hundred and sixty years. Impeachment was a clear channel for the general discontent. Impeachment provided a victim, it gave every Commons member a chance to air his views. Between 1621 and 1715, Parliament would stage fifty impeachments. (Since that date there have been only four.) Among the ruined would be, in 1624, Lionel Cranfield, the man who confessed that he had set Bacon's indictment afoot.

On March 22, 1621, the Commons reported three new complaints against the Lord Chancellor. (It was rumored also that when suitors came to Chancery, their lawyers' first question was, "How are you friended at York House?") Bacon sent a letter to the King, completely candid and very surprised. "When I enter into myself, I find not the materials for such a tempest as is comen upon me . . . I have been no avaricious oppressor of the people. I have been no haughty or intolerable or hateful man, in my conversation or carriage. I have inherited no hatred from my father, but am a good patriot born. Whence should this be? For these are the things that use to raise dislikes abroad."

To Bacon it was impossible that he would be ruined for taking New Year's gifts, or gratuities from suitors. Did not every man in public office the same? He had done nothing in secret, concealment had not occurred to him. "When the book of hearts shall be opened," he wrote, "I hope I shall not be found to have the troubled fountain of a corrupt heart in a depraved habit of taking rewards to pervert justice; howsoever I may be frail, and partake of the abuse of the times. . . . I pray God to give me the grace to see to the bottom of my faults, and that no hardness of heart do steal upon me, under shew of more neatness of conscience than is cause." Bacon indeed seemed stricken, helpless, "with such extremity of head-ache," he wrote the King, "upon the hinder part of my head, fixed in one place, that I thought verily it had been some imposthumation . . . that either it must grow to a congelation, and so to a lethargy, or to break, and so to a mortal fever or sudden death. Which apprehension (and chiefly the anguish of the pain) made me unable to think of any business."

King James showed a disposition to take the case in his own hands. None knew better than James that no public official could live without accepting gratuities — by whatever name they went. "If," James had told the Venetian Ambassador, "I were to imitate the conduct of your republic and begin to punish those who take bribes, I should soon not have a single subject left." Were the matter handled by the Commons alone, Bacon would never escape. Too many barristers desired to see Chancery humbled, let alone the Chancellor. Moreover, political assemblies, once the horn has sounded, bay for the taste of blood. James proposed to name a special commission for Bacon's trial, consisting of six members of the Upper House and twelve of the Lower. Easter vacation was at hand; the commission could do its work during the week of Parliament's adjournment.

To the Commons the offer was tempting; they were to outnumber the Lords two to one. Several members approved. It was Edward Coke who rose to object. The petitioners and complainants against the Lord Chancellor had appealed, Coke said, not to the King but to the Commons; it was the Commons therefore who should proceed in the case. Coke had observed the work of royal commissions; they had a high-handed way of carrying things as they saw fit. "Let us take heed," Coke warned, "the King's Commission do not hinder our Parliamentary proceedings."

During Easter vacation, Bacon recovered sufficiently to rise from bed and go to the King at Whitehall, first writing out a note of preparation for the interview. Concerning bargain or contract to pervert justice, *pendente lite,* he was as innocent in his heart, Bacon said, "as any born upon St. Innocent's Day." It was true he had accepted gifts after judgment, but he conceived it to be no fault; if in error, he wished to be better informed. "I must likewise confess to your Majesty that at newyears tides and likewise at my first coming in (which was as it were my wedding), I did not so precisely as perhaps I ought examine whether those that presented me had caused before me, yea or nay." The scene at the palace is lost to us. But from a letter Bacon wrote afterward to James, we know that the King "shed tears." Whatever this strange monarch's faults, he was faithful to his friends. Actually, James had done all he could for Bacon; further intervention would only fan the flame.

There is reason to believe that Buckingham had consented to this impeachment from the first, though Bacon at this stage seems not to have suspected it. The great Lord Chancellor Clarendon declared (1641) that Bacon had been sacrificed "to gratify a private displeasure," hinting broadly that the displeasure was Buckingham's, as it was Buckingham's displeasure which brought on the subsequent impeachment of Cranfield in 1624. Buckingham knew the Commons must have a victim for their anger over the monopolies — their anger also over Buckingham's closeness to the King and Prince. To throw them so grand a sop as a Lord Chancellor would pacify them, for this session at least. Bacon's behavior concerning the marriage of the Marquis's brother to Coke's daughter a few years before had been arrogant and clumsy; very likely Buckingham still smarted from it. Since his Chancellorship, moreover, Bacon had pushed and poked into delicate matters such as retrenchment in the royal household· and the Navy. Buckingham as Lord Admiral could have enjoyed neither of these activities. Financial savings to the royal treasury indicated financial losses to the King's favorite. "My Lord of Buckingham," wrote a contemporary, "never did undo any of his enemies, but he ruin'd many of his friends."

Without some hint or assurance from Buckingham, the Commons would have been taking a desperate risk. Lacking precedent, a road to follow, they knew that if the House of Lords should judge against their findings they would be in far worse position than if they had not started the business. New petitioners appeared. It was testified that the Lady Wharton, with a decree pending in Chancery, drove to York House with a hundred pounds in a purse. "My Lord asked her," reported Phelips, "what she had in her hand. She replied, 'A purse of my own working,' and presented it to him; who took it and said, 'What lord could refuse a purse of so fair a lady's working?'" Later, the lady sent two hundred pounds more, which Bacon received in the presence of several of his retinue. "Strange to me," remarked Sir Edward Coke, "that this money should be so openly delivered." As witnesses piled up, the Commons were hard put to handle the affair. There were solemn quotations in the Biblical manner: "Corruption in justice destroyeth the land. . . . Bribes blind the eyes of the just. . . . If the fountains be muddy, what will the streams be? If the great dispenser of the King's conscience be corrupt, who can have any courage to plead before him?"

News spread in the City, correspondents exchanged tidbits. One Samuel Albyn said he had heard "a very wise gentleman" offer twenty angels to ten that the Chancellor would retain his place, yet "in the general opinion he was thought to be utterly lost and ruinated forever." The House of Commons, wrote Chamberlain, "is fallen into another labyrinth (whence they see no way out) of briberies and extortions in matters of justice, and the first tempest is fallen upon my Lord Chancellor, against whom there come in daily more petitions and accusations than they can overcome. . . . Many indignities are said and done against him, and divers libels cast abroad to his disgrace, not worth the repeating as savouring of too much malice and scurrility. God send him patience and that he may make the best use of this affliction."

It was nearly May before all witnesses were examined and the charges drawn up. The list is bewildering; there is something grotesque about the incidents: "A dozen of gold buttons in the cause of Hodie and Hodie, worth £50 . . . In the cause of Kenneday and Vaulore, a cabinet worth £800 . . . Of Vaulore, borrowed at two times, £2000. In the Lord of Montagu's cause, £700 borrowed and more promised at the end of the cause . . . In a cause between Reynell and Peacock, £200 in money and a diamond ring worth £5 or £600 . . . In a business between the grocers and apothecaries, he had of the grocers £200, of the apothecaries £500, (besides a rich present of ambergris). . . . Of the French merchants, to constrain the vintners of London to take 1500 tuns of wine; received, £1000 . . . Lastly, that he gave way to great exactions by his servants, in respect of private seals and injunctions."

Bacon had not yet seen these charges. But he had been told enough to know there would be no refuting the particulars. He had in truth accepted these gifts and favors, always in the presence of his household or staff; secrecy in the matter apparently had not occurred to him. Only in one way could Bacon defend himself: by attacking the entire system and Buckingham with it — patently an impossibility. At York House he remained in bed; a news letter from London gave out the Chancellor was "all swollen in his body and suffering none to come at him. Some say he desired his gentlemen not to take any notice of him, but altogether to forget him and not hereafter to speak of him or remember there was ever such a man in the world."

Sure that he was dying, Bacon wrote his will. It was a cry from the heart, submissive, wholly humbled, yet with no note of abjectness. "I bequeath my soul to God above. My body to be buried obscurely. My name to the next ages, and to foreign nations." In a solemn prayer, Bacon made his peace with God. "Remember, O Lord, how thy servant hath walked before thee: remember what I have first sought, and what hath been principal in mine intentions. . . . As thy favors have increased upon me, so have thy corrections; so hast thou been always near me, O Lord; and ever as my worldly blessings were exalted, so secret darts from thee have pierced me; and when I have ascended before men, I have descended in humiliation before thee."

Was the Lord Chancellor recalling, as he wrote, the melancholy that had visited him always when prosperity came? Were these the "secret darts," and was Bacon indeed one of those men who feel guilty under success, unworthy to rise to the heights their fathers have obtained? Now he had fallen, and his father's name would suffer with his. In his extremity, Bacon addressed his God: "I confess before thee that I am debtor to thee for the gracious talent of thy gifts and graces . . . which I have misspent in things for which I was least fit; so as I may truly say, my soul hath been a stranger in the course of my pilgrimage. Be merciful unto me, O Lord, for my Saviour's sake, and receive me into thy bosom or guide me in my ways."

But Francis Bacon did not die. Two days later he wrote out his submission, to be presented to the House of Lords. It was a statement extraordinary in its candor. Bacon said he would make a very strange entrance into the matter. "For in the midst of a state of as great affliction as I think a mortal man can endure (honour being above life), I shall begin with the professing of gladness in some things.

"The first is, that hereafter the greatness of a judge or magistrate shall be no sanctuary or protection of guiltiness; which, in a few words, is the beginning of a golden world.

"The next is, that after this example, it is like that judges will fly from any thing that is in the likeness of corruption (though it were at a great distance), as from a serpent; which tendeth to the purging of the courts of justice, and the reducing them to their true honour and splendour.

"And in these two points God is my witness, that, though it be my fortune to be the anvil whereupon these good effects are beaten and wrought, I take no small comfort. . . .

"It resteth therefore that, without fig-leaves, I do ingenuously confess and acknowledge, that having understood the particulars of the charge, not formally from the House, but enough to inform my conscience and memory, I find matter sufficient and full, both to move me to desert the defence, and to move your Lordships to condemn and censure me. . . . Neither will your Lordships forget that there are *vitia temporis* as well as *vitia hominis* [sins of the times as well as sins of man]."

Their Lordships, went on Bacon, were not simple judges but parliamentary judges, with more arbitrary power than most courts of law. By that same token they had more freedom on points of mercy and mitigation. . . . "And therefore my humble suit to your Lordships is, that my penitent submission may be my sentence, and the loss of the Seal my punishment, and that your Lordships will spare any further sentence, but recommend me to his Majesty's grace and pardon for all that is past."

Is it weakness, when a man does not rise to do battle? Bacon seemed incapable of bearing malice, except toward Edward Coke — and with Coke it had been open war from the beginning, both sides using the weapons at hand. In persistence, Bacon was any man's equal, but he did not relish overt combat. At Gorhambury there were "breeding swans and feeding swans," Bacon had said — but as to malice, he had "neither bred it nor fed it." Revenge he held to be barbaric. "A kind of wild justice," he said, "which the more man's nature runs to, the more ought law to weed it out. . . . A man that studieth revenge keeps his own wounds green." In defeat and agony, in humiliation and obloquy, it was not his enemies whom Francis Bacon sought to conquer, but himself. Long ago, in the little essay called "Colours of Good and Evil," he had written that when evil comes to a man from without, "there is left a kind of evaporation of grief, if it come by human injury. . . . But where the evil is derived from a man's own fault, there all strikes deadly inwards and suffocateth."

In his chamber at York House, Bacon looked into himself, searching his soul not only as to present grief but according to the long reaches of his life. He had been reared by a Puritan mother, a father who followed the safe and middle way — the Queen's prudent servant, on whom she could rely. "Your Majesty may have heard somewhat that my father was an honest man." So Bacon had written to King James. The blow struck deadly inwards. Yet a man does not die for the wishing it. Bacon's written submission went to the Lords — in itself a tactical error; the Commons showed offense because the letter had not been addressed to both Houses. "The Chancellor's great stomach," they said, "would not vouchsafe to take any notice of them." The Lords on their part complained that the Chancellor had created himself a judge to give his own sentence, which was loss of office and nothing more. Further, to the charges of bribery Bacon had replied only in general terms, nor was the word corruption included, but only the phrase "likeness of corruption."

There was reason for Bacon's vagueness. The bill of charges had never been sent to him; for his information he had had to rely on hearsay. He knew that from first to last procedure had been experimental, with no sure example to follow. The Commons were feeling their way. The Chancellor's household included several who sat as members of the Commons, among them his secretary and faithful friend, Thomas Meautys. Day by day, Meautys must have told his master of the debates, of the Commons' fumbling and uncertainty, their sudden shifts from timidity to truculence. "The House of Commons," a member had declared proudly, "is like the Grand Jury for the whole commonwealth!"

On the face of it, a glorious boast. Yet a grand jury can do no more than make presentment. Only a court of record can judge or punish. Repeatedly, the challenge had come up: Did the Commons dare to call itself a court of record? Edward Coke settled it for the moment, bringing up rather doubtful precedents and finally thundering out, in all his authority of learning and experience: "He who questions this House is a Court of Record, I would his tongue might cleave to the roof of his mouth!"

That the Commons were in themselves a court of record was a dazzling thought. Aided by it, Parliament would one day reconstruct a kingdom, bring heads to the block and a royal government to ignominy — not, however, until procedure had been further invented and stabilized. In Bacon's impeachment, members had queried if it were lawful to admit, as the only witnesses against a man, the bribers themselves. These witnesses had one and all been promised protection — in particular the original complainant, Churchill, who was already a dismissed delinquent when he testified. Should not such testimony be held suspect? Nor had anyone called upon England's judges for a definition of judicial bribery. No statutes had been invoked. Edward Coke, who loved to quote Magna Carta, had somehow refrained from letting fly with Chapter 29: *"Nulli vendemus:* to no man shall we sell justice or right" — (Before long, Coke would quote it fully in a second judicial impeachment, to follow Bacon's.) The pertinent question had not been debated, "What is customary, what is acceptable, what do other judges do in our courts?" The point had indeed been raised by the lawyers Finch and Alford, but quickly passed over, no example offered since the safely vanished era of Henry VIII. And indeed it would have been a dangerous exploration — one which, if pursued, would have implicated the entire judiciary.

In Bacon's impeachment it was as if the Commons were holding trial not of the past but of the future — as if they were judging, not *What has happened in our courts and what is happening,* but *What should happen, what ought to happen henceforth?* (In our own day we have seen similar procedure in the Nuremberg Trials.) Yet the law is in essence prognostic, prophetic; all legislation is for the future. In times of evil and corruption, the man first accused pays the penalty.

On the twenty-fourth of April, 1621, Bacon received from the House of Lords — and for the first time — the full indictment against him. There were twenty-eight separate charges. Bacon read them and knew there could be no denial. He had accepted the gold buttons; he had taken the purse from Lady Wharton and the cabinet worth £800, the "rich present of ambergris" — and all of it before witnesses, in the presence of his household. That the course of justice had not thereby been altered was beside the point, nor was it to the point that the complainants had been persons whose suits in Chancery had been lost, not won. Bacon took up his pen:

To the Right Honourable the Lords Spiritual and Temporal [he wrote], in the High Court of Parliament assembled:

The Confession and humble Submission of me, the Lord Chancellor.

Upon advised consideration of the charge, descending into my own conscience, and calling my memory to account so

[199]

far as I am able, I do plainly and ingenuously confess that I am guilty of corruption; and do renounce all defence, and put myself upon the grace and mercy of your Lordships.

The particulars I confess and declare to be as followeth. . . .

Francis Bacon had been in the law some forty years; he knew the courts from every angle. And from no angle did he take a stand to defend himself, though as he read the bill of particulars, he demurred at one or two. Articles 24, 25 and 26 charged the Chancellor with accepting a gift for arbitration between the company of apothecaries and two companies of grocers. The parties, declaring themselves satisfied, had rewarded the Chancellor. This was no judicial business, said Bacon, but an open gift from all three companies. In the cause also of the French vintners from whom he had taken a thousand pounds, there had been no bill or suit pending in the courts. The King himself had intervened, demanding arbitration because the business concerned his customs house and Navy.

One mild defense, Bacon did attempt. "Those that have an habit of corruption," he wrote, "do commonly wax worse and worse." Whereas among these charges were none but were almost two years old. Could not their Lordships here draw inference?

The twenty-eighth and last charge stated that "The Lord Chancellor hath given way to great exactions by his servants, both in respect of private seals, and otherwise for sealing of injunctions." Bacon was aware that he had been a careless householder. "I confess," he wrote, "it was a great fault of neglect in me, that I looked no better to my servants." The defection of his household secretaries and gentlemen dependents must have been to Bacon a sickening blow. Making his way through York House great hall during the proceedings, he had seen his servants stand as he approached. "Sit down, my masters," he said. "Your rise hath been my fall."

At the outset of the accusations in Parliament, one of Bacon's gentlemen retainers — the young engineer they called Button Bushell — had fled to the Isle of Wight and lived with the fishermen, doing penance. "I must ingenuously confess," Bushell wrote later, "that myself and others of his servants were the occasion of exhaling my Lord's virtue into a dark eclipse. We whom his bounty nursed, laid on his guiltless shoulders our base and execrable deeds, to be scann'd and censur'd by the whole Senate of a state, where no sooner sentence was given but most of us forsook him, which makes us bear the badge of Jews to this day." The Lord Chancellor, Bushell added, loathed bribery; his household had been at pains to keep their peculations secret.

The trouble with this dramatic confession is that Button Bushell, busy, talented (afterward a friend to Charles I), was known everywhere as a charming liar, never out of debt. Long ago, when Bacon and his brother Anthony lived as students at Gray's Inn, their Puritan mother had warned against her sons' servants and followers: *Wasteful knaves, proud villains swarming ill-favouredly*. It had been Bacon's great fault that as he rose in public life he lived too much as a private man, choosing his friends not always wisely, preferring entertainment to reliability in his house.

Carefully, in anguish of spirit, Francis Bacon went down the list of charges, signing his name to each as confessed. (I have seen a copy in a contemporary hand, a document extraordinarily moving, with Bacon's name against every count—"*Confessed . . . confessed . . .*") "This declaration," Bacon wrote finally, "I have made to your Lordships with a sincere mind; humbly craving that, if there should be any mistaking, your Lordships would impute it to want of memory, and not to any desire of mine to obscure truth, or palliate any thing; for I do again confess, that in the points charged upon me, although they should be taken as myself have declared them, there is a great deal of corruption and neglect; for which I am heartily and penitently sorry, and submit myself to the judgment, grace and mercy of the court."

A committee of twelve peers was sent to York House to inquire if the Lord Chancellor's confession were indeed his own and if he would stand to it. They found him still sick in bed. From Bacon there issued now the cry that has come down in history as the very symbol of a ruined man. "My Lords, it is my act, my hand, my heart. I beseech your Lordships, be merciful to a broken reed." On the first of May, Bacon was visited by a commission of four, named by the King to fetch the Great Seal from the Chancellor's keeping. "We wish," they said politely, "it had been better with you."

"The worse the better," Bacon replied wearily. He saw them lift the Great Seal from its place by his bed. "God gave it, by my own fault I have lost it," he said—and said it in Latin: *"Deus dedit, mea culpa perdidit."* Next day the Sergeant-at-Arms from the Upper House, the gold-headed heavy mace on his shoulder, handed Bacon a summons to appear in Parliament and hear sentence pronounced. He was too ill to come, Bacon said. Were he well he would willingly comply.

Two days later, the Lords sat to decide on punishment. In

short order the Lord Chancellor's guilt was voted, *nemine dissentiente.* Two of Bacon's enemies sat in judgment: the Earl of Suffolk, three years ago dismissed from office on conviction of embezzlement, with Bacon on the Commission against him; and the Earl of Southampton, partner of Essex in the treason of 1601. Lord Suffolk had already endeavored to bring Bacon, ill or well, in person to the Upper House for confession. But it was Southampton who now counseled utmost severity. Sir Edward Coke was absent, not being a peer.

The Lords agreed easily about Bacon's fine and imprisonment. These were routine punishments and not too serious. Men in public life were continually being sent to the Tower; Parliament called it "our prison." Afterward, as like as not the King remitted their fines and freed them in a week, a month. It was on the question of Bacon's degradation that the Lords stuck. Degradation was a technical term, meaning loss of name, in this case of the honorable titles, *Baron Verulam* and *Viscount St. Alban.* Degradation put an offender on a par with traitors; it was a terrible moral censure, from which a man's heirs could be freed only by an Act of Parliament.

Southampton was of the opinion that the Lord Chancellor was fit to be degraded. "We cannot guide our sentence by any precedent, to make an example of this such as posterity may give us thanks for."

There was disagreement. A man may be attainted, Lord Spencer said, "and yet his honor remain. There are precedents of many."

In the end Bacon escaped degradation by two votes, one of which was Buckingham's. When the final question was put, if all punishments should be inflicted as listed: *"Agreed,"* says the official record, with one dissent. The voice was the Marquis of Buckingham's. It was a gesture the Marquis could well afford.

On Thursday morning, May third, the Commons made their way through Westminster Palace to the Lords' Chamber, crowding behind the bar as was their custom. Speaker Richardson, after three low congees, demanded, in the Commons' name, judgment against "a corrupt Chancellor, as the nature of his offences and demerits do require. . . ." Chief Justice Ley rose from his place to give sentence.

Half a mile away, Bacon lay in his curtained bed at York House, waiting. It was well he could not see and hear this ceremony. Sir Edward Coke stood with his colleagues, well to the fore. Had he not headed the important Committee of Grievances, under whose aegis all this had taken place? Tall, grizzled, implacable, Coke waited to hear his enemy brought low.

On the benches the Lords sat robed as for an occasion for state. Chief Justice Ley wore scarlet. Ley was scholarly, influential, though it was said he often borrowed money of the other judges, and he bore the unpleasant nickname of Vulpone. In the silence his voice was clear:

"The Lord Viscount St. Alban to pay a fine of £40,000. To be imprisoned in the Tower during the King's pleasure. To be for ever incapable of holding any office, place or employment in the state or commonwealth. Never to sit in Parliament nor come within the verge of the court."

⚜ V ⚜

A Noble Five Years
1621–1626

CHAPTER FIFTEEN

A Noble Five Years

O N THE LAST DAY of May, 1621, the Sheriff of Middlesex
called for Francis Bacon at York House water-stairs. It
was early morning and the current was right to shoot the
narrow arches of London Bridge. From his long garden, green
with spring, Bacon stepped into the barge; the river carried
them swiftly eastward. . . . Past Durham House, past Essex
House and Temple Gardens, past the crowded City, with
Paul's Church towering on its hill. The eel boats stood at anchor; swans sailed with the tide. As the barge emerged from
under London Bridge, Bacon saw the foreign caravels stand
high, pulling at their anchor chains.

It was an awful journey, yet it had at least the virtue of privacy. Had they gone by land, Bacon must have endured the
scorn and curiosity of City crowds. Below gray walls their
barge was met by the Tower Lieutenant. Bacon went ashore,
a prisoner "at the King's pleasure." Behind him the long teeth
of Traitor's Gate closed down.

Four weeks had passed since Bacon received his sentence from
Parliament. He had lain seriously ill. In the House of Lords,
the Earl of Southampton had risen to complain: If the Lord

Chancellor were permitted to remain longer at York House, the world might think their sentence was in vain. (Southampton knew whereof he spoke, having himself been two years prisoner in the Tower after his prosecution in the Essex treason.) After Bacon's sentence, Parliament had been furiously busy. They had impeached Sir John Bennet, Judge of the Prerogative Court of Canterbury, "of so many corruptions," wrote Chamberlain, "that by his side the Chancellor seems an honest man." Edward Coke's friend, Sir Henry Yelverton, recently suspended from the Attorney Generalship, was haled from prison to answer for various offenses, all patently political in nature. Defending himself in Parliament, Yelverton made a reckless attack on Buckingham. The Commons may have agreed in their hearts; they would soon agree openly. But they were fearful, repudiated Yelverton's testimony and returned him to the Tower. Buckingham at the palace boasted openly that he was Parliament-proof. The next victim was an elderly Catholic, named Floyd — no member of Parliament — who had been overheard jesting about King James's Protestant daughter, Elizabeth, wife of the Elector Palatine. The Commons at the news went quite crazy with Protestant piety, urged that Floyd's tongue be slit, that he be whipped through the City and hot lard dropped upon his wounds, "with every lash."

The Lower House, in short, was having a field day. A bill for the reformation of Chancery disabled that Court altogether; the King refused to sign it. Lord Treasurer Montagu remarked pertinently that "the example of the late great judge was more effectual than twenty laws." (Montagu, it will be recalled, was the man who paid £20,000 for his office.) Francis Bacon observed these maneuvers, and in his private notebook

expressed himself in Greek characters; "Of my offence, I will
say that [which] I have good warrant for, they were not the
greatest sinners in Israel upon whom the wall of Shilo fell."
And further, in cipher, "I was the justest judge that was in
England these fifty years: But it was the justest censure in Parliament that was these two hundred years." On his first day in
the Tower, Bacon sent a letter to the Marquis of Buckingham;
written, he said, *de profundis:*

> GOOD MY LORD,
> Procure the warrant for my discharge this day. Death, I
> thank God, is so far from being unwelcome to me, as I have
> called for it (as Christian resolution would permit) any time
> these two months. . . . And howsoever I acknowledge the
> sentence just, and for reformation sake fit, [I was] the justest
> Chancellor that hath been in the five changes since Sir Nich-
> olas Bacon's time.

Three days later, Bacon was free. Prince Charles had been
his friend; late at night Bacon was conveyed to a house at Ful-
ham belonging to one of Charles's retinue, Sir John Vaughan.
Bacon thanked the Prince. "The sweet air and Sir John's loving usage," he wrote, "have already much revived my languishing spirits." He asked leave of the King to return to York
House until July, in order to settle his business. The King refused, and Bacon went home to Gorhambury. Late in June,
Parliament was adjourned, upon which James promptly re-
quested Bacon's advice concerning reformation in the courts
of justice and other grievances that the Commons had expressed so vehemently. Under the circumstances it is extraordinary that James would make such a gesture. Bacon's reply
is no less surprising. "Go on with the reformation of your

courts of justice," he wrote, "and make an open declaration: that you purpose to pursue the reformation which the Parliament hath begun. . . . All great reformations are best brought to perfection by a good correspondence between the King and his Parliament."

Five years of life remained to Francis Bacon. Looking back, a writer of the eighteenth century was to call them the *nobile quinquennium,* the noble five years. Even Lord Macaulay gave praise. During these years, says Macaulay, "amidst ten thousand distractions and vexations Bacon commenced a Digest of the Laws of England, a History of England under the Princes of the House of Tudor, a body of Natural History, a Philosophical Romance. He made extensive and valuable additions to his Essays. He published the inestimable Treatise *De Augmentis Scientiarum.* The very trifles with which he amused himself in hours of pain and languor bore the mark of his mind. The best collection of jests in the world is that which he dictated from memory, without referring to any book, on a day on which illness had rendered him incapable of serious study."

The *De Augmentis* is, of course, a Latin translation of the *Advancement of Learning,* with seven new parts added, the Philosophical Romance was the *New Atlantis.* The collection of jests is Bacon's book of *Apophthegms* — surely the most uncompromising joke-book in existence; grim, witty, conducive rather to mental shock than to laughter, and some of it unforgettable.

Bacon was scarcely out of prison when he launched into authorship. Still earlier that spring, in the midst of impeachment, lying ill upon his bed he had written the King that he who has taken bribes is apt to give bribes. He would go further, he said, and present his Majesty with a bribe. "For if your Majesty give me peace and leisure, and God give me life, I will present your Majesty with a good history of England, and a better digest of your laws." A brash statement; already, Bacon's eye was on the morrow. By October, 1621, four months after his conviction, Bacon had completed a *History of the Reign of Henry VII*, a book of 248 pages. Typically, it was planned as the first of a series, to be followed by a history of Henry VIII (which Bacon did not live to write).

Bacon's punishment, his official sentence would not permit him within twelve miles of London. He lacked therefore the essential tools of historical research, though Sir Robert Cotton was generous in sending manuscripts to Gorhambury. Modern history was altogether a new conception. Until 1600, history in the universities had meant only classical history, tales of Greece, Rome, the Bible. With Elizabeth's great reign and her death had come a surge of national consciousness and pride that called for a history of England. Scholars had gone at it obliquely, in bits and patches. Sir Walter Ralegh in prison had written a *History of the World* (no less), but he never progressed as far as modern England. William Camden published (in Latin) his *Britannia* and his *Annals*. John Stow got out his marvelous *Survey of London*. William Lambarde's *Perambulation of Kent* had started the fashion of local histories; John Speed published his maps and prospects of Britain. Sir Robert Cotton, Sir Henry Spelman, haunted the muniment rooms in the Tower of London; scholars learned Anglo-Saxon in order to translate old documents.

"It is," said Bacon, "an ability not common to write a good history. . . . In no sort of writing is there a greater distance between the good and the bad." The customary annals and journals, "antiquities, memorials and commentaries," Bacon looked on as a kind of "unperfect history." Perfect history meant chronicles, lives or full narrations. And concerning lives, Bacon found it strange that their publication was not more frequent in his time. Lives, he said, have a commixture of actions great and small, public and private, "and must of necessity contain a more true, native and lively representation." Sir Walter Ralegh in the Tower of London read what Bacon had to say, and in the Preface to his *History of the World* remarked that the laws and kinds of history had "been taught by many, but by no man better and with greater brevity than by that excellent learned gentleman, Sir Francis Bacon."

Scholars today differ as to the worth of Bacon's *History of Henry VII*. Some say that Bacon flattered King Henry in order to please Henry's great-great-grandson, James I. This is hard to believe. The dedication to Prince Charles carries a note of plainness and honesty. "A wise man and an excellent King," Bacon says of Henry VII. "I have not flattered him, but took him to the life as well as I could, sitting so far off, and having no better light." The book is lively and informal, the descriptive passages have a beguiling intimacy. Bacon is not content with flat statements of fact. Wishing to tell us that Henry felt distress, Bacon writes of "those privy stitches which the King had had long about his heart, and had sometimes broken his sleeps in the midst of all his felicity."

Had not Francis Bacon, too, suffered those same privy stitches about his heart, in the midst of high felicity? God's secret darts, he had called them, which pierced when a man ascended before his fellows.

Bacon's contemporaries were charmed with the book. "It is a pity," wrote Chamberlain, "the late Lord Chancellor should have any other employment. . . . If the rest of our history were answerable to it, I think we should not need to envy any other nation in that kind." John Selden, the legal scholar, declared that Camden's *Annals* and Bacon's *Henry VII* were the only books of their kind to reach real excellence. Except for them, wrote Selden, "we have not so much as a public piece of the history of England that tastes enough either of the truth or plenty that may be gained from the records of the kingdom."

In the autumn of 1621, King James remitted Bacon's fine of £40,000 to "persons the Viscount of St. Alban himself shall nominate." This meant that though Bacon was not pardoned, creditors were prevented from closing in to claim what was left. The King's favorite, Buckingham, now decided that he wanted York House for himself. Recklessly, Bacon refused to sell, refused also an offer from the Duke of Lennox, the King's cousin. "York-House," Bacon wrote, "is the house where my father died, and where I first breathed, and there will I yield my last breath if it so please God, an the King will give me leave. . . . At least no money or value will make me part with it." Buckingham retaliated by delaying Bacon's full pardon, which had been drawn up by the Attorney General for the King's signature. Bacon's friends intervened, warning him that he followed a dangerous course. Early in 1622 therefore, Bacon let the house go to one of Buckingham's friends — though it would be another two years before the King signed his full pardon.

It is not easy to ascertain if Bacon, after his fall, was rich or poor. He continued in debt, worried about money and as usual did not hesitate to borrow from friends. Yet the King allowed him a pension of twelve hundred pounds; Bacon is said indeed to have enjoyed about two thousand pounds a year, more than

[213]

most noblemen could count on. From Gorhambury his coach rolled forth, smart with footmen and outriders. "Do what we can," said Prince Charles, "this man scorns to go out like a snuff." Bacon refused to part with Gorhambury woods; he said he "would not sell his feathers." The Provostship of Eton fell vacant, and to the general surprise Bacon asked James for the post. (No previous Lord Chancellor had aspired to a place so lowly.) Secretary of State Conway reported his Majesty's reply: "He could not value you so little, or conceive you would have humbled your desires and your worth so low." Long ago, when Bacon was Solicitor General, he had noted in his private journal that it would be well to hold a position in some school or college, where he could find scholars to help with his *Novum Organum.* "Laying for a place to command wits and pens," he had written.

It seems strange that Bacon, in 1622, would have expected the King to name a disgraced man as provost of a famous school. The King refused, and the post went to Bacon's old friend Sir Henry Wotton, former ambassador to Venice. Bacon's most valued friends continued faithful, though at the time of impeachment there had been a vast falling off. Tobie Matthew, now in Spain with Prince Charles, wrote letters full of concern and affection. Ben Jonson stated outright that Lord Bacon was "one of the greatest men and most worthy of admiration that had been in many ages." Count Gondomar sent a graceful, sensitive message, saying that he longed to salute Bacon now in his adversity, yet feared lest he give offense. He would, with Bacon's permission, ask the King of Spain to intervene with James in Bacon's behalf.

Bacon's two most faithful friends were Dr. William Rawley, his chaplain, and his secretary, Thomas Meautys, both of whom still served him. Meautys would later be knighted, act as Clerk of the Privy Council to Charles I, and marry Bacon's niece. "Let me claim of your Lordship," wrote Meautys, from London, "to do me this right as to believe that which my heart says, or rather swears for me; namely, that what addition so-ever (by God's good providence) come at any time to my life and fortune, it is in my account but to enable me the more to serve your Lordship in both; at whose feet I shall ever humbly lay down all that I have or am, never to rise from thence other than your Lordship's in all duty and affectionate reverence."

The *Novum Organum* (published in 1620) had had time, now, to become known in Europe; Bacon received letters and visits from foreign savants. At Gorhambury he played at bowls, rode horseback; his friends came to him from London when they could. Yet he was lonely. "If you listen to David's harp," he wrote, "you shall hear as many hearse-like airs as carols." Say what he would, philosophize as he might, now in his sixties Bacon could not accustom himself to his altered station. Long ago, he had said that men will not or cannot retire from great-ness, "but are impatient of privateness, even in age and sick-ness, which require the shadow: like old townsmen, that will be sitting at their street door, though thereby they offer age to scorn."

What should a man do in adversity, and how behave? In a letter to his old friend Lancelot Andrewes, now Bishop of Win-chester, Bacon wrote that he had been searching history to find how great men, overtaken by calamity, had conducted them-selves — "to the end that I might learn by them, and that they might be as well my counsellors as my comforters . . . De-mosthenes, Cicero, Senece — all three, persons that had held chief place of authority in their countries; all three ruined, not by war, or by any other disaster, but by justice and sentence, as delinquents and criminals; all three famous writers, insomuch as the remembrance of their calamity is now to posterity but as a little picture of night-work, remaining amongst the fair and excellent tables of their acts and works."

A little picture of night-work. It is altogether Baconian — and time has proved it true. For ten persons today who know of Bacon's *Essays* and his *Advancement of Learning*, not two remember his impeachment and disgrace. These examples from history, went on Bacon, had confirmed him in a resolution to spend his time wholly in writing, "and to put forth that poor talent, or half talent, or what it is that God hath given me." He planned therefore to proceed at once with some new parts to the *Instauratio Magna*, although he had just cause, he said, "to doubt that it flies too high over men's heads."

Bacon had been worried over finding a Latin translator for the *Advancement of Learning*, as well as for the *History of Henry VII* and his *Essays*. English was too private a tongue, excluding many readers. "These modern languages," Bacon had told Tobie Matthew, "will at one time or other play the bankrupts with books; and since I have lost much time with this age, I would be as glad God shall give me leave to recover it with posterity." Sending to Prince Charles a Latin version of the *Advancement of Learning*, Bacon wrote that it was a book which he thought would live, "and be a citizen of the world, as English books are not."

Early in 1623, John Chamberlain gave out news of the fallen Chancellor: "That Lord busies himself altogether about books and hath set out two lately, *Historia Ventorum* and *De Vita et Morte*, with promise of more." Written by Bacon in Latin, these were designed as parts of the *Great Instauration*. They were to be not theoretical but practical, presenting experiments, observations of nature and such axioms as might be drawn therefrom. Only actual practice, said Bacon, would show the student how mistakes of reasoning were to be righted not by logic, as heretofore, but by investigation. Years earlier, Bacon had thought to have attracted a body of students to do this part of the work; he had purposely published his *Novum Organum* before it was completed, in hopes that fellow-workers, reading, would join him.

When no one came forward, Bacon decided he must collect his own materials for a *Natural History,* though he knew it was a desperate venture. "Plainly a work for a King or Pope," he wrote, "or some college or order." Carefully he planned his schedule. In the ensuing six months he would publish experiments in the History of Winds; in Density and Rarity; Heaviness and Lightness; Sympathy and Antipathy of Things; Sulphur, Mercury and Salt; Life and Death. "I pledge mankind in a liquor strained from countless grapes," he wrote. . . . "For I am building in the human understanding a true model of the world, such as it is in fact, not such as a man's own reason would have it to be. . . . I form a history and tables of discovery for anger, fear, shame and the like; for matters political; and again for the operations of memory, composition and division, judgment and the rest; not less than for heat and cold, or light, or vegetation, or the like."

In November of 1622 the *History of Winds* appeared. "Describe the winds," wrote Bacon; "what winds are annual, or periodical, and in what countries. Carefully mark the differences between sea and land winds. . . . Let the inquiry pass on . . . to rain and showers. For as they perform a dance, it would be pleasant to know the order of it." Let the motion of the winds in the sails of the ships be studied, and their fountains of impulse, to derive rules for increasing and strengthening this motion. Study the prognostics of winds, of rain and fair weather.

The *History of Life and Death* appeared a few months later. The book is a fascinating mixture of medieval lore and farsighted prophecy. "Inquire," wrote Bacon, "into the length and shortness of life in animals, with the proper circumstances which seem to contribute to them. . . . Inquire into the length and shortness of men's lives, according to the times, countries, climates and places in which they were born and lived. . . . And according to their parentage and family . . . their food, diet, manner of living, exercise and the like, with regard to the air in which they live and dwell. Inquire carefully into the differences of the state and faculty of the body in youth and old age; and see whether there be anything that remains unimpaired in old age."

Bacon went on to record his own observations concerning the durability of bones, horns, teeth, vegetables when gathered, skins, hides, stones facing north and stones facing south; different species of trees, shrubs, bushes, whether snow is a preservative, and salt and oil. It is wonderful to read Francis Bacon on the longevity of animals, as the lion, the fox, the sheep, the camel — "a lean sinewy creature which commonly reaches fifty and sometimes one hundred years." The swan is examined, the phoenix, the stork. Surely the stork must be long-lived, says Bacon, if the old story be true, that storks would not go to Thebes "because that city was so often captured. . . . But all things," Bacon adds, "are full of fables," and "it is strange how men, like owls, see sharply in the darkness of their own notions, but in the daylight of experience wink and are blinded."

The task was enormous, endless. "I have heard his Lordship speak complainingly," wrote Dr. Rawley, "that his Lordship (who thinketh he deserveth to be an architect in this building) should be forced to be a workman and a labourer, and to dig the clay and burn the brick; and more than that (according to the hard condition of the Israelites at the latter end) to gather the straw and stubble over all the fields to burn the bricks withal."

Bacon knew that he could not finish, knew that he would not live to complete his plans. There is a grandeur of optimism in his titles and printed apostrophes: "To the Present and Future Ages, Greeting!" says one. Nor are all of Bacon's scientific conclusions merely quaint, poetic or medieval. His observations on winds and ocean currents, while wrong in their conclusions, were valuably suggestive — von Humboldt said later — of certain interdependencies among the elements, upon which modern meteorological theories are based. Reading Bacon's reports of his experiments, one is struck by this continual prophetic search for unity in nature, for the relating of matter to matter where hitherto only difference and antipathy had been noted and credited, as between body and mind, heart and spirit, earthly and celestial phenomena. "Strife and friendship in nature," says Bacon, "are the spurs of motions and the keys of works . . . these fabulous divorces and distinctions, . . . beyond what truth admits of, will be a great obstacle to true philosophy and the contemplation of nature." In the human mind also, Bacon desired to see a marriage between the empirical and the rational faculties, "the unkind and ill-starred divorce and separation of which has thrown into the confusion all the affairs of the human family."

Bacon now began to suffer from almost chronic illness. Yet he kept on with his work. "Life without an object to pursue," he once had said, "is a languid and tiresome thing." The quality of despair, Bacon saw as one of the most powerful causes of delay and hindrance to the progress of knowledge. Let the scientist then put away despair. And if he does despond, Bacon wrote ingenuously, let him then look at Francis Bacon, "of health not very strong (whereby much time is lost), and in this course altogether a pioneer, following in no man's track nor sharing these counsels with any one, who has, by resolutely entering on the true road, submitting his mind to Things, advanced these matters as he supposes, some little way." And let men look ahead to a time when scientific efforts will be combined and then artfully distributed, one man taking charge of one thing and another of another, working together in their labors and industries. In that day, said Bacon, scientists will begin to show their strength.

Less than two years of life remained to Francis Bacon. Dr. Rawley observed him and was moved to set down some reflections of his own. "I have been induced to think," wrote Rawley, "that if there were a beam of knowledge derived from God upon any man in these modern times, it was upon him. For though he was a great reader of books, yet he had not his knowledge from books but from some grounds and notions within himself." Dr. Rawley had seen the birth and growth of the *Instauratio Magna;* he knew the scheme of it, from the *Advancement of Learning* through the *Novum Organum* to the *Natural History*. And like his master, Rawley was aware the work would never be completed. "Have faith, and pursue the unknown end." Three centuries would pass before these words were spoken (and by an American), yet they seem the very voice of Francis Bacon.

As a young man and in middle age, Bacon had been something of a valetudinarian, fussing over his health, writing prescriptions for the apothecary to fill and drinking numerous evil mixtures which he thought conduced to health and longevity. John Aubrey, in his *Brief Lives,* tells how "in April, and Springtime, his Lordship would, when it rained, take his coach (open) to receive the benefit of Irrigation, which he was wont to say was very wholesome because of the Nitre in the Aire and the Universal Spirit of the World." Everything considered, one marvels that Bacon lived as long as he did, what with the purgings and courses of physic he gave himself, the clysters and electuaries, the "astringents, openers and cordials" which he recommended as "instrumental to health." To close the bowels, Bacon advised laying scarlet cloth or young whelps upon the stomach, also the drinking an infusion of "sealed earth, snake's blood, coral, pearls, the shell of the fish dactylus." Yet now at sixty-four, broken in health and often dispirited, he expressed no fear of death. "Nothing," he once had written, "is to be feared except fear itself." There was a plague that year in England, worse than the visitation of 1603 — the worst, men said, since the Black Death three centuries before. At the Cathedral of St. Albans, three miles from Gorhambury, bells tolled for the dead. Bacon fell seriously ill, his recovery was despaired of. Long ago, he had said that "death comes to young men and old men go to death. That is all the difference."

Yet he recovered, and in 1625 he saw publication of the third edition of his *Essays*. Twenty new pieces had been added, making fifty-eight in all. Bacon wrote Of Revenge, and Of Adversity. "The virtue of Adversity is fortitude." At Tobie Matthew's instigation he wrote further Of Friendship. "No receipt openeth the heart but a true friend. . . . For a crowd is not company, and faces are but a gallery of pictures, and talk but a tinkling cymbal, where there is no love." He wrote Of Vain Glory, Of Anger, Of Building. He wrote Of Masques and Triumphs. "Let the songs be loud and cheerful," he said, "and not chirpings or pulings. Let the music likewise be sharp and loud and well placed. The colours that show best by candle light are white, carnation, and a kind of sea-water-green."

Nothing was too slight or too great for this man's attention. He wrote Of Judicature, Of the True Greatness of Kingdoms and Estates, and he wrote Of Gardens. "God Almighty first planted a garden," he said. "And indeed it is the purest of human pleasures. . . . I do hold it, in the royal ordering of gardens, there ought to be gardens for all the months of the year; in which, severally, things of beauty may be then in season. . . . For March there come violets, specially the single blue, which are the earliest; the yellow daffodil, the daisy, the almond-tree in blossom, sweet briar. In April follow the double white violet, the wall-flower, the stock-gilly-flower; the cowslip, flower-delices and lilies of all natures, rosemary flowers; the tulippa, the double peony; the pale daffodil; the French honeysuckle; the cherry tree in blossom; the white-thorn in leaf. In May and June come pinks of all sorts, specially the blush pink. . . . And because the breath of flowers is far sweeter in the air (where it comes and goes, like the warbling of music) than in the hand, therefore nothing is more fit for that delight, than to know what be the flowers and plants that do best perfume the air."

Bacon proceeds to tell us. We read, and the scent of musk rose rises, the scent of crushed strawberry leaves, of honeysuckle, sweetbriar and gillyflowers.

In this year of 1625, King James died, to be succeeded by his son Charles, slight, fair-haired, destined to die on the executioner's block. King Charles's young bride came over from France: Henrietta Maria, escorted by the Marquis d'Effiat, who hastened to call upon Bacon, having read his works. In the four years since Bacon's impeachment, the political wheel had come full circle. The man who had brought the first charges — Lord Treasurer Lionel Cranfield, now Earl of Middlesex — had himself been impeached by Parliament for corruption in office. Even Sir Edward Coke had never liked Cranfield. Coke was seventy-two, and if possible more vigorous than ever. "Bribes!" he exclaimed in the House of Commons. "Double fees taken in the Court of Wards!" When Cranfield's conviction and punishment were voted, Coke cried out, "Oh, Parliaments work wonderful things!" Coke himself, since Bacon's impeachment, had spent six months as prisoner in the Tower of London. Sent there for defying the King and Buckingham, Coke roared his distress like a captive lion. Bacon's successor in Chancery, Lord Keeper Williams, was removed from his place. A diarist wrote that no man pitied his fall.

Heads were bowed, great men changed places. In London, Bacon's fortunes were discussed as on the rise. "My Lord St. Alban," wrote a gentleman, "is like to come again to the council table." Bacon's name was returned from Parliament, but he did not attend. In December of 1625 he made his will. From first to last it was a characteristic document. Bacon was to die some £22,000 in debt. Yet he made grand bequests to friends and servants — to the poor of nine parishes in which he had lived, to Tobie Matthew, to Dr. Rawley and Thomas Meautys. (Bacon at the moment owed Meautys £1200.) The executors were directed to sell Bacon's chambers at Gray's Inn and give the proceeds to needy students at Oxford and Cambridge. Two university lectures in natural philosophy were endowed — a splendid gesture, the money to be taken, Bacon said, from "the good round surplusage" which he expected after the sale of his lands and leases. Actually, these brought £7000.

There was the well-known codicil, brief and cogent. To his wife, Alice, Bacon had earlier bequeathed, in detail, what would make her "of competent abilities to maintain the estate of a viscountess." The codicil revoked all this. "Whatsoever I have given, granted, confirmed or appointed to my wife, in the former part of this my will, I do now, for just and great causes, utterly revoke and make void, and leave her to her right only."

No further explanation was offered. But in Bacon's household lived a gentleman usher, Sir John Underhill, about whose character and looks we unfortunately know very little. Three weeks after Bacon's death, his widow, then thirty-four years old, was to marry Sir John. It is pertinent to add that the marriage was not a success.

Bacon's last months had not the comfort of a wife's companionship. Alice lived probably at Gorhambury, Bacon in his little house at Gray's Inn. He seems to have drifted back to the city without permission and without censure; we find letters dated from London beginning as early as 1622. He worked ceaselessly, adding to his *Natural History,* conducting his experiments and trying vainly to encompass a task which called for many hands and brains. Once Bacon had written, "He that dies in an earnest pursuit is like one that is wounded in hot blood, who for the time scarce feels the hurt."

Sir Francis might have been speaking of himself; his own death was to come in almost this fashion. "As he was taking the air," wrote Aubrey,* "in a coach with Dr. Witherborne (A Scotchman, physician to the King) towards High-gate, snow lay on the ground, and it came into my Lord's thoughts, why flesh might not be preserved in snow, as in salt. They were resolved they would try the experiment presently. They alighted out of the coach and went into a poor woman's house at the bottom of High-gate hill, and bought a hen, and made the woman exenterate it, and then stuffed the body with snow, and my Lord did help to do it himself. The snow so chilled him that he immediately fell so extremely ill, that he could not return to his lodgings (I suppose then at Graye's Inn) but went to the Earl of Arundel's house at High-gate, where they put him into a good bed warmed with a pan, but it was a damp bed that had not been lain-in in about a year before, which gave him such a cold that in 2 or 3 days as I remember Mr. Hobbes told me, he died of suffocation."

Bacon's illness must have been bronchitis or pneumonia. The Earl of Arundel, an old friend, at the moment was a prisoner in the Tower of London; he had committed the serious indiscretion of letting his son marry privately a woman of the royal blood. Bacon wrote to Arundel; the letter is the last word we have from his pen: "My very good Lord," he said; "I was likely

* John Aubrey had his account from Thomas Hobbes the philosopher, once Bacon's amanuensis.

to have had the fortune of Caius Plinius the elder, who lost his life by trying an experiment about the burning of the mountain Vesuvius. For I was also desirous to try an experiment or two, touching the conservation and induration of bodies. As for the experiment itself, it succeeded excellently well. But in the journey between London and Highgate, I was taken with such a fit of casting as I knew not whether it were the stone or some surfeit or cold, or indeed a touch of them all three. But when I came to your Lordship's house I was not able to go back, and therefore was forced to take up my lodging here, where your housekeeper is very careful and diligent about me. . . . I know how unfit it is for me to write to your Lordship with any other hand than mine own; but in troth my fingers are so disjointed with this fit of sickness that I cannot steadily hold a pen."

Bacon lay in the great spare bed at Arundel house — but he did not die unfriended. Nearby lived Bacon's nephew by marriage, Master of the Rolls in Chancery and a member of King Charles's Privy Council, who bore the odd name of Sir Julius Caesar, and whom Bacon had named a supervisor of his will. Sir Julius was known as the kindest man in England; his coach could scarcely get through City streets for the beggars who swarmed when they saw him coming.

In his uncle's extremity, Sir Julius came to him. On the morning of April ninth, Easter Day, Francis Bacon died in his nephew's arms.

What did Francis Bacon's contemporaries say of him when he was gone? What name did he leave with his countrymen, this disgraced Lord Chancellor? "In the business of life," Bacon had written, "a man's disposition and the secret workings of his mind and affections are better discovered when he is in trouble than at other times."

It was an observation made when Bacon himself was experiencing not failure but success. Yet during his last five years the world observed the fallen Lord Chancellor, and at his death a flood of eulogy poured out — from friends and strangers, from playwrights, historians, political pamphleteers. Ben Jonson wrote that after this lord's fall he never could bring himself to condole with him "in a word or syllable . . . In his adversity I ever prayed that God would give him strength, for greatness he could not want." Thomas Fuller, the historian, spoke of "this peerless Lord's everlasting memory, much admired by English, more by outlandish men . . . None," said Fuller, "can character him to the life, save himself." "A rare man," wrote James Howell, "a man recondite, and I think the eloquentest that was born in this isle."

There was a spate of Latin poems, addressed to the late Lord Chancellor. They came from the Inns of Court — from Gray's Inn, the Middle Temple and Inner Temple, from Trinity College at Cambridge: flowery effusions, typical of the age, yet bearing their message clearly in the opening lines:

> *Weep ye now truly, Clio, and Clio's sisters,*
> *Ah, fallen is the tenth Muse, the glory of the choir!*

And another:

> *Thou bold exemplar of how far the human mind may rise,*
> *Thou talented deliverer of thine age!*

One poem is signed, "William Atkins, Household Servant of his Lordship." One is signed, George Herbert:

> *Only in April, surely, couldst thou die,*
> *That here the flower with its tears,*

There Philomel with her laments
May follow only thy tongue's funeral train.

Europe — France in particular — had never believed in the
Lord Chancellor's guilt. A French edition of one of Bacon's
works expressed indignation at the treatment accorded a man
who by his wit had "given the death blow to boredom." Bacon
would have enjoyed this notion, so essentially Gallic in its
values. England, too, protested the Lord Chancellor's treatment
at the House of Commons. Bacon's champions seemed im-
pelled to versify, sometimes in private notebooks, sometimes as
preface or introduction to editions of Bacon's writings. Men
who had personal knowledge of Sir Francis spoke out affectionately. His household apothecary and Latin secretary, Peter
Boener, wrote that his master "was always the same both in
sorrow and in joy, as a philosopher ought to be." Dr. Rawley
wrote a brief biography, devoted and wonderfully revealing.
At Gorhambury or York House dinner table, said Rawley,
guests used notebooks to take down what they heard — though,
added Rawley, his lordship "was no dashing man," to put
others down as some men are, "but ever a countenancer and
fosterer of another man's parts. Neither was he one that would
appropriate the speech wholly to himself, or delight to outvie
others, but leave a liberty to the co-assessors to take their turns.
Wherein he would draw a man on and allure him to speak
upon such a subject, as wherein he was peculiarly skilful, and
would delight to speak. And for himself he condemned no
man's observations, but would light his torch at every man's
candle."

After Bacon's death, Dr. Rawley, while chaplain to Charles I
and Charles II, found time to edit and publish many of Bacon's
works, among them the *New Atlantis,* the collection called

Sylva Sylvarum, the compendium entitled *Certain Miscellany Works,* and the *Resuscitatio,* which includes Bacon's brief biography, together with additional *Apophthegms* of Bacon's that Rawley himself had heard from his master and remembered.

With Bacon's own generation and with the younger men who lived on after his death, the Lord Chancellor's reputation shifted, it seems, according to current political views and inclinations. Simonds D'Ewes, Puritan Parliamentarian, enveighed against the Lord Chancellor for excessive pride and "vices stupendous and great." On the other hand Dr. Heylyn, biographer of Archbishop Laud, declared that King James had made a wrong step when he gave up "this great minister" to the Parliament. *Britannicus,* writing in 1725, believed that Bacon "came to a censure for the most simple and ridiculous follies that ever entered into the heart of a wise man. My Lord Bacon fell with a general pity. He had provok'd but a few suitors of the Court, with taking extorted perquisites."

David Mallet, poet and pamphleteer, voiced a general theory when he said that public rage, directed at Buckingham but not yet daring to declare itself, in Bacon had found a scapegoat. King James, said Mallet, absolutely commanded the Lord Chancellor not to be present at his trial or to plead for himself, fearing that in defending himself, Bacon might further expose Buckingham's already dangerous position. There seemed no end to the speculations. Thomas Tenison, later Archbishop of Canterbury, in 1679 published a book entitled *Baconiana, or Certain Genuine Remains of Francis Bacon.* "Such great wits," wrote the Archbishop, "are not common births of Time. Nature gives the world that individual species, the phoenix, but once in five hundred years. . . . I do not here pretend to speak of an angel but of a man. And no man, great in wit and high in office, can live free from suspicion of both kinds of errors. For that heat which is instrumental in making a great wit, is apt to disorder the attention of the mind, and the stability of the temper. This Lord's fall will be to posterity but as a little picture of nightwork, remaining amongst the fair and excellent tables of his acts and works."

It is pleasant to read the Archbishop, paraphrasing Bacon's own words in his defense. His fall this lord foresaw, wrote Sir William Dugdale. "Yet he made no shew of a base and mean spirit. . . . It appeared not by any thing during all the time of his eclipse of fortune, that there was any abjectness of spirit in him."

Scientific minds were even more lenient to the Lord Chancellor. Robert Hooke mentioned how "poor Galileo was put into the Inquisition. . . . Thus it happened also to Roger Bacon, and, I am apt to suspect, to the far greater man, the Lord Chancellor Bacon, for being too prying into the then receiv'd philosophy." Bishop Sprat, in his *History of the Royal Society,* makes no mention of Bacon's fall but only of his genius, "searching and inimitable . . . a man of strong, clear and powerful imaginations." No further proof was needed, said Sprat, "than his style itself; which as for the most part of it describes men's minds, as well as pictures do their bodies, so did his above all men living. . . . The course of it vigorous and majestical, the wit bold and familiar." Abraham Cowley wrote an ode to the Royal Society, it is often quoted. . . .

> *Bacon, like Moses, led us forth at last,*
> *The barren wilderness he past,*
> *Did on the very border stand*
> *Of the blest promis'd land*

And from the mountain's top of his exalted wit,
Saw it himself, and shew'd us it.

Almost a century and a half later, still another poet spoke out — a man far greater than Abraham Cowley. What Shelley said is more pertinent perhaps and more perceptive than any tribute Sir Francis has received. "Lord Bacon," wrote Shelley, "was a poet. His language has a sweet and majestic rhythm which satisfies the sense, no less than the almost superhuman wisdom of his philosophy satisfies the intellect; it is a strain which distends and then bursts the circumference of the reader's mind, and pours itself forth together with it into the universal element with which it has perpetual sympathy."

Bacon is buried where he asked to be, near his mother's grave in St. Michael's Church at St. Albans, Hertfordshire. Thomas Meautys at his own expense erected a statue to his master above the chancel. It is there today. A soft slouch hat is on Bacon's head; patently, he is meditating — one hand is at his chin, one hangs carelessly over the chair arm. Under the statue an inscription is cut in Latin; Sir Henry Wotton composed it:

Francis Bacon, Baron of Verulam, Viscount St. Alban
Or by more conspicuous titles,
Of sciences the light, of eloquence the law,
Used to sit thus.
Who, after he had unfolded all the secrets
Of natural and of civil wisdom,
Fulfilled Nature's decree:

Let compounds be dissolved.
In the year of our Lord MDCXXVI
Aged LXVI

To the memory
Of so great a man,
Thomas Meautys,
Who honored him in life,
And admired him in death,
Set up this memorial.

St. Michael's Church is small and very old, set in a country churchyard. In the summer the door stands open. Outside, among the graves, yew trees raise their branches, like candles pointed at the sky. There is the sound of bees, and in the morning, rooks call. A parish school is just beyond the hedge; at noon the children run and laugh and scuffle. In the little museum nearby, one can see Roman remains of Old Verulam — mosaic floors, vessels for cooking and eating, pieces of the city wall. The centuries are spread out, here before us; the old Britain, the medieval, and the new and young. A proper resting place for Francis Bacon, with his prescient consciousness of time — a resting place more suitable somehow than the great Abbey at Westminster, among the elaborately monumented dead.

Francis Bacon is gone. We take our farewell of him, with his suffering, his sins, and his cheerful, irrepressible genius. *Sic sedebat,* says the monument: "Thus he used to sit." Thus he meditated, thus he wrote his books, thus propounded his philosophy of learning, so new to the world, so little to be believed and credited in his time. If he lived today, what would men think of Francis Bacon? Surely he would be very much at home, here in America. Manned rockets, journeys to the moon and to the depths of the sea or to the even deeper reaches of men's minds and hearts — these would not surprise Francis Bacon. "Lastly," he had written, "even if the breath of hope which blows on us from that New Continent, were fainter than it is and harder to perceive, yet the trial (if we would not bear a spirit altogether abject) must by all means be made. For there is no comparison between that which we may lose by not trying and by not succeeding. . . . There is hope enough and to spare, not only to make a bold man try, but also to make a sober-minded and wise man believe."

Author's Note

THE AIM OF THIS BOOK is introduction, evocation; an accurate
title would be *Invitation to Francis Bacon*. I have attempted a
more intimate portrayal than has hitherto been offered and to
this purpose I have culled and taken from the existing material such facts and scenes, be they large or trivial, as may re-
veal the man. My chapters are cast in biographical form, yet
they are in essence essays of opinion, the expression of one
person's thinking about Francis Bacon. To encumber such a
book with scholarly apparatus seemed superfluous. Conversations, excerpts from letters, et cetera, are fully documented.
No alterations of the original texts have been made beyond
deletions as indicated by ellipses or in footnotes.

Readers of *The Lion and the Throne* have met in this present volume the dramatis personae a second time, I hope with
deeper understanding. For me it has been a quite extraordinary
experience, and greatly revealing, to study character and ideol-
ogy, scene and action, from two such sharply angled view-
points as those of Bacon and Sir Edward Coke. Occasionally I
found it expedient to repeat a bit of historical dialogue or correspondence from book to book, even a descriptive phrase or
two of my own where it seemed pertinent; surely an author
may plagiarize her own work.

[235]

For the final question of the Lord Chancellor's moral guilt or innocence under the charges brought in 1621, let the reader, having surveyed the scene, decide for himself, if such exercise renders him more comfortable. To me the decision seems beside the point; this was a man in whose debt the world is proud to live.

Every biographer is greatly beholden to the academic scholars. It is with pleasure that I acknowledge the generous help of Professors Caroline Robbins, Elizabeth Foster and Margaret Hastings; for specific queries, Doctors Walter C. Michels, physicist; Stuart Mudd, microbiologist, and Thomas R. S. Broughton, historian and classicist. Among my friends the librarians I want especially to thank Howell Heany and Ellen Shafer of Rare Books, Philadelphia Public Library; Dorothy Mason of the Folger Library and Neda Westlake of the Rare Book Room, University of Pennsylvania; the staffs at the Bryn Mawr and Haverford College Libraries and at the Huntington. In London, Mr. Sydney Dalton made my road easier and pleasanter; at Gorhambury House Mrs. King contributed to memorable hours. Allen Woodruff in Philadelphia put at my disposal his distinguished library of Baconiana and his bibliographical experience in the field. I want to thank Danila C. Spielman for letting me read her unpublished doctoral thesis: *Impeachment: 1621-1624;* and Mrs. Martha Sellers for secretarial work beyond the usual call of duty.

For editorial help I am indebted to my publisher, Edward A. Weeks, to John H. Powell, to Denning Miller — and first and last to my friend and literary critic, Barbara Rex, who has borne with me now through the trials and adventures of five books.

Index

ACADÉMIE ROYALE DES SCIENCES, 11
Adams, John, 24
Albyn, Samuel, 193
Alford, Edward, 178, 185, 198
America, 35
American Philosophical Society, 7
Andrewes, Bishop Lancelot, 13, 52, 111, 118, 215
Anne, wife of James I, 140
Aristotle, 35
Armada, Spanish, 55
Arundel, Thomas Howard, Earl of, 225
Ascham, Roger, 34
Astrology, 28
Atkins, William, 227
Aubrey, John, 61, 222, 224
Awbrey, Christopher, 184

BACON, ALICE, LADY (wife of Francis), 114, 115; appearance, 116; James confers precedency upon, 153; and Bacon's will, 224; second marriage, 224
Bacon, Ann, Lady (mother of Francis), 28-29, 81; bust of, 30; interest in religious controversy, 57; sells jewels to aid Anthony in Europe, 57-58; agitated by Anthony's papist followers, 58; admonitory letters

to sons, 58-60; unhappy about sons' friends, 60-61, 201; on Essex's efforts on behalf of Francis, 73; irritated by Francis's high-flown language, 84; later years, 94-95
Bacon, Anthony (brother of Francis), 15, 29; ill-health, 33, 34, 58; at college with Francis, 33-34; leaves Cambridge, 37; goes to Europe, 38, 42; father's bequest to, 40; intelligence work in Europe, 57-58; with Francis at Gray's Inn, 58, 201; grudge against Burghley, 58, 64, 73; friends, 59; and the Earl of Essex, 62, 64, 79, 99; in Parliament, 69; moves from Gray's Inn, 81; Francis's *Essays* dedicated to, 89-90; death, 94; verse quoted by, 159
Bacon, Edward (stepbrother of Francis), 40, 95
Bacon, Francis, Baron Verulam and Viscount St. Alban: prayer by, 3, 194, 195; character, 4-5; 400th anniversary of birth, 7; detractors, 12-13; friends, 13-14, 59, 61, 214; legend concerning, 14-15; letters, 15-16; birth and boyhood, 18-19, 23, 24-25, 29, 31, 33; sisters and brothers, 29; bust of, 29, 30; appearance at

Bacon, Francis (*continued*)
different ages, 30, 66-67, 94-95; at
Trinity College, Cambridge, 33-34,
36, 37; abroad with Sir Amias
Paulet, 37, 38-39; and his father's
death, 39-43; lack of judgment in
money matters, 41, 89, 160-161,
213-214; studies law at Gray's Inn,
46-50; admitted to bar, 50; notes
on his system of philosophy, 50-51;
idea of Great Instauration, 51;
member of Parliament, 52-54; advice to Elizabeth on the Oath, 56;
at Gray's Inn with Anthony, 58,
59-60; alleged homosexuality, 61-
62; and the Earl of Essex, 62, 64,
68, 74, 75-76, 78-80; letter to
Burghley, 64-66; desires to found
school or university, 65-66; suggested by Essex as Attorney General, 69; loses Queen's favor by
speech against triple subsidy, 70-71;
pleads cases in court, 72-73; irked
at Queen's attitude toward him,
73-74; interest in Lady Hatton, 74;
regains Elizabeth's favor, 76-77;
notebook, 81-85; first project for
reforming English laws, 85-87; legal maxims, 86-87; begins to write
essays, 87-89; arrested for debt, 89,
91; rivalry with Coke, 89-93, 101,
125; and *Chudleigh's Case*, 93;
called to be Double Reader at
Gray's Inn, 92-94; illnesses, 95,
163, 188, 194, 202, 207, 219, 221;
on the accession of James I, 98;
seeks favor of James I, 99-100; desires knighthood, 100; thinks of
marriage, 100; knighted, 101; royal
patent as King's Council Extraordinary, 101, 112; sets to work on
his philosophy, 102-107; flatters
James I in dedication, 107-108; in
James's first Parliament, 112-113;
as speaker, 113; asks for post of

Solicitor General, 113-114; marries,
114-117; awaits Solicitor Generalship, 117-118; named Solicitor
General and Clerk of Star Chamber, 118; reaction to promotion,
119; as Solicitor General, 122-125;
and *Calvin's Case*, 123-124; advises
James concerning his plantations,
124; presents Petition of Grievances
to James, 124-125; and Robert Cecil's death, 125-127; seeks Cecil's
vacant positions, 127-128; seeks Attorney Generalship, 129-130; as Attorney General, 130, 133; in judicial struggle, views King as above
the law, 134, 135, 136-139; and
events leading to Coke's dismissal,
139-142; as Privy Councilor, 140,
157; statement of charges against
Coke, 142-143; and Ellesmere's
final illness, 144; urges reformation
of English law, 144-150; charges
to juries, 145; aphorisms, 146; as
Lord Keeper, 151-153, 154-157; as
regent during James's absence, 157-
158; obstructs Coke's plans for
daughter's marriage, 158-159; Lord
Chancellor and Lord Verulam, 159;
lavish scale of living, 160; ideas on
health, 162-163, 221; and the condemnation of Ralegh, 164-166; sixtieth birthday, 172; created Viscount St. Alban, 172-173; persuades
James to summon 1621 Parliament,
173; presides over House of Lords,
177; indebted to Buckingham,
181; Commons committee works
against interests of, 183-184; letters
to Buckingham, 187-188, 209;
charged with receiving bribes, 188;
taken ill, 188, 194, 202, 207; pro-
tests charges against him, 189-190,
191; charges against, 193-194, 199,
200; writes his will, 194, 223-224;
writes out submission, 195-196,

Bacon, Francis (*continued*)
197; receives indictment against
him, 199; confession, 199-202; pronounced guilty, 203; punishment
discussed, 203; sentenced, 204;
taken to the Tower, 207; released
from prison, 209; promises James a
history of England, 210-211; on
writing history, 211-213; fine remitted, 213; financial status after
his fall, 213-214; requests Provostship of Eton, 214; in retirement at
Gorhambury, 215; valetudinarianism, 221; death, 224-226; last
letter, 225; contemporaries' opinions of, 226-230; poems addressed
to, 227; grave of, 231-232
    WORKS: *Advancement of Learn-
ing*, 6, 83, 102-105, 107-108, 109,
111, 112, 166, 210, 212, 216; *Apology in certain imputations concerning the late Earl of Essex*, 100;
Apophthegms, 59, 60, 154, 210,
228; *Certain Miscellany Works*,
228; "Colours of Good and Evil,"
87, 196-197; *Commentarius Solutus*, 120-122, 128; *De Augmentis
Scientiarum*, 146, 150, 210; *Description of the Intellectual Globe*,
8; *Discourse touching the Happy
Union of England and Scotland*,
123; *Elements of the Common
Laws*, 6; *Essays*, 6, 46, 87-89, 117,
221-222; *Great Instauration* (*Instauratio Magna*), 7, 28, 51, 152,
166, 167, 216, 220; *History of Life
and Death*, 218; *History of the
Reign of Henry VII*, 211, 212-213;
History of the Winds, 8, 217-218;
In Felicem Memoriam Elizabethae,
80; *Maxims of the Law*, 86-87, 88;
Natural History, 8, 39, 167, 217-
219; *New Atlantis*, 7, 167-171,
210, 228; *Novum Organum*, 6, 8,
11, 83, 107, 152, 167, 171-172,

215, 217; "Of Deformity," 126-
127; *Of Dense and Rare*, 8; *Of Hot
and Cold*, 8; "Of the Ebb and Flow
of the Sea," 8; *The Pacification and
Edification of the Church*, 113;
*Promus of Formularies and Ele-
gancies*, 81-85, 122; "A Proposi-
tion touching the Compiling and
Amendment of the Laws of Eng-
land," 145-147; *Resuscitatio*, 228;
"Sacred Meditations," 87; *Statute
of Uses*, 93; *Sylva Sylvarum*, 228;
Use of the Law, 6
Bacon, Jane Fernley (first wife of Sir
    Nicholas), 28
Bacon, Nathaniel (stepbrother of
    Francis), 40, 53, 115
Bacon, Nicholas (nephew of Francis),
    160
Bacon, Nicholas (stepbrother of Fran-
    cis), 40, 53, 115
Bacon, Sir Nicholas (father of Fran-
    cis), 23; land holdings, 25, 27-28;
    has busts of family made, 29; in ill
    health and overweight, 29-30, 155;
    visited by Queen Elizabeth, 31;
    charity, 33; lives in Paris, 38; death
    and will, 40, 42; dislike of long-
    winded attorneys, 155-156
Baconiana (Tenison), 229
Barnham, Alice. *See* Bacon, Lady
    Alice
Bennet, Sir John, 208
Bettenham, Mr., 59-60
Beza, Theodore, 57
Blount, Charles, Earl of Devonshire
    and Baron Mountjoy, 102
Bodley, Sir Thomas, 13, 85, 111
Boener, Peter, 228
Bonham's Case, 135
Boyle, Robert, 11
Bracton, Henry, 47, 141
Brahe, Tycho, 102
Brandon, Charles, Duke of Suffolk,
    23

Britannicus, 229

Bromley, Sir Thomas, 42

Bruce, Edward, Baron Bruce of Kinloss, 99

Bruno, Giordano, 7

Buckingham, George Villiers, Marquis (later Duke) of, 158, 187; Commons opposed to, 174, 181, 182, 183; spectacular rise of, 180-181; apologizes to House of Lords, 183; and Bacon's impeachment, 191-192; votes against degradation of Bacon, 204; attacked by Yelverton, 208; desires York House, 213

Burghley, Lady Mildred, 32

Burghley, William Cecil, Baron, 15, 26, 27; house, 32; Chancellor of Cambridge, 33; on sending young men to Europe, 38; Bacon's letters to, 50; fails to help Bacon's career, 52, 63-64, 66, 67; as administrator for Elizabeth, 54; makes use of Anthony Bacon's dispatches, 57, 58; credited by Queen for work done by Anthony Bacon, 58; Anthony Bacon bears grudge against, 58, 64, 73; Bacon's last appeal to, 64-65; blamed for Bacon's failure to gain Solicitorship, 73; death, 94

Bushell, Thomas "Button," 13, 128, 201

CAESAR, SIR JULIUS, 226

Calvin's Case, 123-124, 134, 141

Cambridge, in 1573, 34-37

Camden, William, 85, 211; *Annals,* 211, 213

Campanella, Tommaso, 7

Campbell, John, Baron, quoted, 17-18

Carew, George, Baron of Clopton, 173

Carlyle, Thomas, quoted, 5-6; on Bacon, 14-15; on Spedding's work, 16

Carr, Robert, Viscount Rochester, Earl of Somerset, 122, 128

Case of Commendams, 135, 137-138

Castlehaven, Mervyn Touchet, Earl of, 116

Cecil, Robert, Earl of Salisbury, 15; Bacon seeks advancement through goodwill of, 50, 122; chosen Secretary of State by Elizabeth, 64; Bacon blames, for his loss of post of Solicitor General, 73; gives financial aid to Bacon, 89; proclaims James I, 97; influence on James I, 98-99; created Baron Cecil of Essendon, 100; Bacon sends copy of *Advancement of Learning* to, 111; probable antipathy toward Bacon, 118; in Upper Chamber, 124; death of, 125-126; Spanish pension, 180

Cecil, William. *See* Burghley

Chamberlain, John, 107, 208; on Bacon's *History of Henry VII,* 212-213; on Bacon's works in progress, 216

Charles I, King of England: as Prince, proposed marriage to Infanta of Spain, 157, 182; secures Bacon's release from Tower, 209; *History of Henry VII* dedicated to, 212; on Bacon, 214; becomes King, 223

Cheke, Sir John, 34

Chudleigh's Case, 93

Churchill, John, 184, 186, 198

Clarendon, Edward Hyde, Earl of, 191

Clavius, Christopher, 102

Coke, Anne, 90

Coke, Sir Edward, 24, 26, 53, 120; *Institutes,* 6; *Reports,* 6, 139, 140; as bitter rival of Bacon, 14, 89-93, 101, 125; devotion to common law, 48-49; first session in Parliament, 55; obvious candidate for Queen's Attorney, 69, 70; granted Attorneyship, 72; prosecutes Essex, 78; writings, 85; knighted, 101; promotion to judgeship rumored,

Coke, Sir Edward (*continued*)
113; marital battles, 115; as Chief Justice of Common Pleas, 117, 125; dramatic trials make reputation of, 122; moves up to King's Bench, 129-130; judicial struggle against Ellesmere, 134-135, 137; suspended as Privy Councilor, 139; events leading to dismissal of, 139-141; statement of charges against, 142-143; seeks to recover royal favor, 158; affair of daughter's proposed marriage, 158-159; restored to Privy Council, 159; and Ralegh, 165, 166; opinion of *Novum Organum*, 171-172; in Commons, 177, 178; Bacon mistrusts motives of, 182; and investigation of corruption in Chancery, 186, 187, 188; and Bacon's impeachment, 141, 188, 189, 190-191, 192, 196, 198, 203, 204; and Cranfield's impeachment, 223; in the Tower, 223
Coke, Frances, 158
Coleridge, John Duke Coleridge, Baron, 86
Comenius of Moravia, 11
Commendams, Case of, 135, 137-138
Commons, House of: grievances of, 178-180, 181; threaten to make reforms, 181-182; Committee for Inquiring into Abuses, etc., 183-184, 204
Conway, Edward Conway, Viscount, 214
Cooke, Sir Anthony, 29
Copernicus, 36
Cotton, Sir Robert, 13, 85, 211
Cowley, Abraham, 230, 231
Cranfield, Lionel, Earl of Middlesex: helps effect economies in royal budget, 157; and Commons committee of inquiry, 183-184; impeachment, 89, 191-192, 223

DARWIN, CHARLES, 12
De Rege Inconsulto, 135, 139, 143
Dee, Dr. John, 28, 36-37
Demosthenes, quoted, 108
Descartes, René, 11, 12
Devereux, Robert, Earl of Essex. *See* Essex
Devonshire, Charles Blount, Earl of, 100
D'Ewes, Simonds, 61, 85, 228
Digby, Everard, 37
Digges, Sir Dudley, 188
Doddridge, Sir John, 87
Donne, John, 115
Drake, Sir Francis, 35, 53
Dugdale, Sir William, 230
Durham House, 24
Dyer, Sir James, 148

EFFIAT, ANTOINE DE RUZÉ, MARQUIS D', 223
Egerton, Edward, 185-186, 188
Egerton, Sir Thomas, Baron Ellesmere. *See* Ellesmere
Elizabeth, daughter of James I, 208
Elizabeth I, Queen of England, 17, 24; councilors of state, 25; army and navy, 26; belief in astrology, 28; and Sir Nicholas Bacon, 30; notices young Bacon, 30-31, 46; at Gorhambury manor, 31; favors Cambridge, 34; Bacon in service of, 37, 41-42; names Sir Amias Paulet Mary Stuart's jailer, 38; and Bacon's admission to the bar, 50; regard for Bacon mentioned by him, 52; and Parliament, 54-55; triumphal procession after defeat of Armada, 55; excommunicated by Pope, 55; Bacon's letter to, on religion, 56; pursues middle way in religion, 56; on Anthony Bacon, 57; profanity, 60; and Essex, 62, 77, 79-80; outraged by Bacon's stand on subsidy vote, 70; Essex

Elizabeth I (*continued*)
 pleads with, for Bacon's appointment as Attorney General, 71-72; grants Attorneyship to Coke, 72; considers Bacon for Solicitor General, 73; names Fleming Solicitor General, 74; takes Bacon back into favor, 76-77; approves legal reform, 86; plans visit to Coke's country house, 90; receives gifts from Bacon and Coke, 90; reign comes to end, 94, 96; death, 97; promises Star Chamber post to Bacon, 101; does not sit in Star Chamber court, 136; deems preambles to bills unnecessary, 147; and Ralegh, 164
Ellesmere, Thomas Egerton, Baron, 77, 100, 117, 133; judicial struggle with Coke, 134-135, 139; in *Calvin's Case,* 141; final illness, 144, 151; recommends Bacon as his successor, 144
Encyclopedists, 11
Erasmus, Desiderius, 34
Essendon, Baron Cecil of. *See* Cecil, Robert
Essex, Robert Devereux, Earl of, 14; friendship with the brothers Bacon, 62, 63; and Elizabeth, 62, 77, 79-80; Bacon as friend and adviser to, 68-69, 74; urges Bacon for Queen's Attorney, 69, 71; seeks post of Solicitor General for Bacon, 73; ambition to go to Ireland to subdue Tyrone, 75; refuses to heed Bacon's advice against going to Ireland, 75-76; rebellion, 78; trial, 78-79, 91, 188; public confession, 79; and James I, 98-99
Eton, Bacon requests Provostship of, 214

Fernley, Jane, 28
Field, Theophilus, 188
Finch, Heneage, 178

Finch, John, 185, 187, 199
Finch, John, Baron Finch of Fordwich, 87
FitzGerald, Edward, 16
Fitzherbert, Sir Anthony, 47
Fitzherbert and Rastell, *Terms of the Law,* 85
Fleetwood, William, 52
Fleming, Sir Thomas, 74, 128
Floyd, Edward, 208
Fortescue, Sir John, 47
Foulis, Sir David, 99
Freud, Sigmund, 9
Frobisher, Sir Martin, 35
Fuller, Thomas, 80, 226
Fuller's Case, 134

Galilei, Galileo, 7, 8, 11, 102
Gardiner, Samuel Rawson, 136
Gawdy, Sir Francis, 117
Gilbert, William, 8, 103
Glanville, Ranulf de, 47, 178
Gondomar, Count Diego, 13, 153-154, 156, 165, 214
Gorhambury House, 27-28, 29, 31, 33, 36, 39, 161
Gray's Inn, 46; Bacon at, 45-47, 58, 81, 224
Gresham, Thomas, 103
Greville, Sir Fulke, 13, 73
Guise, Francis, Duke of, 79

Hacket, John, quoted, 177
Hakewill, William, 178
Hallam, Henry, 15
Hariot, Thomas, 8, 120
Harvey, William, 8, 14, 103, 166
Hastings, Sir Francis, 53
Hastings, Sir George, 184, 185
Hatton, Sir Christopher, 48, 53
Hatton, Lady Elizabeth (Cecil), 14, 74, 158, 159
Henrietta Maria, wife of Charles I, 223
Henry VIII, 23, 25

Henry of Navarre, 57
Herbert, George, 13, 227
Heylyn, Peter, 229
Hilliard, Nicholas, 41
Hobart, Sir Henry, 117, 121, 129, 130
Hobbes, Thomas, 12, 162, 224*n*.
Holdsworth, William S., 94
Hooke, Thomas, 230
Howard, Henry, Earl of Northampton, 128
Howell, James, 227
Humboldt, Friedrich, Baron von, 10, 219

INNS OF COURT, 47

JAMES I, King of England, 6, 14, 18; proclaimed King, 97-98; appearance, 98; knights created by, 100-101; grants pension to Bacon, 101; *Advancement of Learning* dedicated to, 107-108; interest in *Calvin's Case*, 123, 124; not unpopular as King, 133; and the judicial struggle, 135-136, 137-139; plans to rid self of Coke, 139, 140, 142, 143; sees no need of preambles to bills, 147; confers precedency on Lady Bacon, 153; desires son's marriage to Spanish Infanta, 157; and the marriage of Coke's daughter, 158-159; refuses Ralegh a public hearing, 165; and the *Novum Organum*, 171, 172; summons 1621 Parliament, 173-174; dislike of Parliaments, 178-179; lacks funds, 178, 179-180; lavishes money on favorites, 182; rebukes Commons for disrespect, 183; intervenes for Bacon, 190, 191; requests advice of the impeached Bacon, 209; remits Bacon's fine, 213; death, 223
Jonson, Ben, in praise of Bacon, 4, 214, 226-227; as friend to Bacon,
13, 118; on Bacon's speaking in Commons, 113; verses for Bacon's sixtieth birthday, 172

KEELING, RICHARD, 186
Kepler, Johannes, 102
Knollys, Sir Thomas, 53

LAMBARDE, WILLIAM, 211
Law, common, 47, 49; struggle concerning review of decisions of, 133-138
Leibnitz, Gottfried, 11, 12
Lennox, Ludovick Stuart, Duke of, 213
Ley, Sir James, 204
Littleton, Sir Thomas, 47
Locke, John, 12
London, in 1561, 23-24

MACAULAY, THOMAS BABINGTON MACAULAY, Baron: condemns Bacon as treacherous to friends, 5; verdict on Bacon's champions, 15; angry essay reviewing Bacon biography, 16; on Coke, 187; on Bacon's last five years, 210
Maitland, Frederic William, 85
Mallet, David, 229
Marks, manor of, 40
Martin Marprelate, 56
Matthew, Tobie, as friend of Bacon, 13, 61, 118, 216, 221; meets King James, 98; reads manuscript of *Advancement of Learning*, 111; in Spain with Prince Charles, 214; Bacon makes bequest to, 223
Meautys, Sir Thomas, as friend of Bacon, 13, 214-215; erects monument to Bacon, 13, 231; speaks before the Commons on Bacon's behalf, 186; in Bacon's household, 197; Bacon makes bequest to, 223
Michell, Sir Francis, 182

Mill, William, Clerk of Star Chamber, 101, 118, 119
Mompesson, Sir Giles, 182
Montagu, Henry, Viscount Mandeville, 193, 208
Montaigne, Michel de, 57, 87
More, Sir George, 89
More, Sir Thomas, 154, 167
Mountjoy, Charles Blount, Earl of Devonshire and Baron, 100

NEWTON, SIR ISAAC, 12
Northampton, Henry Howard, Earl of, 128
Northumberland, Henry Percy, Earl of, 99, 120
Novae Narrationes, 86
Noye, William, 87, 178, 186, 188

OLDENBURG, HEINRICH, 11
Owen's Case, 143

PAKINGTON, DOROTHY, LADY, 114, 116
Pakington, Sir John, 114
Parliament, Elizabeth and, 54-55. *See also* Commons, House of
Paulet, Lady, 39
Paulet, Sir Amias, 37, 38, 42
Peacham's Case, 135, 139, 143
Peel, Sir Robert, 146
Percy, Henry, 60, 62
Phelips, Sir Robert, 184, 188, 192
Philip, King of Spain, 26, 55
Pleas of the Crown (Stamford), 85, 86
Plessis, Madame du, 57
Plutarch, quoted, 163
Pope, Alexander, 4
Popham, Sir John, 78
Postnati, 122, 123
Prentise, servant of Anthony Bacon, 60
Puckering, Sir John, 53, 73
Pym, John, 179

RALEGH, SIR WALTER, 14, 24, 53, 188; efforts to retain royal favor, 18; out of favor with James I, 99; marriage, 114-115; imprisoned, 120; son Walter, 164; hearing and execution, 164-166; pays Buckingham for release from Tower, 181; *History of the World*, 211, 212
Rawley, Dr. William, on Bacon's fame, 11; editor of Bacon's works, 13, 228; as loyal friend to Bacon, 13, 215; on Bacon's fainting fits, 163; on Bacon, 219, 220; Bacon makes bequest to, 223; biography of Bacon, 228
Rich, Penelope, 79
Richardson, Sir Thomas, 204
Rochester, Robert Carr, Viscount, 122, 128
Royal Society, ode to (Cowley), 230
Royal Society of London for Improving Natural Knowledge, 11

SAVILE, SIR HENRY, 13
Selden, John, 13, 85, 213
Shakespeare, William, 4, 75
Shelley, Percy Bysshe, on Bacon, 4, 230-231
Sidney, Sir Philip, 53
Simpson, goldsmith, 89
Somerset, Robert Carr, Earl of, 122
Southampton, Henry Wriothesley, Earl of, 203, 207-208
Spedding, James, 16-17
Speed, John, 211
Spelman, Sir Henry, 87, 211
Spencer, Robert Spencer, Baron, 203
Sprat, Thomas, 230
Stamford, *Pleas of the Crown*, 85, 86
Stevinus, Simon, 103
Stowe, John, 211
Stuart, Mary, Queen of Scots, 38, 55
Suffolk, Charles Brandon, Duke of, 23

Suffolk, Thomas Howard, Earl of, 202, 203

TENISON, THOMAS, 229
Tennyson, Alfred Tennyson, Baron, 16
Terms of the Law, Fitzherbert and Rastell, 85
Thackeray, William Makepeace, 16
Theobalds, 32, 173
Tottell, Richard, 85
Twickenham, 95
Tyrone, Hugh O'Neill, Earl of, 62, 75

UNDERHILL, SIR JOHN, 224

VERULAM HOUSE, 161-162
Vieta, François, 103

Villiers, George, Earl of Buckingham. *See* Buckingham
Villiers, Sir John, 158, 209

WALSINGHAM, SIR FRANCIS, 57
Wentworth, Thomas Wentworth, Baron, 173
Wharton, Lady, 192, 199
Whitgift, John, 34
Williams, John, 223
Woolwich Marsh, Bacon inherits, 40
Wotton, Sir Henry, 214, 231

Year Books, 85
Yelverton, Sir Henry, 208
York House, 23, 25, 42; Bacon makes extensive repairs on, 159-160; Bacon refuses to sell, 213